Praise for

THE MOTHER-DAUGHTER BOOK CLUB

"What a great idea! . . . I hope the idea will spread."
—*Beverly Cleary*

"A wonderful idea."
—*A*

"This
book
Mot
adul
child

"*The*
wond
taken
cataly

The

MOTHER-DAUGHTER
Book Club

The

MOTHER-DAUGHTER
Book Club

TENTH ANNIVERSARY EDITION

*How Ten Busy Mothers and Daughters
Came Together to Talk, Laugh, and Learn
Through Their Love of Reading*

SHIREEN
DODSON
with Teresa Barker

HARPER

NEW YORK • LONDON • TORONTO • SYDNEY

HARPER

HarperCollins books may be purchased for educational, business, or sales promotional use. For information please write: Special Markets Department, HarperCollins Publishers, 10 East 53rd Street, New York, NY 10022.

First Harper paperback published 2007.

Designed by Nancy Singer Olaguera/ISPN Publishing Services

Library of Congress Cataloging-in-Publication Data has been applied for.

ISBN: 978-0-06-089034-6 (pbk.)
ISBN-10: 0-06-089034-7 (pbk.)

07 08 09 10 11   ISPN/RRD   10 9 8 7 6 5 4 3 2 1

To my daughter and my friend Morgan,
who was the inspiration for it all;
to my daughter Skylar,
for continuing the journey;
and to my son, Leroy III,
who reminds me that it is all a blessing

CONTENTS

CONTENTS

THE ORIGINAL MOTHER-DAUGHTER BOOK CLUB
1996

Cheryl Brown and Ashley (age twelve)

Linda Chastang and Rebecca (age eleven)

Alexis Christian and Jamexis (age twelve)

Shireen Dodson and Morgan Fykes (age eleven)

Winnie Donaldson and Tiffany (age eleven)

Leslye Fraser and Brittney (age ten)

Grace Speights and Ashley (age ten)

Alice Lacey Thomas and Holly (age ten)

Kathie Thompson and Jihan (age twelve)

Joyce Yette and Maya (age nine)

SKYLAR'S MOTHER-DAUGHTER BOOK CLUB
2005

Linda Adams and Jesse Greenblatt (age sixteen)

Sherry Bindeman and Brooke and Hannah Kahn
(twins, age sixteen)

Shireen Dodson and Skylar Fykes (age fifteen)

Kris Heinz and Sylvie Stein (age fifteen)

Irene Klores and Molly (age sixteen)

Jane Prelinger and Joanna Rothkopf (age sixteen)

Amy Reingold and Celia (age sixteen)

Pam Riley and Riley Collins (age fifteen)

Maria Volpe and Ari (age sixteen)

PREFACE TO THE
TENTH ANNIVERSARY EDITION

Ten years ago, in the fall of 1996, I started a mother-daughter book club with my daughter Morgan. The following February, in celebration of Black History Month, a reporter who knew one of the moms wrote a wonderful human interest story about our Mother-Daughter Book Club. The story mentioned that I worked at the Smithsonian Institution, and my phone at work began to ring off the hook. People wanted to join my Mother-Daughter Club; they wanted to talk about what a great idea they thought a mother-daughter book club was, and if they could not join my club, they wanted to know how to start their own mother-daughter book club. The response was so overwhelming that I started collecting contact information with a promise to send a one-page write-up on how to start a mother-daughter book club. So when eventually I received a phone call from an agent asking, "Have you ever thought about writing a book?" I was prepared. In 1997 *The Mother-Daughter Book Club* was published.

Many pages later, Morgan's younger sister, Skylar, watched and waited to have her own Mother-Daughter Book Club. She and I began the Bookworms when the girls were eight and in the third grade, just starting to read chapter books. Thinking that girls so young could not sustain a meaningful discussion, we added a related craft activity to the meetings. Were we ever wrong! The discussions, though shorter, were rich and insightful. The Bookworms stayed together for six years, into the beginning of eighth grade. As they anxiously anticipated high school, their activities became more centered on their individual schools and the Bookworms drifted apart. I mourned the loss of my secret weapon for getting through the difficult high school years. Had we laid enough foundation? Who was I going to discuss books with?

I received my answer to those questions in the fall of 2004, when Skylar entered high school and I found myself at the back-to-school potluck for ninth graders. A mom new to the area mentioned that she had read my book several years before. She regretted that as her girls' childhoods were waning, she had never followed through on her intention to participate in a mother-daughter book club. She wondered if it was too late for the girls to be interested in such a club. That was all it took for me to galvanize and start an all-new group with and for our daughters who were all just entering high school. Once again Skylar pulled together a wonderful group of ten girls who shared an enthusiasm and passion for reading. The girls all attend Georgetown Day School, known for its academic rigor; but somehow they always manage to juggle their book club reading, schoolwork, and extracurricular activities. They come each month ready to tackle tough issues and their insights never cease to cause the moms to pass secret silent smiles of relief from one to another. Our girls are growing up just fine!

Meanwhile, in the summer of 2005, I received another phone call, this time from my publisher, saying, "You know, it's been almost ten years—have you thought about updating *The Mother-Daughter Book Club*?" It seemed impossible that ten years had flown by. So much in my own life had changed: My son had graduated from college and answered the call into ministry; Morgan, who was my original catalyst, was twenty and a college sophomore; my role with my aging parents had reversed, as I was now caring for them; I was separated from my husband of twenty-seven years; and Skylar was no longer the baby but a nearly grown young lady. The one constant through it all was the joy that I experienced from reading and sharing books with my daughters.

When I received the call to do a new edition, I had just finished year one of Skylar's new Mother-Daughter Club. I was fully immersed again in the world of young adult literature, talking, laughing, and learning through books. It felt wonderful. So it was without hesitation that I agreed to this tenth anniversary edition of *The Mother-Daughter Book Club* in which you will get to know Skylar and the other members of Skylar's Mother-Daughter Book Club. The voices of the very first Mother-Daughter Book Club, which lasted until the older girls went off to college, are still here of course. At our annual Christmas holiday reunion the original members looked back on their book club years, and their reflections have been added as well. But you will also meet the members of Skylar's club, who give new meaning to just how special a Mother-Daughter Book Club can be.

The world has changed a lot in the past ten years. Oprah started her famous television book club, and adult book clubs became hugely popular. J. K. Rowling introduced Harry Potter and children's literature has not been the same. Girls—and to everyone's amazement, boys—were suddenly racing through 700-page books with complete rapture. This new edition includes complete discussion guides for books we've discovered in recent years—books that deal with terrorism and peer pressure and all manner of topics of interest to a more grown-up generation of mother-daughter readers. And this book has inspired thousands of mother-daughter book clubs around the world! Not a week goes by that I do not hear from some mom who has discovered the joys and is reaping the benefits of participating in a mother-daughter book club. Some of their heartwarming stories are included in this tenth anniversary edition. It is wonderful to have a place where girls can be girls, and explore their present lives while dreaming out loud about their futures.

With this book, I invite you to join us in Mother-Daughter Book Club country. I think you will agree that a one-page write-up would never have been adequate to capture the beauty and magic of this very special place.

Shireen Dodson

2007

INTRODUCTION

Everyone needs to take time off and spend time away. You need that special place where you can cleanse your mind and renew your soul. For me that time is our annual family vacation and the place is Martha's Vineyard. We try to go for at least two weeks in August, and often we can squeeze in three weeks. Not only do I use the time to search inside myself, but I also have a chance to reconnect with my three children, Leroy III, Morgan, and Skylar. We talk: We review the past school year and then look ahead. How are they looking at the world around them, and what are they thinking about the year ahead? It is surprising what emerges from your children when you slow down from the hustle and bustle of the usual school and extracurricular routines, step back, look, and listen. I am amazed at how much we can discuss in the absence of normal everyday interruptions. At the end of each August, I am always a little bit sad as we drive home, to be leaving behind the opportunity to relate to my children in such a relaxed way. Our vacations create a haven for positive interaction to occur spontaneously. I think I was unconsciously trying to figure out a way to carry that feeling back into our regular lives.

During our 1995 summer vacation my morning routine included a walk with a new friend and her daughter along the water's edge. There was something so beautiful and calming about the ocean that conversation just seemed to flow. My friend and I walked and the girls Rollerbladed on an adjacent path, which gave us a chance for private conversation. Our talk often turned to our daughters and an only half-joking question: How were we ever going to survive their growing up? After all, children do not come with an instruction manual. And since there is something unique about the mother-daughter relationship, especially as girls approach adolescence, directions of some kind would surely be useful.

So these walks with my friend were comforting confirmation that I was not alone in my difficulty understanding my daughter. Morgan was my middle child, and while she was beautiful, bright, and normally very self-confident, she could be vulnerable and moody. In taking stock that summer, I realized that I often mistook Morgan's self-confidence and intellect for maturity, and would sometimes forget that she was only nine. We would argue over every little issue and did not really talk. That's not exactly accurate. We talked a lot. The problem was that we were not communicating. We talked at each other, and while neither of us particularly enjoyed this ongoing power struggle, we didn't know how to change our way of relating. My friend was engaged in a very similar prickly relationship, and though the individual skirmishes were different, the struggle was the same.

Like many women I know, I think things through by talking about them. One morning my friend and I were brainstorming aloud about how she could communicate more effectively with her daughter. I was asking all kinds of questions about what she and her daughter liked and didn't like to do. I thought an activity and conversation might flow from some common interest.

Neither of them was into sports, and both had very busy schedules. But they both liked to read. Suddenly I heard myself saying, "Why don't you start a mother-daughter book club?"

An idea was born! My friend was intrigued, so I continued to talk it through as we completed our walk. Eventually our conversation moved on to other things, and soon the vacation itself came to an end.

I did, however, mention the idea to my husband, Leroy, on the drive home. This time, when I heard myself talking about a mother-daughter book club, I thought of Morgan and me. Morgan and I both loved to read. As the previous discussion with my friend flooded back into my mind, I realized that all the comments about her and her daughter also applied to Morgan and me. I made up my mind right then to start a book club—and soon. I felt a sense of wonder and hope for the upcoming year. Our experience was gratifying.

Yes, Morgan and I still had an occasional fight, but the atmosphere at home improved. We no longer had to wait for August and Martha's Vineyard to find a peaceful haven. The Mother-Daughter Book Club offered us that kind of harmony all through the year.

Just as we occasionally invited guests to our Mother-Daughter Book Club meetings, it seemed natural to invite guests into our book to share their wisdom on the subject of literature and the lives of girls and women. They joined us enthusiastically. These authors, educators, counselors, and others, through interviews or letters, contributed an abundance of practical tips, candid advice, personal memories, and suggestions for reading, all of which are here for you to savor.

With this book in hand, then, welcome to a very special meeting of the mother-daughter book club.

Shireen Dodson
December 1996

PART ONE

ONE

Why Start a Mother-Daughter Book Club?

TO OUR MOTHERS AND GRANDMOTHERS, AUNTS AND GREAT-AUNTS. TO ALL THE WOMEN WHO STOOD BEFORE US, TELLING US ABOUT WHERE THEY CAME FROM, WHAT THEY SAID, DID, AND IMAGINED. THEY LET US KNOW THEY STOOD FOR US. TALKING, THEY COMBED OUR HAIR, ROCKED US TO SLEEP, SANG TO US, TOLD US TALES OF THEN AND NOW—AND TOMORROW. THEY WORRIED ABOUT US. THEY HOPED FOR US AND SHOWED US THE WAY. THEY CARED.

—VIRGINIA HAMILTON, *dedication*, Her Stories

Morgan Fykes & The Original Mother-Daughter Book Club

Hello. My name is Morgan Fykes. When I started the book club with my mother, Shireen Dodson, I was nine years old. Two years later we were publishing a book and doing a book tour together. Since then a lot has changed between my mother and me. The older I get, the more our relationship has become a friendship. We've been through a lot together in these past ten years: deaths in the family, seeing my friends' parents and now my own parents separate, and of course high school, which was a unique experience. While change can be hard, we have gotten through it all with grace, and I cannot imagine how different our relationship would be had we never had the book club. It is not just the relationship that I have developed with my mom that has changed my life growing up; it is also the closeness I have with my friends' moms. I would never hesitate to pick up the phone and call them if I ever needed anything. That is an amazing feeling. Another wonderful aspect of the book club was that it included people from different aspects of my life so I have been able to maintain relationships with people that I might otherwise have lost touch with over the years.

Over the life of our club, mother-daughter pairs moved away and others lost interest and dropped out. We wanted to make sure we would always have a critical mass when we met so over the years we added new members: Jennifer Green and her mom, Cheryl; Shannon Sanders and her mom, Monice; Brittany Lattisaw and her mom, Ardawn; Nikki Jourdain-Earl and her mom, Judy; Rachel Charity and her mom, Gail; and Mariel Fernandez and her mom, Nurial, all joined us on our journey.

I am now twenty years old and a sophomore at Cornell College in Iowa where my majors are Psychology and possibly Business. I am currently treasurer of the Black Awareness Culture Organization at my school as well as a member of the cheerleading squad and the women's golf team. I work on the Alumni Phone-a-thon, which is a blast because

I get to talk to students from the past about Cornell. The most interesting are the people who attended Cornell before the OCAAT (One Course at a Time) was instituted. OCAAT is what attracted me to Cornell. You take one class at a time for three and a half weeks and then you have fours days off (Block Break). After each block break, you start all over again with a new class. Since most of the classes are capped at twenty-five students, I enjoy a classroom setting that is personal and intimate. Cornell is a great fit for me because it works really well for how I learn.

While our book club is no longer active, we have started having an annual holiday party during our Christmas break from college. It is a fun time, where we all get together and talk about what everyone has been doing and current issues in our lives. This year we even pulled out some of the old tapes from the first book tour. It was a great time for all the girls and moms to relax and catch up.

Here is what some of the voices throughout the book are now doing: Brittney Fraser is a sophomore at Stanford and loving it. Rachel Charity, one of my best friends who joined after we wrote the book, is a freshman at Clemson and is really enjoying the South. Jamexis Christian is a junior at Boston College and just finished spending a semester in London. Jen Green is a sophomore at Hofstra and is majoring in Marketing. Rebecca Chastang just moved back to D.C. from New Jersey and is in her junior year at Brown. Shannon Sanders is a junior, at Spelman along with Nikki Jourdain-Earl who is also a junior and they are both doing great. Maya Yette is a freshman at Wake Forest with a focus on Communications. Ashley Speights is a sophomore at the University of Virginia and recently pledged Delta Gamma. Mariel Fernandez is a sophomore at the University of Chicago. Brittany Lattisaw is currently at Haverford. Holly Thomas is a freshman at McDaniel, majoring in History.

While so much has changed, one of my favorite books is still *The Ear, the Eye, and the Arm* by Nancy Farmer, which was the first book the original Mother-Daughter Book Club read.

What mother doesn't have a secret agenda as we go about plotting good times for our children? The family vacations, the slumber parties, the new diary. Sometimes we yearn to give them what we didn't have at their age. Sometimes we hope to fan an ember of memory into a glow to warm the rest of their lives. No matter what we had in mind, the reality always holds some surprises.

When I first thought of organizing the Mother-Daughter Book Club, I'll admit I had an agenda. It wasn't creating memories that motivated me, although I hoped that would be a benefit. And it wasn't as if I had some soulful longing for literary discussion, though I've always enjoyed the company of women and girls. No, my motivation was planted very firmly in the here and now.

My daughter Morgan had just turned nine years old, and we enjoyed the full range of emotions and dialogue you might expect of two creative, determined females with a generation between them. It seemed we were constantly butting heads over everyday things. More and more, I realized that I needed—and wanted—to find a way to spend some special time with Morgan that would help us understand each other better and give us a close relationship as she grew up.

"I spend time with each of my children, one-on-one, but I like the Mother-Daughter Book Club because it is not just you and the child, but a group of peers and parents all having something in common. And all of us are interested in wanting to build more of a relationship between mother and daughter."

Alice

WHAT IS IT ABOUT GIRLS . . .

Like a lot of other mothers, I was beginning to ask myself: "How do you know what girls are actually thinking about? How do you plant the seeds of the values you want to take hold in their lives if they won't listen to you when you talk to them one-on-one?"

Another mother of a preteen daughter put it this way: "We can be standing on the same square foot of earth, looking up at the same sky, and we still manage to see things differently. We get along fine, but I suspect that when it comes to knowing what she's really thinking about things, the truth is often I don't have a clue."

All of us—mothers and daughters alike—do see things differently. Not only that, we actually *see different things*. It's like what happens at the checkout line at the supermarket when you're waiting there, confronted with tabloids and magazines with headlines that shout about every conceivable angle on life: how to get a man, how to please a man, how to diet, how to dress for success from the boardroom to the bedroom, how to have great sex, how to flatten your stomach, thin your thighs, quit smoking—the headlines go on and on and on. I'm gazing at those covers and not giving them a second thought. I know fact from fiction when it comes to suggestions about my body, my relationships, and my life. But when Morgan, or the girl behind us, reads those covers, what happens to all those lifestyle messages, those images of flawless supermodels and carousing celebrities? Our girls don't need books to be readers. They're reading the world everywhere they go, from the checkout line to the television screen. All day our daughters are gathering images and ideas about the world, about themselves, and about their futures.

ON READING AND DISCUSSION

It's really good to get children actively reading. Their minds are working all the time, so ask them a question and encourage them to go a bit further.

"Every now and then, in the structured, yet informal, atmosphere of our book club, we reveal to one another some bit of personal, family, or world history that we never shared before. Those, to me, are among the most precious moments of the Mother-Daughter Book Club experience."

SHERRY

"Our generation shares its experiences and views, and our daughters have a very different generational perspective. In some discussions, this generational divide is apparent, and in others, personal attitudes that have nothing to do with age generation drive the conversation."

KRIS

It's especially meaningful for a girl, because I think in school girls still tend to be a little reticent and hesitate to speak up. In this safe setting, talking about literature with friends and with her mother, the child can learn how to express her ideas and feelings openly. The experience of being listened to is terribly important. If a mother can do that for her daughter, then she is helping her develop the basis for confidence in her own power to think and to look at things.

Sometimes children are locked into their own realities. They can become trapped in their own perceptions. One of the great positive and liberating things about discussing a rich story is seeing all the different ways of looking at it that people in the group bring. It can be highly motivating, a kind of revelation for the child.

Start with their ideas and show that you really value what they have to say, and then gently go beyond the initial response. Ask, "Can you explain that further, show us where you got that idea?" a very gentle but consistent drawing out.

Generally, children really do blossom when they're listened to.

— ALICE LETVIN, FORMER PRESIDENT,
The Great Books Foundation

As caring mothers, we want to know what they're making of it. Sometimes we do know. Sometimes we just wish we did, maybe with the hope that if we knew what they were thinking we could cheer on the conclusions we like and change the ones we don't. Direct questions don't get you anywhere, either. What does a girl think about the glimpses of life she sees or hears each day in advertising, on television, and in popular music? What does she make of it all?

> "You always have these great goals of doing something special with your child, and then the laundry comes up. Having the structure of the book club seems like a nice way to spend some time with your daughter and her friends and see what they're thinking about."
>
> Leslye

"Nothing," shrugs Morgan, then eleven.

I don't believe that. But I do believe that's precisely what most girls would say if you asked them. They *don't* know what they're making of it. As their mothers, we're finding out the hard way—from our own experiences or those of families around us—that the culture imposes harshly on our girls' views of themselves, of us, and of their prospects for the future.

In *Reviving Ophelia: Saving the Selves of Adolescent Girls*, author Mary Pipher, a clinical psychologist, tells us something most of us already know in our hearts:

"In order to keep their true selves and grow into healthy adults, girls need love from family and friends, meaningful work, respect, challenges, and physical and psychological safety. They need identities based on talents or interests rather than appearance, popularity or sexuality. They need good habits for coping with stress, self-nurturing skills and a sense of purpose and perspective. They need quiet places and times. They need to feel that they are part of something larger than their own lives and that they are emotionally connected to the whole."

Other formal studies deliver similar conclusions. Despite some differences in cultural attitudes among girls of different races or ethnic groups, one common theme comes through loud and clear: Life circumstances and the messages girls absorb from their world shape their attitudes about themselves and other girls.

So, if our life circumstances include the scream of high-tech audio-video-electronic cultural influences, how can the calm, purposeful pursuit of books and conversation begin to make a significant difference?

> "In the group, I can be the mom, or the professional, or the 'aunt,' if you will, to the other girls—and they get to see various sides of me—we see different sides of each other, and that is good."
>
> *Alexis*

WHAT IS IT ABOUT BOOKS . . .

Books have always been a refuge, a place where we put aside the routine of the day and step into someone else's story, where we can laugh, cry, gasp, or wonder at the goings-on without being responsible for any of it. The story's success doesn't depend on our wisdom or patience; the main character isn't waiting for us to drive her to dance class or pick up poster board for a homework assignment.

Books are a great equalizer. You may not have the money to travel the world, but with a library card as your passport your horizons for exploration and self-discovery are unlimited.

MOTHERS AND DAUGHTERS CREATING A CIRCLE OF CARING, SHARING

I would like to think that the Mother-Daughter Book Club would be a time for mothers to share stories of their own childhood. I look at my own nieces and nephews and I tell them stories, and they look through our family album and they laugh. There is a time perhaps for some sharing to go on.

In *Addy* there's a part about double Dutch jumping rope, you know, and when I'm talking to groups of moms and girls, the jumping rope is something these mothers remember from when they were girls. But a lot of the kids are shocked to learn that their mothers jumped rope—that they learned double Dutch. They kind of look at you as being grown, and a woman, and they never see you were a child, a child with weird hair and weird clothes. And you can say, "I've gone through what you're going through."

There's that age when they start to believe that their lives are drastically different from any other life on the planet and they need to understand that their moms went through the same things.

It's natural to start pulling away at that age—you're forming who you are—and sometimes there needs to be some distance to let you be the woman you're going to become, but if you've formed that bond, you can come back to it. That bond will still be there after all that. My mom is one of my best friends. I can talk with her about anything—men, work, anything.

There's this popular culture thing going on where it's, "I hate my mother." Our girls don't have to get that popular notion.

I was talking to a little girl, and we were talking about extended family. She described extended family as "not someone you were born to, but someone who loves you like they were." I really think that's been a continuing part of many communities, a sense

that other people look out for you, care about you. And it's benefi-
cial for everybody, having people who have entered the family that
way. That's what's been lost in society today. We need to find ways
to bring it back.

—CONNIE PORTER, AUTHOR,
The American Girl Collection, Addy series

BOOKS TO GROW ON

Books of undeserved obscurity,
I call them:

The Mouse and His Child
Russell Hoban

The Gammage Cup
Carol Kendall

Drop Dead
Julia Cunningham

Jingo Django
Sid Fleischman

Elidor
Stan Garner

Goody Hall
Natalie Babbitt

—CYNTHIA VOIGT, AUTHOR,
Homecoming

You can visit cultures from around the globe and learn about *anything* that interests you.

Reading can be emotionally freeing as well, as one woman shared with me: "I was a very sick child, alone a lot, and books became my friend," she said. "If you come to a sad place in a book, you can cry and the book doesn't tell you to stop. You can laugh, reading a book, when you might not be able to laugh with other people. If you're shy or sick or just alone, you can experience emotions you couldn't experience any other way."

If you've ever read a book and chatted about it with someone or enjoyed a lively group discussion, then you know that books can be bridges as well. Book talk fills the gentle open spaces of time and distance between friends. It can span generations, and criss-cross the textured geography of differing cultures. It makes a neat, quick plank for conversation with someone new. You don't have to know someone to talk books with them, but when you talk books with someone, you're getting to know them.

When we share the experience of reading with our children, books create a garden, a special sunlit corner where our relationship can grow alongside but apart from the crowded landscape of everyday life.

That's what the Mother-Daughter Book Club is all about. Staking out that special garden space, tending it lightly together, inviting a handful of others to join in, and sharing the harvest of pleasure and discovery. And the growing season never ends!

WHAT IS IT ABOUT LIFE . . .

Our daughters need this growing space. They are partners with us in family life, but as they grow, so does their excitement at the very prospect of growing up and the independence that comes with it. As they search for their own authentic life view, the voice that comes from their own heart, they're listening to the voices all around them: those of family, friends, and teachers, as well as magazine covers, fashion and lifestyle trends, news headlines, and the din of popular culture.

At school—no matter how good the program—they make their way in that tangled wood, on a good day exercising their minds and developing their talents as the culture permits. The forest is thick with the undergrowth of social, emotional, and developmental issues, and it grows thicker as each year progresses.

Academics? In studies conducted by the American Association of University Women, researchers have described the typical school culture as one that teaches our daughters to silence themselves, discounting their learning styles, curbing their questions, and focusing instead upon striving to please.

In short, the confident girl who spoke up with a math answer in September may only occasionally be raising her hand by November and will feign ignorance by December to avoid being branded a "brain."

Even so, the desire for recognition is there and the competition is fierce. Especially as they become increasingly sensitive to boys' reactions, girls may become reluctant to take the intellectual risks—with the potential for failure—that are necessary to build confidence and competence. And the pressure is on whether the girls attend school with boys or with girls only. In their preteen years, girls can become cliquish in the worst ways, imposing social suffering on other girls who differ in any way from the in-group's power brokers that day.

At the end of a long school day, many girls step out the door and into a rush of after-school classes where they pursue their special interests. We juggle car pool duty or on our own get them where they need to go: dance, soccer, music, swimming, drama, art, gymnastics. If

---

BOOKS TO GROW ON

My first memory is *Go, Dog, Go*, the part about the hat. I remember being fascinated by *James and the Giant Peach*.

James and the Giant Peach
Roald Dahl

The Borrowers
Mary Norton

Charlotte's Web
E. B. White

Go, Dog, Go
Philip D. Eastman

Little Women
Louisa May Alcott

—JAMIE LEE CURTIS,
ACTRESS, AUTHOR,
*Tell Me Again About the
Night I Was Born*

we see them at all, it's to pump them up with a snack, pop them into a car, and, between traffic lights, practice our gentle art of motherly interrogation to learn something, *anything*, about their day:

"What did you learn today?" I would ask Morgan on the way home from school. Her reply: "I don't know. Stuff."

Direct questions just never get you anywhere.

Evenings are prime time for conversation. But there's housework, homework, and other preparations for tomorrow's return to the hubbub of work and school. Fortunately for me, Morgan was a night owl, and we shared our reading and chat time at an hour when most of her friends were already asleep. After a typical day, most mothers and daughters we know consider the night a success if they can squeeze in time for a hug and a kiss on the way to sleep.

So, how could *another* organized activity—and a group one, at that—be so satisfying and rewarding? I think it's because a mother-daughter book club doesn't *require*, it *invites*. Instead of obligations, it offers enrichment. It takes what we bring to it—a love

> "When they're on their own and it's girls only, there are different dynamics than in a mixed group with boys. There's a lot more honesty, connecting and sharing."
>
> *Whitney Ransome,*
> *National Coalition*
> *of Girls' Schools*

of reading, lively conversation, and friendship—and amplifies those pleasures. The club format provides just enough structure so we can relax. And into the comfortable familiarity of our circle, it introduces with each book a raft of new characters, with their own ideas and experiences, to broaden our view.

WHAT IS IT ABOUT A MOTHER-DAUGHTER BOOK CLUB . . .

It doesn't matter if you haven't taken time to read a novel in years. Or if your daughter seems to read only when it's assigned at school. Whether or not you or your daughter is a devoted reader, the Mother-Daughter Book Club works because it isn't just about books. And it isn't just about reading or mastering analytical skills. It's about mothers and daughters, girls and women, and how reading and talking together can enrich our relationships with one another and strengthen our daughters' courage to be themselves.

The benefits are real, and we see them in action not only at our meetings, but in the girls' lives at home, at school, and all around.

THE CLUB ENCOURAGES READING

The girls read because they want to. The club motivates the girls to read. Some love reading anyway. But others read because they want to be prepared for the discussion and any activities planned around the book.

"They're not all girls who like to read and have great analytical skills, but they all are excited about coming to socialize," says Linda Chastang. "For the girl who doesn't like to read so much, if she wants to come to that meeting, she's going to read that book."

The before-and-after snapshots of our girls as readers provide some convincing evidence:

"Prior to the Mother-Daughter Book Club, Tiffany's only craving for books was *Goosebumps*," says Winnie Donaldson. "I was glad she was reading anything. But over the past year, the club has encouraged her to want to read other books. She's become a more serious reader. It truly is important to her that she reads the book club book so she'll be prepared to participate in discussion at the meetings."

The girls' approach to reading changes and improves, too, we've noticed.

"She's become a very active reader," says Grace Speights, about her daughter, Ashley. "She'll stop and say something like. 'That's stupid,' or 'Why did that character do that?' and she'll ask about similes or metaphors she doesn't understand. She really asks questions. And I can tell she enjoys it because she'll ask, 'Are we going to read tonight?' and she'll be standing there with the book in hand."

> "Maya and her friends were beginning to have more frequent 'whispered conversations.' Reading the same books has helped us to have more in common as she approaches the age when children begin to distance themselves from their parents."
>
> *Joyce*

CRITICAL THINKING SKILLS GET A WORKOUT

Through discussions of the plots, characters, and authors' writing styles, the girls are learning how to take an idea and pull it apart to see what makes it tick, build on it, question it, find evidence to support their opinion of it, and use that experience to reflect in greater depth on their own lives or the lives of others.

"These kids are really reading these books and connecting things," says Leslye Fraser. "They'll say things like, 'I'd give it an 8.5,' and they'll analyze the good and the bad, and they'll say the author should have done this or that. It's been nice watching

BOOKS TO GROW ON

This is a list of books from my childhood, which was a long time ago, since I am now ninety. Today's children, it seems to me, are missing so much not reading more folk and fairy tales.

English Fairy Tales and *More English Fairy Tales*
Joseph Jacobs

Grimms' Fairy Tales
Jacob and Wilhelm Grimm

Blue Fairy Book and *Red Fairy Book*
Andrew Lang

Heidi
Johanna Spyri

The Secret Garden
Frances Hodgson Burnett

Little Women
Louisa May Alcott

Jane Eyre
Charlotte Brontë

Dandelion Cottage
Carroll Watson Rankin

Downright Dencey
Caroline Dale Sneder

—BEVERLY CLEARY, AUTHOR,
Ramona the Pest

them be in charge, assuming the leadership role with no problem, no fear. And they encourage each other."

It seems like we each see a success story unfolding in our daughter's life.

Alice Thomas recalls how impressed she was the first time she heard her daughter, Holly, hold forth on the book of the day: "I knew she was getting the story okay, but when we got to the meeting and I heard her talking about all these details in the story, and tying them together to make a statement about the character, I was just amazed—I had no idea she was thinking that deeply about it—and I was proud."

These girls, who can't remember to close the door on their way out, nonetheless remember intricate details of plots and characters that pass through our discussion circle:

"I'm always pleasantly surprised at how girls compare characters from book to book, or reflect on different writing styles," says Joyce Yette. "Maybe I should get used to the fact that they're bright and curious, but I wouldn't have imagined these kinds of discussions."

A FRIENDLY FORUM FOR DISCUSSING IMPORTANT ISSUES

By talking about the impersonal—plots, characters, and author's choices—we've heard the girls' candid thoughts on important issues like death and illness, friendship and marriage, family relationships and school and social issues.

"What's been nice is gaining some insight into how they think," Leslye says. "We sometimes take for granted that our children share our life experience—for instance, some of the unhappy things we could all remember from our childhoods—but their comments make it clear that those experiences aren't necessarily part of their lives. That has been a pleasant surprise."

"Some of the issues in the books have been a little delicate, but we talk about them anyway," says Alexis Christian. "If we don't talk about it, who else will? Who do we want the girls to talk about sensitive issues with, if not us?"

A CHANCE TO SEE FRIENDS, MAKE FRIENDS OUTSIDE SCHOOL

The smaller group size and the emotional comfort level of a mother-daughter book club makes it a safe, supportive place for a girl to venture outside the lines she draws for herself each day at school. The combination of laughter, play, and talk creates a natural habitat for learning within a circle of caring mothers.

"It gives the girls an opportunity to discuss books without being under pressure like they are at school, wondering if this is the answer the teacher is looking for," says Kathie Thompson. "In our book club there are no right or wrong answers. You can say what you feel."

Even the girls who are a bit shy, who typically might be reluctant to say what they feel, are finding a voice in our circle.

"This close, supportive setting has provided an excellent opportunity for Maya, who has always been so shy and quiet, to express herself," says her mom, Joyce. "With each meeting, her voice has become a little louder, her eye contact has become a little more direct, and her confidence has grown a little stronger."

Morgan likes the speak-up-and-be-heard atmosphere, too. Says she: "It's much easier than school because you're not writing; you're just talking. A lot of the kids in the club like to talk a lot, so it's nice because that's what we're *supposed* to do!"

STRENGTHENS THE MOTHER-DAUGHTER RELATIONSHIP

Relationships are built on understanding, and this is an easy, gentle way to gain understanding. There are very few regular opportunities in our lives to relax and enjoy one another's company and express our feelings or ideas about what goes on in the world without lecturing.

"One thing I like is that we're able to look at things from a different perspective and try to start helping them think from a different perspective," says Cheryl Brown. "Often the way we phrase our questions is deliberately done so we generate some new thoughts. You don't want to provide answers for the girls, but kind of help them see it differently. A mother can rephrase things, pull ideas out and focus on them, and ask some thought-provoking questions."

Whatever our differences in perspective, the time we share talking at meetings and at home brings us closer to our daughters in ways that feel right.

"The relationship between mothers and daughters in those teen years can get a little strained," Alexis says, "but at this stage, it's a wonderful opportunity for me to actually sit down with Jamexis, even a chance to touch her—stroke her hair, make sure she's okay—it's some real time we can share and be best friends

Takoma Park Mother-Daughter Book Club

The Takoma Park Mother-Daughter Book Group is a club of seven girls and seven mothers, formed when our daughters were six and seven years old. Our girls are now seven and eight and in second and third grade.

We started by reading *The Wheel on the School* by Meindert DeJong and knew at that first meeting that something very special had happened and that this would, indeed, be a journey we would continue on with these girls. They amazed us with their thoughts, their ideas, their enjoyment of the book, their maturity, their memories (!), and their enthusiasm. Since that first book we have met on an almost monthly basis and have enjoyed a variety of books, some more popular than others, but all loved in their own way. After reading *James and the Giant Peach* this summer, we went to a children's performance of the book at Imagination Stage. We had a great discussion afterward about how the characters were brought to life, what the girls would have done differently had *they* been staging it, what they missed from the book, and so on.

We hope we can keep our book group going as long as possible. It is a joy to all of us—mothers and daughters.

Thanks again for the inspiration! My mother bought me your book when my daughter, Eleanor, was born and I was so thrilled when she got to the age where we could think about forming a group.

—*Becky Linafelt, Founder, Takoma Park*
Mother-Daughter Book Club,
Takoma Park, Maryland

because women can become best friends, and hopefully she'll understand she can tell me anything because I plan to tell her everything."

We all share that desire for emotional closeness with our children, and the challenge of creating ways for it to grow.

"It's difficult, because in the normal flow of the parent-child relationship at this age the parent is viewed as the authoritarian who will be angry or upset if you say something wrong," Grace says. "It's hard for them to cross the line—they're thinking, 'This is my mom, but she's also my friend,' and until you have some kind of relationship where you can show that side in a natural way, it's a hard thing to do. This gives us a chance to do that. I want Ashley to view me as a mom who is open and willing to talk about anything that she wants to talk about, no matter what the subject."

> "The funniest thing that happened at a meeting was when we discussed the folk tales in *Her Stories* by Virginia Hamilton, and our moms asked us to describe the man that we would like to marry. Although we had all been very talkative at every meeting, this question from the moms just caused us to giggle."
>
> *Ashley S.*

A WHOLESOME FEELING OF BELONGING

Along with the fun, the group provides affirmation—a feeling of recognition and acceptance—that our adolescent girls need. A story I heard one evening at a Girl Scout board meeting left me and a room full of others in tears, and it tells me we're right to be concerned and we're on the right track with our book discussion club. The speaker told us of a letter she had received from a

HOW CAN WE HELP OUR CHILDREN BECOME ENTHUSIASTIC READERS?

On the one hand, you leave them alone, and on the other, you read with them. Don't force books on children. When I was a child, all my reading was done without any kind of organization, and I try to approach reading in a similar way with my daughter. If I really want her to read something, I may just slip it into her room, but seldom more than that. Because if they discover it on their own, it's what they want.

And don't be too worried about what they choose. There are protests from time to time about certain children's books: Parents think they are too cruel, too this, too that. Usually, these are the books that children love most. Children really do want to know how to deal with life; they want those truths. And you have to let them discover a book that gives them a way to incorporate such lessons into life, and that also gives them some pleasure in the hard truth.

The second part of the solution is to read with them. It sounds so corny, but it's true: If you make that time to sit down and read them something, and not just when they are little and can't read, but when they are older and can read, and you read together, it makes all the difference in the world.

Eventually, they will get to the point where they think it's uncool to do that. Then you find something that's really funny, and you read it aloud in parts. Or, when you find that they don't want you to read something to them, then you just read it, too. So you say: "We're going to read this book: You read it, and I'm going to read it, and then we can talk about it." Now of course, when you talk about it, you don't do it in any kind of quiz way, you just talk about it. I've found that this really works.

For instance, my daughter is now falling into the *Star Trek* age, and she is reading some of those books, and they are horrible books. But I'm reading the *Star Trek* books, too, because then I can talk to her about them. And when we talk about those, then we can also talk about *Sophie's World* and the other good books, which she also reads. I try not to convey any sense that I'm too good to talk about those other books. And if I feel tempted, as I sometimes do, to say something like: "You know, these are really terrible books," I remember my comic books and *Mad* magazine, and I bite my lip.

—RITA DOVE, FORMER U.S. POET LAUREATE

college girl—a former Girl Scout. The young woman had written that she was sitting at her desk at 3 a.m., her roommate in the throes of an emotional crisis, feelings of despair thick in the dormitory room. She wrote about the emotional tempests of college life, but added that she was keeping an even keel, and concluded that it was her experience as a Girl Scout that had given her a strong, sure belief in herself. There really are very few places where girls get that message of affirmation in a continuing way. Our Mother-Daughter Book Club does that for our daughters.

The Mother-Daughter Book Club provides a kind of balance to the life our girls experience at school and the view they see of mothers at home or at work. They even experience *each other* differently than they do in other settings.

"We don't all go to the same school and see each other every day, so when we get together, it's like a party, and you play and play until it's time to go home," says Holly Thomas, ten. "The book discussion is fun, so it's like part of the party."

"It's really nice if you like reading *and* if you want to make more friends *and* if you want to get to know people better," says Maya Yette, ten. "It's fun to get to play at other people's houses more."

> "It gives you the chance to talk about the books so you're not just reading them and putting them down. You're really understanding."
> Maya

Those simple thoughts ring true. Even the girls who knew one another well have seen their relationships flower around our meeting discussions.

"My favorite part of the book club meetings is the social part, when we eat and talk and play games," says Rebecca Chastang, eleven. "The books are okay, too."

Our reading, meetings, and discussion allow our girls the freedom to focus on:

SHARING INSTEAD OF COMPETITION: There's eagerness in the discussion but never a race to see who can "win" the race to give a right answer. "In school, there's always a right and wrong answer, so usually I don't answer if I think I might get it wrong,'" says Brittney Fraser, ten. "This was new to me—I was nervous at first because I thought everybody was going to say 'No!' like they do in class. But they didn't."

REFLECTION INSTEAD OF PERFORMANCE: By posing questions that draw on the girls' experience as well as their understanding of a story, the discussion invites thought and comment. It encourages reflection, because the more thought you put into an answer, the more everyone responds to it, and that's an immediate source of enjoyment for everyone. "When we read the book *The Friends* by Rosa Guy, I liked that book," says Ashley Brown, twelve. "The fact that it talks about friendship and how there are problems sometimes, but you can work things out. It made me think about my friends."

ACCEPTANCE INSTEAD OF JUDGMENT: Discussion offers a safe haven for expression. Since every perspective is valuable in an open discussion, each person's comments receive the same respect and acknowledgment. Some comments lead to more vigorous discussion than others, but it's not because the comment is good or bad. It's the chemistry of the moment, and the girls quickly become comfortable in that judgment-free zone. "I never knew it was so easy to express your opinions," says Ashley Speights, ten. "I used to be very shy about that, but now it doesn't seem so hard to say what I think about something."

📖 **EXPLORATION INSTEAD OF MASTERY:** The shy one can speak without fear of ridicule, and the perfectionist learns to share her full rainbow of ideas instead of narrowing her contributions to just "the right answer." The careful exploration of ideas helps girls develop a sense of mastery, a comfort level with critical thinking skills that they need to hold their own in other circles or circumstances. "When we're all talking about the same book, some people have different ideas and it opens up a new perspective you didn't even think about, and then you listen and understand it." says Jamexis Christian, twelve.

📖 **EXPERIENCE INSTEAD OF OBJECTIVES:** In most other realms of our lives we face a constant pressure to achieve results: meet deadlines, make good grades, meet expectations of our own or of others. You can't make an A in the Mother-Daughter Book Club: There is no performance review. The experience is what there is, all there is, and it is the experience that teaches us the most about the books and about ourselves. "Discussing the book is my favorite part of the meeting," says Jihan Thompson, twelve. "Sometimes the mothers might bring up a topic, and people will say how they feel about it or give their views on the book. It's really fun to get different people's insights on it."

📖 **SEEING MOTHERS AS INDIVIDUALS INSTEAD OF EXPERTS OR MANAGERS:** Mothers enjoy the same respectful treatment as every member of the discussion group, and that sense of equality in this setting allows our girls to see us more as individuals, as interesting women with thoughts to share. Here, our years of life experience don't make us "boss." Our experience only adds to the richness of the conversation.

It didn't take Morgan long to warm up to some real conversation. "At our very first meeting, some of us weren't so

BOOKS TO GROW ON

Some of these came from my "Women Writing in French"
course. Others came from my work on women and girls and
general reading.

So Long a Letter
Manama Ba

Mother to Daughter, Daughter to Mother
edited by Tillie Olsen

*Meeting at the Crossroads: Women's Psychology
and Girls' Development*
Lyn Mikel Brown and Carol Gilligan

The Book of the City of Ladies
Christine de Pizan

The Lais of Marie de France
Marie de France

Women's Friendships: A Collection of Short Stories,
edited by Susan Koppelman

Between Mothers and Daughters: Stories Across a Generation,
edited by Susan Koppelman

—ELLEN SILBER,
Director of the Marymount Institute for
the Education of Women and Girls

used to doing things like this with our moms, but once we got started talking, it just started flowing and then it was just great," Morgan says. "Now it's always that way."

The fact that we're all so busy, mothers and daughters alike, makes it a special experience when we simply sit down in a place together to talk—instead of *to get something done.*

"I have homework, and she has work and Girl Scouts," says Tiffany Donaldson, eleven, whose mother, Winnie, is a Girl Scout leader, among other things. "When I'm home, I'm reading or working on homework and she's doing Girl Scouts and other stuff, so I pretty much don't get to talk to her. I like hearing her ideas about our books at the meetings."

What's in it for us, the mothers? Some of the benefits are those we had in mind when we started—dreams come true:

📖 We express ourselves as individuals, beyond our roles in the family, community, or workplace.

📖 We treasure this special time with our daughters outside the flurry of family life.

📖 We enjoy the company of women and girls with a similar interest in exploring literature and the world of ideas and intellectual exchange. "As we explore places we probably will never visit, talk about things that probably would not come up in the ordinary course of our lives, get to know characters unlike any we'd ever meet, and share our thoughts and experiences with other mothers and their daughters," Linda says, "we have grown closer and we have learned a lot about each other—how alike and different we are, and how much we learn from each other."

MOTHER-DAUGHTER BOOK CLUB:
OPEN MINDS, OPEN VOICES

Look at a group of eleven-, twelve-, thirteen-year-old girls—it's a hoot! They laugh, they're spontaneous, they're joyful, they're loving, they take pleasure in a wide variety of things. Girls go through a critical passage from age eleven to fourteen—fifth grade through ninth grade. They begin with a tremendous amount of interest and enthusiasm, pleasure in the things around them and themselves.

Then, as they start to make the transition between girlhood and young womanhood, it's like walking through a minefield, in terms of the images before them about how they should look, how they should act, what they wear, what they think, what they do. All of that begins to narrow and limit how they perceive themselves. They don't start out that way. It's our job to help them keep that spontaneity.

—WHITNEY RANSOME,
COEXECUTIVE DIRECTOR,
National Coalition of Girls' Schools

> "I like sitting in a room filled with girls and their moms and knowing that I will not be judged for what I say. I don't have to worry about whether others agree with me or not. At book club meetings, nothing you say can be wrong, whereas in school, there is often only one right answer. In book club, we find a way to take in what each member says and see it all as the right answer. Your voice can always be heard."
>
> BROOKE

Beyond those gifts was a surprise that I never anticipated that day I took my quiet agenda of hope and put it into action: the experience of discovering *myself*, the *woman* at the heart of the mother, daughter, wife, sister, colleague, and friend that I am to others. Through reading and chatting with Morgan, and exploring our stories together with the women and girls in our group, it's as if we're picking up our threads of experience, some old, some new, and weaving them into the fabric of our lives today. It is a comfortable cloth, with texture and color, and it has the feel of truth.

A mother-daughter book club gives you and your daughter the space in your relationship and your schedules to do all this, and you don't have to be an "expert" to make it happen. You don't need a college degree in literature, and your daughter doesn't have to get A's in reading at school to enjoy a mother-daughter book club. You've already got all you need: a desire to spend some quality time with your daughter and a willingness to do something about it!

ENDNOTES

📖 Literature and discussion can strengthen the bond between mothers and daughters.

> "My mom and I can also discuss the books outside of the meetings, which helps us learn about each other in ways we might not otherwise. I share a new bond with my mom due to the book club and the discussions and ideas that come out of it."
>
> *Brooke*

"It has helped me because we can relate to one another better. Now we have all these little things to discuss and argue about. The material from book club gives us an outlet, a chance to sit down and focus so we don't have to be worrying about all those little things."

Sylvie

📖 A mother-daughter book club encourages reading.

"Being in a book club has pushed me to read books I would not otherwise read, and I am glad."

Riley

"Until our mother-daughter book club read *The Curious Incident of the Dog in the Night-time* by Marc Haddon, I would have never known I had an interest in mysteries."

Celia

📖 The reading club format gives girls a chance to develop critical thinking skills outside the classroom.

📖 An intimate circle of mothers, daughters, and friends provides a sense of affirmation and a place to be heard.

"I actually enjoy talking in big groups of people and letting my ideas be heard."

Jesse

"I feel so comfortable talking about books with our book club because I know the people around me genuinely care what I have to say."

Hannah

TWO

How to Organize Your Book Club

THE READING AND DISCUSSION GROUP IS AS ENDURING AS THE WRITTEN WORD, FOR AS LONG AS WORDS HAVE BEEN WRITTEN, PEOPLE HAVE READ, CONTEMPLATED AND GATHERED TO TALK ABOUT THEM.

—ALAN MOORES, RHEA RUBIN
"Let's Talk About It," American Library Association

Skylar Fykes & Shireen Dodson

Hi, my name is Skylar Shireen Fykes. I'm fifteen and a sophomore at Georgetown Day School in Washington, D.C. I have a sister, Morgan, who is twenty. Everyone says we look just alike, but I don't see the resemblance at all. I also have a brother named Leroy, who is twenty-five. I enjoy being the youngest because I have been able to learn from my older siblings' mistakes.

I don't have a favorite book. I have read so many books that I love that I cannot choose one to call my favorite. There are also too many different kinds of books, "magical" books as opposed to books about real people in real situations. When it comes to "magical" books, I loved the Harry Potter books (I was one of those crazy kids lined up at midnight to see the movie, too); I also loved *The Golden Compass, The Subtle Knife,* and *The Amber Spyglass* by Philip Pullman. I also like "trashy" books like the Gossip Girl series and *The A-List* by Zoey Dean. I loved *The Sisterhood of the Traveling Pants.*

Most of the time the books that I read inspire me to do things I wouldn't have done otherwise. For example, I might be tempted to try foods or music mentioned in the book. *The Sisterhood of the Traveling Pants* inspired me to create traveling pants with two of my best friends from camp. We met at debate camp over the summer at Stanford University and we were really sad about leaving each other. We collectively came up with the pants idea. The pants were Hadley's, who lives in Missouri. The third sister is Audrey, who lives in California. Every month, we mail the pants to each other along with letters of what happened while we were wearing the pants. But unlike the book we do wash the pants! It's our way of keeping in touch with each other.

I am active in organizations inside and outside of school. In school I am in Black Culture Club, Young Women of Color, Step

Team, Monday Night Tutoring, Rapture (a gospel singing group), Debate Team, and I take photos for the *Augar Bit*, my school newspaper. I also play varsity soccer and track. Outside of school I am in Jack and Jill, where I am the co-head of the community service group.

My favorite groups are the Step Team, Rapture, and soccer. I love performing more than anything. It gives me such a rush when I am on stage stepping or singing. There is nothing comparable to the feeling you get when the crowd goes wild. There is a similar feeling when I score a goal in a soccer game and the adrenaline is pumping. I love any type of competition because I am a very competitive person.

I love eating and shopping. I love all types of food. It's all amazing. There must be four billion different ways to cook chicken, and before I die I want to try them all. I love shopping because who doesn't? I love bargains. A $100 pair of shoes on sale for $30. Yes! It just doesn't get any better than that. Also who doesn't love a good party? It's amazing when friends get together to hang out, dance, eat, sing, watch a movie, cry. It's all good.

My mom is Shireen Dodson. As you have already read, she is the mom behind the whole mother-daughter book club movement. My middle name is my mom's first name, which is pretty cool because Shireen is a pretty name. My mom and I disagree a lot on what I am allowed to do, but it has gotten better since the beginning of the mother-daughter book club. It's easier to talk to her now because I have a better understanding of some of the things that she has been through as a person. My mom and dad have just recently separated so we have been spending more and more time together. I'm not going to lie; it has been frustrating especially when articles like "The Secret Life of Teens" come out in a local magazine and my mom wants to talk about the same issues over and over again. But I must admit usually after we have a discussion about the issue at hand we have reinforced another layer of trust.

If you've ever planned a birthday party, you can organize a mother-daughter book club.

I don't mean to make it sound overly easy. It does take some careful thought and planning. But organizing a book club is actually simpler than the administrative job most of us do each week to juggle everyone's schedules and expectations. And there are some very nice differences: First, the organizing task itself is something enjoyable to do with your daughter. And second, unlike the cluttered closets, family meals, or after-school activity schedule, your book club needs to be organized only once!

> "The books are long and they're boring in the beginning. But they get interesting in the middle and the end."
>
> *Brittney*

It helps to think about your Mother-Daughter Book Club in its essential terms right from the start. What is "the most important thing" about your club? What do you want it to accomplish?

My reasons for wanting to start a book discussion club were fairly straightforward. I saw a mother-daughter book club as a way to spend some special time with Morgan, doing something that would get us talking and listening to each other and enjoying the company of other mothers and daughters with similar reading interests. Surprisingly, ten years later, my reasons for starting a club with my second daughter would be exactly the same.

Think about your reasons. Whatever they are, it's important that you keep them in mind as you organize your club, inviting members, establishing meeting times, compiling a book list from which the girls will choose their selections. Each of these choices will influence the personality of your club and the direction it takes over time. Each step deserves some careful thought.

YOUR MOTHER-DAUGHTER PARTNERSHIP: READY, SET . . .

First impressions are important. The way you introduce the idea of the mother-daughter book club to your daughter may make or break your case, so think about the best way to present it to get the response you want—that excited "yes!"

We all bring more enthusiasm to things when we feel we've made a choice to be involved. The partnership you need with your daughter to start a mother-daughter book club will work only if your daughter wants to do it. If your daughter routinely rejoices at your suggestions for how she should spend her free time, then consider yourself indeed blessed and carry on. If, however, your daughter routinely or even occasionally resists activities you request, or even those you simply suggest, then don't do either. Try wondering out loud. In politics, they call it "floating a trial balloon." To test a potentially controversial idea at a safe distance from any negative fallout, politicians will see to it that somebody leaks the idea to the media. If it gets a positive response, they run up to claim it and carry it forward. If it gets a negative response, they listen from a distance and use the criticism to guide them as they modify the idea for a more successful introduction.

For mothers, that process boils down to one step: Choose

> "Nobody ever says, 'That's dumb.' The moms and girls encourage each other."
>
> *Joyce*

Tips from the Girls on Organizing a Mother-Daughter Book Club

"It is important not only to pick books consistently that are fun to read and discuss, but to also have a group of women who enjoy each other's company."
— BRITTNEY

"Have a good number of people because sometimes some people don't show up."
— JIHAN

"I would plan to have the girls close in age or grade. There is a big difference between a sixth grader and a fourth grader, in terms of their interests and reading abilities. However, it has been nice to get to know and socialize with the younger girls in our book club."
— REBECCA

"Good food is important."
— MORGAN

"Make sure the meeting time is consistent."
— RACHEL

words that make it easy for your daughter to say yes. If your experience is anything like mine, that means making an idea attractive to your daughter, never mind all the reasons that make
it an attractive idea to you.

For example, here are two different ways to suggest to your
daughter that you two start a mother-daughter book club. As
you read them, imagine your daughter's reaction:

STYLE # 1

*Mother: "I've got a great idea. Let's start a mother-daughter
book club. We can assign books that are better literature
than those paperbacks you read all the time. It'll give us all
a chance to talk about the really important issues in life. And
when you hear the other mothers' opinions, you'll see I'm not
the only one who thinks the way I do."*

I can hear the footsteps fade as she runs in the other
direction.

STYLE # 2

*Mother: "What would you think of inviting a group of your
friends and their moms to read books, and then have a get-
together with refreshments where you girls could relax and
we'd all get to share what we thought about the story and do
some fun activity with it?"*

Style #2 was my choice, and Morgan took off running—to
get the pencil and paper to make her list and start her invitations.

"I thought it was a good idea because usually you don't
get to spend a lot of time with your mom, so I liked having

"Murch" Mother-Daughter Book Club

We began in the spring of 1998—the girls were second-semester fourth graders, about nine and a half years old. There were five girls and their moms. We were all at Murch elementary school in upper northwest, Washington, D.C. I had a friend who was in a mother-daughter book club and I had heard about your book. I began to think about starting a club and talked to a couple of moms, and we got it going. The girls all knew each other, but they weren't each other's best friends. We met about every six weeks on Sunday afternoons, rotating houses. The host girl came up with discussion questions. In the beginning the girls were quiet and would raise their hands to answer. As they got older, they were more comfort-able with free-form discussion. We moms had to be careful some-times not to talk too much. Our meetings generally lasted about sixty to ninety minutes with a good forty-five minutes spent discuss-ing the book. The rest of the time the girls played and talked among themselves while the moms had time to chat with each other over cookies or brownies.

By the time the girls were in sixth grade, two girls attended different schools, but everyone stayed in the book club, which was a way for them all to remain connected. Some of our best meet-ings were those at which we acted out scenes from the book. For example, we read *Tom Sawyer* one summer (we didn't meet in July and August). On Labor Day weekend we got together at a house with a pool. The pool became the Mississippi River and an air mat-tress became the raft, and the girls acted out various scenes. When we read *Jacob Have I Loved*, each group member drew a name of a character and answered questions and participated in the discus-sion "in character." One time we went to hear Virginia Euwer Wolff read and talk about her book—*True Believer*. We all enjoyed that book and then went back and read *Make Lemonade*, the sequel. I particularly liked these two books because the mother was such a strong character. In several of the books we read, such as *Speak* and *The Woman in the Wall*, we moms wondered, "Where are the parents?"

We generally chose books the girls had not read. I did a lot of prereading of many children's/young adult literature and referred to *100 Books for Girls to Grow On*. It was important that at least one adult read the book so we knew what we were getting into. As the girls got older and their school work increased, they had less time for pleasure reading. By the time they started the eleventh grade, they all had busy schedules and it was harder to get together. For our final meeting the moms reminisced about how much our daughters had grown, how much we all enjoyed getting together, how the girls all still got along, and we resolved to get together one more time after they graduated from high school.

Some of our favorite books were *Out of the Dust, Baby, Stargirl, Walk Two Moons, Speak, The House on Mango Street*, and *The Lovely Bones*. A Wrinkle in Time was not popular among many of the moms—science fiction wasn't a favorite of our club.

—*Monica McGowan, Founder, "Murch"*
Mother-Daughter Book Club
Washington, D.C., 2005

something where I could spend time with my mom and with my friends." Morgan says.

What if your daughter hands you a negative response even with a positive introduction? She wouldn't be the first skeptic in the crowd.

"I thought, 'Oh no, here goes another thing,'" recalls Brittney. "I thought piano was going to be fun, and it turned out not to be. I thought basketball was going to be fun, and it turned out not to be. I thought soccer and softball were going to be fun, and they weren't. And I thought swimming was supposed to be fun, and it turned out to be quite boring. So I thought, 'Oh no, another thing I have to go to.'"

If your daughter balks, find out why. Listen to her reasons. You may discover that she doesn't understand the idea or thinks it would be more challenging or demanding than it really is. You may discover that she has personal reservations about reading or about socializing that deserve your attention. You both may discover that through talking about her response, you can identify the parts of the idea that *do* sound exciting, and use those to define the terms for your mother-daughter book club. If she really seems opposed to the idea, then drop it! Suggest the idea to another mother, and see if your daughter changes her mind when she gets an invitation in the mail to join her friends.

> "Our Mother-Daughter Book Club has been everything I thought it might be, and maybe a little more, because I didn't imagine in the beginning that the girls would bring about the depth of discussion that they have."
>
> *Alice*

My point here is not to tell you how to talk with your

daughter but to suggest that our efforts to communicate with our daughters work best when we try to see the moment through their eyes. That's a big part of what the Mother-Daughter Book Club is about—listening to our girls and truly sharing the experience instead of directing it. As a woman and mother with a take-charge habit, it has taken me some time, and practice, to learn when to hit my pause button and listen: *listen* to my daughter's words and, with a caring heart, *hear* what she is saying.

Once the idea has the unanimous approval of the two of you, it's time to find some good company.

GIRL BY GIRL, MOM BY MOM: BUILDING A DISCUSSION GROUP

We're always instructing our girls to be inclusive, to keep the circle open as they play at recess or after school, or as they make their way through life. And I bristle when I hear about girls and cliques at school, or remember them from my own girlhood.

So when Morgan and I sat down to discuss whom to invite to be in our Mother-Daughter Book Club, the fact that we were "picking" people seemed right and wrong at the same time. Why not invite all of Morgan's closest friends? Why not include those mothers with whom I had a close friendship, even if the girls weren't particularly close? Our "open door" policy had always served us well in the past. Why select a group now?

For the answer, go back to your original reasons for wanting to start a mother-daughter book club. For us, one of my motivations was the thought that this group would give Morgan and me an opportunity to spend time with each other and some friends we didn't see very often, exploring a common element of

BOOKS TO GROW ON

I've simply selected books that I enjoyed reading at the time and that I find returning to my thoughts again and again. All of the books are thought-provoking and should be great discussion books. They range from serious to whimsical, from fact to fantasy. Although *Mrs. Mike*, published in 1947, may seem a bit out of place, I had to include it as it was my favorite book as a young girl. I first read it when I was in sixth grade and continued to read it at least once a year well into college.

Mrs. Mike
Benedict Freedman

The Giver
Lois Lowry

The Man from the Other Side
Uri Orlev

Dealing with Dragons
Patricia C. Wrede

Louisa May: The World and Works of Louisa May Alcott
Norma Johnston

Grace
Jill Paton Walsh

The Bomb
Theodore Taylor

Running Out of Time
Margaret Peterson Haddix

—BARBARA J. MCKILLIP,
FOUNDER AND PRESIDENT,
The Libri Foundation

our lives—our African American heritage. At first we planned to focus completely on books by African American authors or about the black experience. Our reading selections quickly expanded beyond that original idea, to reflect our full range of interests. But the composition of the group—all African American mothers and daughters—has become a wonderful source of support and experience of our cultural heritage, a theme that is missing from the girls' school programs and extracurricular activities, where they most often are a small racial minority.

> **BOOKS TO GROW ON**
>
> These are books from my childhood that I still love to read:
>
> *The Bible*
>
> *Winnie the Pooh*
> A. A. Milne
>
> *The Secret Garden*
> Frances Hodgson Burnett
>
> *The Yearling*
> Marjorie Kinnan Rawlings
>
> *A Tale of Two Cities*
> Charles Dickens
>
> —KATHERINE PATERSON, AUTHOR, *Bridge to Terabithia*

Whatever your vision for the group, whether you plan to invite only girls and mothers you know well or post your invitation on a library or Sunday school bulletin board for an open enrollment, you're hoping that the individuals who respond will be a "good fit." That doesn't mean they should all think alike. It does mean that they need to share the vision or goals you have for your group; they should be able to participate in the group's reading, discussion, and activities in a meaningful way, and they should be able to follow through on any commitment they make to host or help coordinate the group meetings.

Some qualities that contribute to a "good fit" include:

📖 An interest in reading

📖 Reading skill level that makes reading a pleasurable activity

📖 Age or grade level close to the others

📖 Maturity level in the range necessary to participate fully in the reading, discussion, and related activities

📖 Comfort in discussion

📖 A cooperative attitude

📖 An acquaintance or friendship with others in the group

📖 An interesting mix of viewpoints for the mothers, including differences of opinion shaped by each woman's life experience. It's best if every mother can be up-front about any personal sensitivities—religious, political, or otherwise—that would influence her enjoyment of the group or otherwise affect the group.

📖 If you want to create a group that shares a special interest or objective, think of girls who bring that particular life experience or reading interest to the group. (See Chapter Nine: "Using Themes to Guide Choices.")

This process of selecting whom to invite is an opportunity to help your daughter learn about team building. They get plenty of experience in team*work* in their other school and after-school activities: cooperative learning projects at school, dance class, soccer teams, Girl Scouts. All of them offer wonderful opportunities for girls to gather together and experience the challenges and delights of playing, performing, or working toward a goal in a cooperative way.

BOOKS TO GROW ON

Over the years there have been a number of books that my daughters and I have enjoyed. The following is a list of some of our favorites:

Little Women
Louisa May Alcott

Anne Frank: The Diary of a Young Girl
Anne Frank

Charlotte's Web
E. B. White

The Nancy Drew series
Carolyn Keene

Little House on the Prairie
Laura Ingalls Wilder

I also recommend the biographies of such influential women as Eleanor Roosevelt, Olympic legend Wilma Rudolph, and Susan B. Anthony, and also the writings of Maya Angelou. The lives of these women can serve as a source of inspiration to us all.

— TIPPER GORE

Team *building* is different. It requires that you think about your goal and think about the qualities needed for the team to work well. In terms of a mother-daughter book club, it's important to aim for a lively yet harmonious blend of personalities and talents. All of our friends have special qualities. It's a matter of thinking about them, and tapping those girls and mothers who seem most likely to enjoy and enable others to enjoy good books, relaxed socializing, and stimulating discussion.

This is another opportunity to listen to our daughters and show some trust, be willing to take a chance on their judgment. Morgan was absolutely determined that one of her younger friends—an eight-year-old girl who was not an avid reader— be invited to join the group. I resisted at first, believing that she simply wasn't quite ready to participate in a book discussion group. As it turned out, the mother and daughter were so enthusiastic about the idea that both were willing to put in extra effort to tackle the challenging reading assignments. And the perspectives and creativity they have brought to the group are cherished. Morgan *knew;* I listened and learned.

THE MORE THE MERRIER . . . UP TO A POINT

When you've got your list of names ready, it's time to do a little simple math. How many girls and mothers should you invite to establish your club?

I can share the advice of experts: The Great Books Foundation, in its suggestions for organizing book discussion groups for young people, suggests starting with eight to ten children. Teachers have recommended that from six to ten or so children makes a group small enough to be comfortable yet large enough to keep a discussion going strong.

> "Our mother-daughter book club discussions allowed Jessica to see that she was not alone in coping with a mother with a laundry list of rules and values."
>
> *Sandra*

I happen to be at ease with large groups, especially a group of girls and women I already know. Even so, when Morgan's list topped out at twenty girls, we managed to whittle it to a more realistic twelve invitations that went out in the next day's mail. One of the mothers in our group has told

> "Raising teens isn't a snap, so sharing the experience with others is a great comfort and support."
>
> *Maria*

me since that when she first heard that invitations had gone out to that many girls, she had second thoughts about joining. Her daughter was one of the youngest in the group, a little shy, and not an avid recreational reader. And the thought of eventually hosting a club meeting that brought twenty-four girls and moms into her home was daunting. Still, she and her daughter came for that first meeting and were pleasantly surprised to find that the number of mothers and daughters who actually signed on was quite comfortable.

While you're thinking about numbers, think again about the vision you have for your club. If having the club meet at members' homes is important to you, then you'll need to aim for a number that fits comfortably into your home settings.

For us, meeting at homes was important because it was where we felt we could most completely relax, reflect, and enjoy our discussion. Over time, we also have come to realize that, for us, sharing our homes has been a way of sharing ourselves, and it gives the girls, especially, a tangible feeling of ownership of the club when they host a meeting. When one of our members felt her town house couldn't handle the crowd comfortably, she asked a friend for the use of *her* home. The request was graciously granted.

The ideal number will be small enough to fit comfortably into your meeting place and large enough to sustain a lively discussion even when a few are absent. I suggest inviting about

A Special Place for Sharing and Growing Together

Reading together is a wonderful idea because it's a positive way to grapple with real-life issues. If these things come up in the context of a book, or a book discussion, then it doesn't seem so personal and it may be easier for the girls to discuss. It feels a little safer. And if the moms are open and they really want to hear what their girls are saying, then there can be a real sharing. You need to watch what the girls do, listen to them, and understand that they are different than we are.

And the girls should be open and listening to what the mothers have to say, too. There is definitely something to learn from both sides.

An all-girl environment such as the one found in the Girl Scouts works so well because there girls really have a chance to be leaders, to show their leadership qualities, be creative, have a real voice, and not be concerned about what a boy will say or have to defer to a boy because of the social pressure. With other girls, a girl feels comfortable trying out different roles and ways of expressing herself.

A girl needs to be able to say what she's really feeling—not just what she's "supposed to feel" or "the right thing"—but what she really feels, who she really is.

The most important thing mothers need to do is really express how much they care about their daughters. They need to show them that. They need to really listen to them and say, "Who is my daughter?" rather than trying to make her into something. And, of course, enjoy—really enjoy her. Parents sometimes take an almost businesslike approach to living instead of looking for ways to have fun together.

It's also very important for girls growing up to have a sense that it's not just their mother who cares, but other adults who care and take them seriously. A Girl Scout leader or someone else's mother could do all those things.

—HARRIET S. MOSATCHE, PH.D., DEVELOPMENTAL PSYCHOLOGIST,
DIRECTOR OF PROGRAM DEVELOPMENT,
Girl Scouts of the U.S.A.

four more girls than the minimum you would hope to have at every meeting. Then if someone misses, or one drops out, you still have a strong core group to keep your club going.

SAMPLE INVITATION

Shireen and Her Daughter Morgan
Invite You to the
Organizing Meeting of the
Mother-Daughter Book Club

Sunday, October 1, 1995
TIME: 4 to 6 P.M.
PLACE: Home of Alexis and Jamexis Christian
RSVP: Shireen or Morgan Fykes

Please bring book ideas and your calendar!

While a written invitation is always nice, the girls say it travels by snail mail. These days e-mail invitations work well, and once the club has settled into a routine date and time a quick e-mail highlighting the meeting location and the book serves as a welcome reminder.

SAMPLE E-MAIL INVITATION

Greetings,

Our Girls have gotten together and the word is they want to start a **Mother-Daughter Book Club**. Skylar and I will host the first meeting. We hope we can count you in on what is sure to be a wonderful journey. So read our book selection (*Whirligig* by Paul Fleischman) and then come on over on **Sunday, March 13, 2005 @ 4:00 P.M.**

Shireen

TAKING THE LEAD: HOW MUCH SHOULD YOU PLAN IN ADVANCE?

When I organize something, I don't like to leave much to chance. So before we sent out our invitations, I called several mothers to be sure they were interested in doing this with us. We talked about the kinds of books we thought would be on-target for our group. And we agreed upon a convenient date for our organizational meeting.

From the moment I knew we were going to do this club, I began scouting the bookstores for books the group might want to read. I must have read fifteen or twenty books in my search for the eight that eventually were introduced to the girls. (See Chapter Four: "How to Find and Read Books.") But my efforts as a previewer paid off for the group. By the time we met for our organizational meeting, we had a good array of books from which the girls could pick one to start, and that made their selection process fairly simple.

There are other ways to blaze the trail to your first meeting and book selection. You might pick the first book yourself and include a copy of it—or simply name it—in the invitation that goes out to your charter members. Then, at your organizational meeting, the group can enjoy its first "official" mother-daughter book discussion.

Every book discussion group is bound to be unique, reflecting the age of its members, their interests, and their life experiences. But our hunt for good books begins at the same place and leads us in the same direction. A wonderful thing—another pleasant surprise—comes out of the process of organizing, of looking for books, reading them, and thinking about the girls, the mother-daughter relationship, the club, the stories and the discussions to come. It becomes absolutely clear that in the hubbub of all this living and literature, a mother-daughter book club is a *right* idea, one that brings us heart to heart, and the prospect of that first meeting becomes truly exciting.

BOOKS TO GROW ON

Ten of my favorite books when I was ten years old:

The Wizard of Oz, L. Frank Baum

Baby Island, Carol Ryrie Brink

Caddie Woodlawn, Carol Ryrie Brink

The Secret Garden, Frances Hodgson Burnett

Understood Betsy, Dorothy Canfield

James and the Giant Peach, Roald Dahl

The Peterkin Papers, Lucretia P. Hale

Misty of Chincoteague, Marguerite Henry

Mary Poppins, P. L. Travers

Stuart Little, E. B. White

Ten books I would now recommend to ten-year-olds:

Sounder, William H. Armstrong

The Secret Garden, Frances Hodgson Burnett

Ramona the Pest, Beverly Cleary

James and the Giant Peach, Roald Dahl

Anne Frank: The Diary of a Young Girl, Anne Frank

A Wrinkle in Time, Madeleine L'Engle

Rascal, Sterling North

Bridge to Terabithia, Katherine Paterson

Roll of Thunder, Hear My Cry, Mildred Taylor

Stuart Little, E. B. White

—ANN MARTIN, AUTHOR,
The Baby-sitters Club series

ENDNOTES

📖 Stay focused on your reasons for starting a mother-daughter book club.

> "The chance to share a laugh, hear a confession, argue
> a not-quite-cogent perspective, compliment a new haircut,
> all grist of friendship and belonging, this is the foundation
> of who we are, my daughter and I. A Sunday afternoon
> gabbing with the girls? Perfect."
>
> *Pam*

📖 Present the idea of a mother-daughter book club to your daughter as fun.

> "We find ourselves laughing a lot and having a good
> time. Sometimes someone will recall a story in one of the
> discussions that makes people laugh. Also the girls always
> laugh a lot when we do our art project or something like that
> after the meeting."
>
> *Brooke*

> "It is great to share a common activity with Sylvie. 'Have
> you read the book yet?' 'Where did you put it?' 'You had
> it last.' Just the mundane interchanges are fun because they
> have us relating more as equals than as mother-daughter."
>
> *Kris*

Choose members who share your vision and goals for the club.

> "Make sure that the participants come together because of a love of reading. While the club offers the opportunity to socialize and make new friends, it will fall apart if the girls don't primarily share the love of good books."
>
> *Sandra*

> "The hardest part about forming a club is picking the right members. Once you do that, the rest is easy. The chemistry is really what will hold the group together."
>
> *Morgan*

> "The most difficult and important part of a book club: You have to make sure to pick a group of mothers and daughters that flow through discussions. The challenge is making sure everyone feels comfortable and no one feels overpowered."
>
> *Skylar*

THREE

The Organizational Meeting:
Prelude to a Great Year

FOR ASHLEY, THE THOUGHT OF A SUNDAY AFTERNOON GET-
TOGETHER WITH FRIENDS, AND OF US READING THE SAME
BOOK AND ACTUALLY SPENDING TIME REFLECTING TOGETHER
WAS JUST VERY EXCITING.

—GRACE SPEIGHTS

Ari & Maria Volpe

Hi, my name is Ari Volpe, I'm sixteen years old and I am in the tenth grade at Georgetown Day School. I have two pets. They are Dusty, the family dog, and my new kitten, Olivia. I also have a sister, Addy, who is seven. I like going to the theater, anything to do with Europe, and the beach, traveling and seeing wonderful sights, relaxing with a great craft, and of course shopping. I also like to play sports; I am on my school's varsity soccer and basketball teams.

I can be very shy but only until you get to know me. I can be very quiet—until I am comfortable in my surroundings, in which case I can be extremely loud. I have a well of empathy for others, which I do not always exhibit openly—and I am pretty sensitive. Though I think I am fairly level-headed about things, I have difficulty making definitive decisions. I am accepting of people and tolerant—unless I feel someone is inexcusably mean. To be honest, I do not fully understand myself yet—sometimes my reactions to situations or things surprise me.

My favorite books are historical fiction, mysteries and, because of book club, I now really enjoy best sellers. I love to read!

I am concentrating on graduating high school and getting into college. After that I hope to pursue a career in medicine or law—or combine the two. (My dad is a lawyer and my grandparents were both doctors.)

My mother's name is Maria and she is a stay-at-home mom. She was born in New York but grew up in Montgomery County, Maryland. She got her love of reading from her mom who regularly took her to the local library for their own special day of mother-daughter bonding through books. They are very close. Once when my mom was traveling with my dad, my grandmother attended one of our book club meetings. She told my mom that she was so amazed at the insights we shared during the meeting.

My mom is a ballet and opera "fanatic," and she shares my enthusiasm for travel. She used to seriously dance when she was growing up and was pleasantly surprised to reunite with another book club mom whom she used to take lessons with. My mom also played sports growing up, and I am lucky that she can come to all of my games: It is like having my own cheering section.

Before the Mother-Daughter Book Club, I might have said my mom and I have absolutely nothing in common. She is very emotional, I'm not; she is very conservative, and I'm not. I love Mexican and Chinese and, well, popcorn! It's a life staple! And Mom loves Italian and French food. Along with doing things we both like a lot—reading, being together, and talking with our friends, our Mother-Daughter Book Club is helping me see we do have things in common and can find common ground on many issues.

I can still feel Morgan's bubbly excitement and remember my own cheerful expectations the night of our organizational meeting. I felt akin to Noah—or perhaps to Mrs. Noah—as two by two they arrived, mothers and daughters. With each tap at the front door, two more beaming smiles, two more partners welcomed into the slowly growing group in the family room. The sound of girls' and women's warm laughter and conversation wafted through the house like holiday music. It felt good. This is the way it should be, I thought: a happy conspiracy of girls and women, books, conversation and sharing.

No matter how familiar everyone is with everyone, we all enjoy a simple icebreaker activity that welcomes us to a new, special circle. The one I chose for our organizational meeting was deceptively simple: Each girl was asked to introduce her mother and tell a little about her, and each mother was asked to do the same for her daughter. Well! Those simple introductions launched us into some remarkable discussion and discovery.

Morgan, for instance, told the group that I worked at the Smithsonian Institution, which was true, but her sense of what I did there was thin on detail: "She mostly sits in a little office and answers the telephone," Morgan volunteered, "and then she comes home and changes clothes and goes out to parties a lot." In my work as a museum administrator, coordinating exhibits and events for the Smithsonian Institution's Center for African American History and Culture, I suppose I *did* sit in my office and talk on the telephone quite a bit. And I *was* expected to represent the Smithsonian—and other organization on whose boards I serve—at many cultural events, often in the evening. But the reality of my work was quite different from the impression that Morgan had developed from her vantage point.

The other mothers enjoyed similar revelations as we discovered, introduction by introduction, that what we did with the days of our lives was not necessarily clear to our daughters. With every introduction—mothers and daughters alike—came some opportunity to set a record straight ("Mom, I don't enjoy music. I take music lessons—it's not the same thing!").

We had great fun with it, but I can tell you as well that it was a perfect lesson in sharing and discovery between the mothers and daughters there. All without a single lecture!

This is also a perfect time to poll each girl on the types of books she enjoys the most. The answers can help guide your search for new titles to bring to her. And her involvement in that process adds to her sense of ownership in the club and the book selection process.

Because the mothers in our Mother-Daughter Book Club had so much in common, it was easy to agree upon some basic objectives of our group. Thus the business—I like to call it *housekeeping*—part of our organizational meeting was fairly short. I welcomed the group, described my reasons for

> ## BOOKS TO GROW ON
>
> *The Twenty-One Balloons*
> William P. Du Bois
>
> *Anne of Green Gables*
> Lucy M. Montgomery
>
> *Ozma of Oz*
> L. Frank Baum
>
> *Homer Price*
> Robert McCloskey
>
> *Centerburg Tales*
> Robert McCloskey
>
> *Anne Frank: The Diary
> of a Young Girl*
> Anne Frank
>
> —NORA EPHRON, NOVELIST,
> SCREENWRITER, DIRECTOR,
> *You've Got Mail*
> *Sleepless in Seattle*

Mothers & Daughters: Appreciating the Differences

We all want to be appreciated for who we are. Daughters want some positive mirroring from their parents—to be seen and heard for who they are and what they are. Mirroring is shorthand meaning somebody really sees the other person—taking in what the other person is putting out, and communicating that we're taking it in. It's like saying, "I hear you," rather than "Why can't you do it the way I did?"

Almost everyone thinks of their life as a rough draft and their child's life as an edited version—and they will be the editor. Of course, people don't articulate it that way. But it's a shock when you discover you're not working from the same manuscript. In these times we live in, when the pace of change is so rapid, the kid's manuscript changes very rapidly.

> "I learned that my mother really wants to hear what I have to say. She respects my opinion"
>
> MAYA

> "I learned that my daughter is much more like me than I realized."
>
> JOYCE

The pace of life itself is not as leisurely as it used to be. Any one member of a family is connected to an electronic device at any given moment—TV, computer, video game. There really isn't unstructured time for easy talk, random talk, for wide-ranging conversations about this or that.

But with a mother-daughter book club, here's this golden opportunity for girls to hear. It's almost like a literary version of the quilting bees, where the little ones would listen and women would talk, which is a terrific way of transmitting wisdom. But the reality is that our children are growing up in the age of the sound bite and MTV, and that's why it's so important that the group is daughter-focused—why it needs to be daughter-focused or they'll lose interest.

Instead of lecturing or pushing your point, it can be useful to point out that you're surprised by the girls' reaction to something: "We thought you would have a lot to say about this or that, but you seemed to move right over it." The girls can ask themselves why, and the girls can tell the moms why they didn't think it was so inter-esting. That's an opportunity for real contact.

—SUMRU ERKUT, PH.D., ASSOCIATE DIRECTOR OF
THE CENTER FOR RESEARCH ON WOMEN,
Wellesley College

BOOKS TO GROW ON

The Nancy Drew series
Carolyn Keene (my childhood favorites)

The Giving Tree
Shel Silverstein

What's Happening to Me?,
Where Did I Come From?
Peter Mayle

Value Tale series
Ann D. Johnson and Spencer Johnson

The Prophet
Khalil Gibran

Roll of Thunder, Hear My Cry
Mildred D. Taylor

Their Eyes Were Watching God
Zora Neale Hurston

Go Ask Alice
Anonymous

Catcher in the Rye
J. D. Salinger

Are You There God? It's Me Margaret
Judy Blume

Stuart Little
E. B. White

The Ramona series
Beverly Cleary

—FAYE WATTLETON,
Center for the Advancement of Women

wanting to establish the club, and asked the members whether they were ready to commit to it for themselves. The answer was a resounding yes, and we were on our way.

Since there are several points that need to be covered in that initial setting-up discussion, it helps to have a

> "I thought this sounded like a great idea—it sounded like fun to get to know my mom."
> *Morgan*

mental agenda or some notes to keep the group on track, making progress. But there's no need to have a formal agenda to hand out, there's no need to have elected officers, and there's no need to run the meetings like a business seminar.

Remember, the important thing about a mother-daughter book club is the sharing and discussion. You don't really *need* a lot of structure, rules, and regulations. Any structure to the group should be for the sole purpose of simplifying the effort so you can focus on enjoying books and one another. Don't worry about building in opportunities for leadership, responsibility, and cooperative effort. In a mother-daughter book club, it *all* happens—*naturally*.

That said, for some minimal structure, points for the group to review and agree upon might include:

📖 **THE GENERAL PURPOSE AND PHILOSOPHY OF THE CLUB.**

📖 **RESPONSIBILITIES BEYOND READING,** such as hosting or researching authors if that's something you want done regularly.

📖 **A LEADER OR COORDINATOR** to facilitate the housekeeping part of the meetings. I've served in that role for our group since I organized it, but it may make sense to rotate that duty, perhaps yearly, among any mothers willing to handle it.

THE CALENDAR CRUNCH — WHEN TO MEET

There isn't a day in the week when most of us have long stretches of time unclaimed and available for a relaxing get-together.

A few tips may help you carve out the calendar space you need to enjoy a mother-daughter book club.

• ESTABLISH THE LENGTH OF THE MEETING AND STICK WITH IT. Start and end on time as a matter of courtesy to the hosting mothers, as well as others who have families or other commitments waiting at home. It's easier to imagine making the time for the meeting if you can depend on it to ask no more of you.

"You want to be careful to keep it simple and not let the food or activities get so complicated that your meetings run over the time you've set aside. When it runs longer, you're running into family time," says Cheryl.

• ALLOW AMPLE TIME FOR HOME READING BETWEEN MEETINGS. Once a month provides a nice stretch of time for reading amid all the other commitments we have. You may need to schedule meetings a little closer or farther apart at times to accommodate holidays and other calendar conflicts. Or you may want to make the meetings quarterly simply because that's the schedule that's most comfortable for you.

• IF YOU MEET AFTER SCHOOL, SEE IF CARPOOLING CAN SIMPLIFY THE PICK-UP PROCESS AT SCHOOL, while off-duty moms drive straight to the meeting house. This makes getting there a little less hectic for the off-duty moms, and a rotating car pool duty means the driving isn't a big deal for anyone most of the time. If your girls go to different schools, look for meeting times that take everyone's situation into consideration.

• IF WEEKENDS ARE A "FAMILY TIME" FOR YOU, look for a pocket of in-between time when your absence for a couple of hours won't be a problem. For instance, our group began meeting the first Sunday of every month, from 2 to 4 p.m. We've expanded it to 3 to 6 p.m. to allow for more social time, but that's remained a comfortable commitment for most of us most of the time.

• EXPECT THAT EVERYONE WILL MISS A MEETING FROM TIME TO TIME. It's virtually impossible to accommodate everyone's schedule all of the time. If you plan to be absent, however, let the hosting mother and daughter know as soon as possible so they can plan accordingly.

WHETHER YOU WANT TO LEAD THE DISCUSSION YOURSELVES or consider asking a professional facilitator to do it. Our girls do it themselves. But expert facilitators, often available through the public library or a bookstore, can be a good idea, especially for a larger, community-based mother-daughter book club.

MEETING DATES. The simplest way is to pick a schedule as a group and stick with it. We established the first Sunday afternoon of each month as our set meeting date. We scheduled around a couple of major conflicts—a Girl Scout camp-out and a national holiday—but otherwise we stick to the plan. That little bit of structure establishes the meeting—and the group—as a priority for one day each month. It means we aren't constantly checking with each other to confirm when the next meeting is, or trying to negotiate changes to accommodate all the variables in everyone's lives. Inevitably, someone can't make it to a meeting now and then. That's life.

A BOOK SELECTION PROCESS. (See Chapter Four: "How to Find and Read Books.")

HOSTING DUTY. Members can sign up for the date that suits them for hosting the Mother-Daughter Book Club, whether it's at their home or an alternate location. Sometimes someone picks a date because they have a special interest in the book—perhaps they recommended it—or a book-related activity. Hosting duty means providing refreshments, being prepared to lead the discussion, and, if you wish, planning a book-related activity. (See Chapter Ten: "Beyond the Books.")

EXPECTATIONS, such as that mothers and daughters attend together, and that both read the book and be prepared to share thoughts about it.

Whatever you do, remember your objectives for the club and the personality of your group. Let your structure and your choices reflect the true desires of the group. Be candid about preferences. Even the discussions of planning details can lead to interesting insights into each other's lives if only we are honest about our feelings.

For instance, if you want the girls to explore new titles— ones that none of the girls has yet read—then the mothers may want to facilitate by providing book options, allowing the girls to make the final choice. There's no need to lecture the girls about the need for mothers to pick out "what's good for them." By contributing to the selection process, you're showing them that you can help them access the world and they can make good choices. It can be a win-win situation.

Depending on the age and interests of the girls, it may work out fine for them to have a more specific say in finding and selecting the titles for the group. Or you may want to ask each mother-daughter team to be responsible for selecting a book and hosting the meeting for that discussion. That gives each girl the chance to see her special choice become the group's pick, but allows for some motherly input in the process. However you decide to pick the club's books, be prepared to experiment with it a bit and let it evolve to reflect the desires of your group.

A nice touch for the organizational meeting is to have take-home materials prepared for each mother-daughter couple. This might be an article of interest from the newspaper, a list of the year's Caldecott Medal, Coretta Scott King, or Newbery awards for children's literature, or simply:

📖 **THE CLUB MEMBERSHIP LIST,** with names, addresses, and phone numbers

SURPRISES — EVEN AMONG FRIENDS
Breaking the Ice

The warmest of friends can still enjoy an icebreaker activity to get a meeting off to a rousing start. Here are two winners:

Mother-Daughter Introductions

Invite each mother to introduce her daughter, and each daughter to introduce her mom.

Suggest that everyone include a brief description of what the other does during the day, and then focus on qualities that make her daughter or mother special — no need to talk about "flaws" or shortcomings here!

Expect a round of giggles and groans from the girls, but don't let them squirm out of it. They'll love hearing nice things about themselves and saying nice things about their moms.

Once the introductions are made, go around the circle of girls and ask what kinds of books they like to read the most. The information will be useful later when the group wants to select new books to read.

To Tell the Truth (or Fiction and Nonfiction!)

Give each mother and daughter a piece of paper and pencil.

Ask everyone to write on the sheet four "facts" about themselves that the others, even close friends may not know — three of the comments should be true, but one should be false. The more believable the false statement is, the more fun the group has trying to sort out the possible truth from the possible fiction.

Going around the group one person at a time, ask each person to read all four of her "facts" aloud and let the group guess which one is false. To conclude her turn, each girl or woman reads her four statements again, this time disclosing whether the statement is true—nonfiction—or fiction.

You may choose to ask mother and daughters to play as partners, coming up with four statements that describe either or both of them—but one statement that is completely false for both.

This activity can be enjoyed more than once. Consider playing it again to add a sparkle to a midyear meeting.

📖 **A LIST OF PHONE NUMBERS** of area bookstores, libraries, or other helpful community contacts

📖 **THE INITIAL SUGGESTED BOOK LIST** for the group

📖 **ANY REMINDERS**

If supplying these materials is too costly or inconvenient, you might consider some simple alternatives:

📖 **KEEP A MOTHER-DAUGHTER BOOK CLUB SCRAPBOOK** for articles or information members bring to share. The materials can be read casually during the nondiscussion portion of the meeting.

📖 **MAKE A DO-IT-YOURSELF MEMBER LIST,** by arranging the girls in a circle or a line, then giving each girl a sheet of paper and asking her to write her and her mother's name, address, and phone number on a line or two. Ask the girls to pass their page on to the girl on their right and write the same information again on the page they now hold. Keep going until the pages have come full circle and each one contains the information from all the girls. Each girl will have a list with her name at the top!

YOU'RE A CLUB NOW: SEE YOU NEXT TIME!

In the sweet children's story *Corduroy*, a little stuffed bear bumbles from one place to another, optimistic but never quite certain if what he has found is the something that he had always imagined and wished for. Finally, at the end of one adventurous day, he guesses right: Snuggled in the arms of a little girl who treasures him, Corduroy muses: "You must be a friend. I've always wanted to have a friend."

BOOKS TO GROW ON

CLASSICS

Alice in Wonderland and *Through the Looking-Glass*
Lewis Carroll

Jane Eyre, Charlotte Brontë

Selected Poems of Emily Dickinson

Little Women, Louisa May Alcott

Pride and Prejudice, Jane Austen

CONTEMPORARIES

A Mother and Two Daughters, Gail Godwin

A Thousand Acres, Jane Smiley

Dinner at the Homesick Restaurant, Anne Tyler

Annie John, Jamaica Kincaid

Foxfire, Joyce Carol Oates

Mother's Love, Mary Morris

Needle's Eye, Margaret Drabble

Quilting: Poems 1987–1990, Lucille Clifton

The Mother Child Papers, Alicia Ostriker

—JOYCE CAROL OATES, NOVELIST, POET, CRITIC,
Big Mouth & Ugly Girl

A Sample Organizational Plan and Meeting Checklist

- THINK ABOUT OBJECTIVES to determine a group identity or theme-based interest.

- CONTACT SCHOOL OR COMMUNITY LIBRARIANS, bookstore contacts, and others for recommended reading. Contact a bookstore about discounts on group purchases.

- CALL AHEAD TO A CORE GROUP of mothers and daughters to confirm sufficient interest. Send out invitations to those and others for an organizational meeting.

- ARRANGE A POTLUCK DINNER OR REFRESHMENTS for an organizational meeting.

- GREETINGS—describe the idea for the club and the vision, theme, or philosophy you have in mind. Ask for a show of hands or voiced responses to signify approval or need for discussion.

- ICEBREAKER GAME: Mother-Daughter Introductions or Fiction/Nonfiction games.

- ESTABLISH YOUR BOOK SELECTION PROCESS. Choose the book for the next meeting, or pick the next two or three books as well, to eliminate the need to spend time on that process at every meeting.

- POLL GIRLS FOR INTERESTS to guide future selections.

- SET MEETING DATES AND HOURS.

- REVIEW HOST MOTHER-DAUGHTER DUTIES, which are to provide meeting space and refreshments, prepare questions about the book to lead discussion, and coordinate or supply materials for any book-related activity.

- CREATE AND DISTRIBUTE A MEMBER LIST with telephone numbers and addresses.

- ESTABLISH A CLUB LEADER OR COORDINATOR to monitor calendar changes and manage other minor coordinating duties for a year.

- ASK FOR A VOLUNTEER MOTHER AND DAUGHTER to serve as communicator, typing up highlights from each meeting to send out to absent members, or calling them to let them know information needed for the following meeting.

By the end of our organizational meeting, Morgan and I felt as if we had truly found the thing that we previously had only imagined could exist. Before that meeting, your idea for a mother-

"It's kind of nice to have it at your house. You get to visit other people's houses, and it's nice to have them to yours."

Jihan

daughter book club was just that: an idea. Now it was real! We had gathered together. We had talked. We had planned. We had enjoyed the meeting immensely. The enthusiasm within the circle of mothers and daughters was unanimous.

This must be a mother-daughter book club. And it was even better than we'd imagined!

ENDNOTES

📖 An icebreaking activity is a fun way to begin.

"When starting a new book club it is important to get to know each other in the beginning." Going around in a circle and saying your name and food is an easy and fun way to get started."

Skylar

📖 Club meetings need minimal structure—sharing and discussion occur naturally.

"Did you like the book, yes or no?" This seems like such a basic question, but we always open up with it and every time the question takes us so much further than yes or no. Usually this is the question that connects us to the rest of the discussion."

Jesse

📖 The basic organization of the club can reflect your group's personality and objectives.

"We usually have a craft project for after the book discussion. I'm an artsy person so I have really enjoyed this activity. Once we decorated little purses with ribbons, buttons, and glitter because our book had a prom theme. It was a big hit! All of my friends in the book club are really creative, so it's fun to see each girl's final product."

Hannah

📖 Include your daughter in the preparations for this and every other club meeting. It's a great way to spend time together.

"My mom and I can also discuss the books outside of the meetings, which helps us learn about each other in ways we might not otherwise. I share a new bond with my mom due to the book club and the discussion ideas that come out of it."

Brooke

FOUR

How to Find and Read Books

READING BOOKS REALLY SHOULD BE FUN, YOU KNOW. IT CAN'T
ALWAYS BE ABOUT IMPROVING, ABOUT LEARNING LESSONS
IN LIFE.

—PAM SACKS, The Cheshire Cat Bookstore

Brooke & Hannah Kahn & Sherry Bindeman

Hi, my name is Brooke. I'm sixteen years old and in tenth grade at Georgetown Day School. I started going to GDS in ninth grade, and right away I loved the school and the people there. I have a twin sister named Hannah, who is also in the book club, and a brother named Ben, who is twelve. Being a twin is a large part of my life, because we share so much and do a lot together. It can be hard sometimes, but I love having her because she is always there for me. Although we share many interests, we are very different.

I play tennis and lacrosse for my school. I love music and I play the piano. I also like singing, dancing, and performing. Outside of school, I love spending time with friends. I enjoy doing anything with them, from shopping to going out to dinner, to listening to music, to just hanging out and talking. I like to scrapbook, when I have the time, because I love collecting pictures and memories.

One of my favorite books is *The Giver* by Lois Lowry. It is an amazing book that is very moving, but fun to read at the same time. It takes place in a society of Sameness, where the people cannot love or experience true happiness. It is hard to imagine a world like this, so this book teaches you to appreciate the world we live in.

It is important to me to have love in a family. I think I am a loving and caring person, who listens to others. I try to get along with everybody. I think I am like my mom in many ways. She is very compassionate and always trying to help. Before I was born, she practiced law as a divorce lawyer and now does all kinds of volunteer work. My mom is my role model, and I look up to her, trying to be as considerate and giving as I can, like she teaches me every day.

Hi, my name is Hannah. I am sixteen years old and am a sophomore at GDS. My fraternal twin sister, Brooke, is older than I am by a minute. I am a friend, a student, a performer, an optimist, and a dreamer.

My two strongest passions are acting and singing. I've been in shows ever since I was little and have always felt comfortable on stage. My favorite roles have been Dorothy in *The Wizard of Oz* and the Cat in the Hat in *Seussical the Musical*. Last year I worked on sets crew, and this year I acted in the fall play and winter one-acts. I am co-head of my school's a cappella group, Eat at Joe's, and am going to be a co-leader this year. When I grow up, I want to be an actress, either on screen or on stage. I know that making it as an actress is not easy, but I am too determined and motivated to give up my lifelong dream. I am not in pursuit of fame or fortune, but just the happiness that comes with doing what I love to do.

I am a member of the GDS Student-Staff Council along with my friend Sylvie, who is also in the book club. I think I make a good representative for my grade because I am friendly, creative, responsible, and have a lot of school spirit (Go Hoppers!). I am a very diligent, hardworking person and always try to do my best.

My "home away from home" is my sleep-away camp in New Hampshire where I have spent the past three summers. Another very important aspect of my life is Judaism, and I am going to be confirmed this year at my synagogue. I love to read and write. My favorite books are *A Tree Grows in Brooklyn* by Betty Smith and *The Giver* by Lois Lowry.

My mother is an amazing woman. Although she has been a stay-at-home mom for sixteen years, she used to be a practicing domestic relations lawyer and spends much of her time doing volunteer work in several schools, organizations, and our synagogue. My mother is compassionate, generous, and loving. She is much more patient and clear-headed than I am, while I am more outgoing and imaginative than she is. My mom has a beautiful voice and we love to sing harmonies together. I think that I get my perception and understanding for people from her. Whenever I need someone to talk to, my mom is always there to listen and provide me with wisdom. She is more than just my mother; she's my best friend.

When I say that I scouted for books in that period before our group met for the first time, that's a dignified way of saying the thrill of the hunt took over my life. On my way to the office I'd stop at this bookstore or that one. I recruited help: My husband would return from his trips to the library laden with offerings from the helpful librarian. On business trips to different cities, I'd find the local bookstores specializing in children's or African American titles; I'd scour the book racks at airports and hotel gift shops. If a friend at the office or in the neighborhood recommended a book, I'd be off and running—and *reading*.

I'd like to be able to tell you that I found the perfect books for your mother-daughter book club or that by using the book lists I've collected here, you're all set. Instead, I'll share the two most important things I learned from my crash course in literature:

THING ONE:
You really can't judge a book by looking at its cover—or even its reputation.

THING TWO:
Always be sure that one of the mothers in the group—or a trusted librarian, bookstore contact, or other knowledgeable adviser—has read a book before you suggest it to your group.

I discovered during my preliminary reading, for instance, that one book that *looked* ordinary enough and sounded interesting from the back-cover description actually dealt with incest. There wasn't a clue on the cover of that book that the story included such a sensitive topic. Some classics were heavy with ignorant or stereotyped images of women or men, or of people of different races, religions, or beliefs. Other books took a more enlightened view but treated complex issues in overly simplistic ways, with plots and characters that were just too tidy.

It's not that these books wouldn't provide points for discussion—of course, they would—but with our limited time together, we wanted to focus on literature that fueled the girls' excitement about reading, gave them some positive images of girls and women making their way in the world, and affirmed their courage to be themselves.

"IT'S A GREAT BOOK"—SAYS WHO?

I love a good bookstore. Any place where books line the walls and fill every flat surface is a place where my heart is at home. Thousands of books all around and every one of them is a treasure, a real find, if you believe what you read on the promotional posters and in book cover comments. In the presence of so many, how do you close in on the few, the books that hold particular promise of reading enjoyment and discussion for your mother-daughter book club?

I found Pam. Pam Sacks was our resourceful contact at the Cheshire Cat Bookstore, a gem of a neighborhood bookstore where I had shopped for children's books for years. She enjoyed being a matchmaker, suggesting books that would be a fit for this child or that one. When I told her about our Mother-Daughter Book Club, and our particular interests, she made a number of suggestions—about books, about children, and about subject matter—so insightful that her wisdom guides us still today. For instance, I told Pam that one of our goals was to strengthen our mother-daughter relationships, and that we'd like a book that would inspire some discussion along those lines. I was expecting her to recommend a book with a strong mother-daughter story to tell. She didn't. Instead, Pam suggested we read *The Man in the Ceiling* by Jules Feiffer, a cartoonist, author, and writer of plays and screenplays—and a man. The good-humored story includes a mother and two daughters, but the main character is Jimmy, a boy cartoonist who grapples with the creative struggle that is part of art and life. The story depicts family life from a child's frank perspective, complete with caring but self-absorbed parents and intentionally annoying, self-centered siblings.

Pam's explanation: The book was wonderfully written, and by focusing more on the little boy's experience of his entire family, especially an unsympathetic father, it would give us a way to *begin* to discuss parent-child relationships without confronting the mother-daughter relationship head-on. The presence of an interesting mother character in the book also carried some potential for discussion if the girls picked up on it.

> "I like to think of what happens to characters in good novels and stories as knots—things keep knotting up. And by the end of the story—readers see an 'unknotting' of sorts. Not what they expect, not the easy answers you get on TV, not wash-and-wear philosophies, but a reproduction of believable emotional experiences."
>
> *Terry McMillan,*
> *Introduction*, Breaking Ice

And that's exactly what happened. All of us enjoyed the book thoroughly. The girls instantly picked up on issues dealing with the rivalry between brothers and sisters, and on how the family members communicated with each other. There was a lot of talk about family relationships and this child's emotional struggle to be himself in a family and world that were too busy to take him seriously. Then a few of the girls took the mother character to task for being "selfish" because she had this little room where she would go and work on her artwork, and she wasn't totally accessible to her kids

> "Many women tell stories about what saved them from the precipice. One girl was saved by her love of books, by long summer afternoons when she read for hours."
> Mary Pipher, Ph.D., Author, Reviving Ophelia

when she was working there. And suddenly we were in the middle of a spirited discussion about mothers, and how it is that if the dad is a workaholic that's okay with everybody, but if the mom focuses on a work project then *she's* selfish. All of us had a good time with that one, and I know it's because the subject came up indirectly. *It was a book and it was somebody else's family.*

Pam's familiarity with children's literature and the way children interact with literature proved an invaluable guide. It helped us understand that sometimes the best approach to an issue is *indirect,* through literature that offers a nonthreatening arena—one with some distance built in—for discussing ideas that otherwise hit very close to home.

Because our Mother-Daughter Book Club members had a special desire to explore more African American literature, Pam also identified authors and books she felt would be of particular interest to us. That's how we discovered Virginia Hamilton, much-acclaimed author of stories that give young readers the intellectual respect they are due.

Whether you look to a favorite bookstore contact, a community librarian, or other adviser for suggestions, your most valuable advice will come from people who know and understand what you're looking for—as well as what you're *not* looking for.

BIOGRAPHIES

Sharing the Can-Do Spirit

Every "famous woman" started out as the girl next door. Joan Franklin Smutny, educator, author, and activist for child-centered education, suggests that the biographies of famous women, as well as the stories of other men and women who have accomplished remarkable things, carry a special message for our daughters. Here are her thoughts:

"Girls need to read stories of women who have done great things and women who have overcome tremendous obstacles—whether it's family background, poverty, educational circumstances, other limitations, or external conditions. They need to see that others have done it.

"Girls today need to hear mothers talk about their lives in everyday conversation. How they overcame adversity. How they managed to reach where they are—wherever they are.

"We can help girls develop a sense of that higher vision, that feeling that says, 'Of course I can,' instead of accepting limitations on their talents or fields of interest. Too often girls themselves accept stereotypes about the college or career choices in which they can expect to be successful. They need to see beyond the traditional opportunities and see that women have achieved greatness in math, science, computers, engineering, law, and medicine.

"Girls are desperately seeking values. Biographies emit them. When you read the life of a great person, or a person who has struggled, for discussion, you can ask:

• Why is this person a great person?

• What did this person contribute to his or her community and the world?

• What were the adversities they met along the way, and how did they overcome those adversities?

• When they were young, did everyone like them? Were they considered successful and popular?

• How did those experiences prepare them to make the contribution they did?

• What were their qualities: their strengths and weaknesses? How did they overcome their weaknesses?

"I think that biography encapsulates values as almost nothing else can. Every family has its own values, but in a larger sense, we all want children to aspire. We want our children to say, 'It can be done. I can do it.' A biography says just exactly that: 'I did it, and this is what I had to do to do it.' And the good biography tells a child, 'You can do it, too.' "

> **BOOKS TO GROW ON**
>
> Favorite books in my youth:
>
> *The Wind in the Willows*
> Kenneth Grahame
>
> *The Wizard of Oz*
> L. Frank Baum
>
> *Smoky, the Cow Horse*
> Will James
>
> *Little Women*
> Louisa May Alcott
>
> *Gone with the Wind*
> Margaret Mitchell
>
> —BETH WINSHIP,
> SYNDICATED COLUMNIST,
> *"Ask Beth"*

We've found that it works well when one of the mothers in our group can "preread" a book and share the story and her impressions of it with us during our moms' portion of the meeting, before we add it to the group of books from which the girls will choose. The previewing activity is fun, and it gives us another way to share a facet of our thinking. Ultimately, it means that even when we drop a book because it isn't a good fit, we've gained insights just from discussing the book and the issues it raises.

MOTHERS: SHARING, TRUSTING, READING

One of the delights of a book discussion group is that everyone brings a different point of view or a different life experience to share, and it's the mix that keeps the talk simmering along. That same intellectual energy can spark some friction when it comes to selecting books, particularly among the mothers. No matter how much you may have in common—friendship, work, religion, ethnic heritage—you're bound to find some differences regarding basic issues you just may never have chatted about before.

These kinds of differences can arise over any aspect of a book—the author, the writing style or language, the plot, the theme, the characters, imagery, and race or gender issues.

> "I just wrote the kind of books I wanted to read as a child."
>
> *Beverly Cleary,*
> *Ramona books*

Language was an interesting point of discussion in our early reviews of selections to put before the girls. Initially, several mothers wanted to avoid books in which the African American characters spoke regional dialects or slang, rather than conventional American English. Others felt the dialects were valuable *if* they contributed to the authenticity of the characters and to the reader's overall experience of the story. After some discussion we all agreed that the quality of the literature should be our guide.

Through our discussion, the mothers in the group were able to share feelings and explore issues in a way we don't often get the chance to do waiting in car-pool lines or on the sidelines of a soccer field. The discussion was interesting in itself, and it helped each of us understand the others just a little better.

Sometimes, as mothers, our feelings vary about different subject matter. It may be that we aren't comfortable with the subject, or it may be that we don't feel it's appropriate reading—just yet, anyway—for *our* daughter. Or it may be a matter of timing: When one father in our group was seriously ill, we decided against one particular book because the death of the father character was central to the book. We didn't avoid every book that included the death of a character. We simply were sensitive to any particular emotional pain or discomfort a story might impose on any one of us.

Beyond those special circumstances, we try not to shy away from great books with difficult or sensitive subjects, as long as the

ON CHOOSING WOMEN AUTHORS

I once had a furious argument with a college president over a book list—I said it needed more women authors. He said, "We do *Anna Karenina* by Leo Tolstoy and all these other books that have women characters." But all the writers were male. "There is a difference," I said, and he started to scream!

The fact that Louisa May Alcott or Jane Austen or other women writers' names are on a book is a very important statement, and we should talk about that: how things were for women writers. Girls need to know what it was like, historically, for women to write. Why, in the Renaissance if a daughter wrote a poem and it was published, it was as shameful as if she had run naked down the street. Women weren't supposed to write. The Renaissance was no renaissance for women.

People will point to books written *about* women, by men, and books written *by* women, and say, "Tell me, what is the difference?" The answer, in addition to the fact that women will be portrayed differently, is to say, "Well, how many books do you know where female friendships are *authentically* portrayed, where childbirth is *really* portrayed, where the mother-daughter relationship is talked about in a *meaningful* way, where women's *real* experience during wartime is portrayed? You could look at what's left out." Virginia Woolf said it so well in *A Room of One's Own*: "Women are inevitably portrayed in men's literature as having to do with men; their lives are seen as centered on men. And how little of a woman's life this is!"

Women have very full lives, and while love and romance may be part of it, they are hardly the center of it everyplace but in the movies. It's very important that girls get a sense of this, and they do get it in literature by women.

—ELLEN SILBER, PH.D.,
Director of the Marymount Institute for the
Education of Women and Girls

presentation is age-appropriate for our girls. (See Chapter
Eight: "Girls Will Be Girls:
Age and Attitudes.") When
the group reads a good book
that contains an element that
we all anticipate will be a bit

> "I was not a good reader
> as a young girl. I became
> a much better reader when
> I began reading to my
> children."
>
> *Sumru Erkut*

touchy, usually one of two things happens. Either the girls pick
up on the topic and enjoy a spirited discussion of their views, or
they skip right past that detail of the story to the aspects of the
story that they find compelling to talk about.

Regardless of the nature of the discussion during group
time, when we bring a book into our circle, we bring its story
into our lives. We add its issues, its images, its messages to our
thoughts. And the reflections can shimmer in conversation far
removed from the circle. It may be during after-school or bedtime chat, or standing in line at the grocery store, but the ideas
do surface again when their time is right.

CREATIVE CHOICES: NOVELS AREN'T THE ONLY BOOKS

Our continuing prowl for good books provides constant reminders that thought-provoking images and ideas come in all
shapes and sizes. In our first year we focused on novels. That
idea of a "book'" seemed familiar and comfortable to the girls
and mothers. Novels just seemed to provide the best story
structure for discussion. Now that we're old hands at the art of
discussion (and you'll be delighted at how quickly that trans-
formation occurs!), we're getting more creative in how we look
at—and look for—a good read.

What a field day! Biographies, poetry, short stories, essays, nonfiction and photo essays. Even picture books can open the doors of discussion in wonderful ways. The more we explore, the more we discover, about the world as well as about ourselves and each other.

READING LISTS: GREAT FOR BRAINSTORMING IDEAS

Books are a refreshing undercurrent of life and conversation almost anywhere I go. In my office, when we're gathered around the conference room table stuffing envelopes for the next event mailing, we're as likely to mention the book we're currently reading, or just finished, or read last year, or heard about from our mother-in-law, as we are any other topic of the day.

A few weeks later, there is always the follow-up conversation: "Did you get a chance to read that book yet? What did you think?" Regardless of the opinion, the discussion instantly taps into our feelings about characters, plots, and ideas the book brought our way. Recommendations are always made with good intentions. Whether the book itself was a hit or a flop, the discussion is always refreshing.

The stream of books and recommendations for reading flows from ancient days, literally, with classics, proclaimed classics-to-be and books that promise a simple good read. Books may rise to fame, sink and surface again in the course of time and the changing context of culture and readers' interests and expectations. With all the possibilities, it's always nice to hear suggestions from friends or others whose opinions we enjoy or respect. As you consider selections for your mother-daughter book club, tap into that reservoir of recommendations for ideas.

Reading lists are a wonderful way to find ideas for book

selections and to share with others a title you feel is special. Our Cheshire Cat Bookstore friend Pam Sacks reminds us, however, that book lists should be used as a starting point rather than an assignment sheet.

"Reading lists should come with a Surgeon General's warning," Pam says. "Just because they were right for someone else doesn't make them right for you."

Pam also points out that reading lists can become dated in ways that affect their usefulness. Some titles go out of print

> ### BOOKS TO GROW ON
>
> *The Souls of Black Folk*
> W.E.B. DuBois
>
> *Narrative of the Life of Frederick Douglass*
> Frederick Douglass
>
> *Incidents in the Life of a Slave Girl*
> Harriet B. Jacobs
>
> *Colored People*
> Henry Louis Gates Jr.
>
> *Coming of Age in Mississippi*
> Anne Moody
>
> —HENRY LOUIS GATES JR.,
> PROFESSOR OF HUMANITIES,
> HARVARD UNIVERSITY; EDITOR,
> *The Norton Anthology of African American Literature*

and copies are difficult to find. Others may be easy to find but not really a match for your group's interests. Remember that "good books" are good for different reasons to different people. Pick and choose the selections based on your own group's interests.

FINDING BOOKS THAT BELIEVE IN GIRLS

Not all "great" books are created equal. Some portray girls and women in ways that ignore the realities of our lives and those of women historically. There are reasons for it, of course.

ON LIFE, LITERATURE, AND THE PURSUIT OF A GOOD READ

Reading at night, summer vacation—it was such an event to go to our library and check out the biggest stack of books I could carry. I'd read Nancy Drew, the Bobbsey Twins, horse stories by Marguerite Henry, light fantasy such as Doctor Dolittle books, *Mr. Popper's Penguins,* and the Roald Dahl books. I loved my mother's Laura Ingalls Wilder books and E. B. White's books. I still have all my childhood books. When I was first leaving home, the majority of cartons I packed were full of my books.

I was a pretty eclectic reader then and now, everything from the series books to the classics and in between. I love Stephen King and gobble his books up, and still read the classics, new fiction and nonfiction and short stories. I think that's how a lot of children read. If the Baby-sitters Club series is all a child is reading right now, I wouldn't be too concerned. I'm sure she's going to go on to something else. I do make sure to include in the Baby-sitters books other existing titles—if I need to mention a book because one of the characters has a book report or project due, I'll recommend one of my favorites for kids.

—ANN MARTIN, AUTHOR,
The Baby-sitters Club series

Some books reflect an era when belittling comments or attitudes about women were the norm in the dominant culture. Other books, in casting boys and men as the action characters, simply leave women out of the picture or portray them as minor characters, when, in historical fact, they played active, important roles in the "story" of real life.

> "You can never foretell, you can never predict, what the outcome is going to be of a reading experience."
>
> *Nina Baym*

In her book *Woman's Fiction: A Guide to Novels by and about Women in America, 1820–70*, author Nina Baym points out that the authors of many traditional classics, and other celebrated books since, would "rather write about vapid angels and maligned temptresses than about what Louisa May Alcott called 'good, useful women'" and that the authors preferred "to present women as men's auxiliaries rather than center them in worlds of their own."

Asked how she would advise mothers in their selection of books for a mother-daughter book club, Nina suggests looking for women authors: "The very spectacle of the woman as a writer is very important to young girls. Sometimes it's the woman as a writer that's even more important than the character of a woman in the story.

"Any story about a young woman or girl who has an inner life is a story that has a lot of possibilities," Nina says, "because one of the real pressures on girls is that they have to live for the outside world, for others. They're 'supposed to' listen and pick up on other people's thoughts, conform themselves, and not show much in the way of an inner life. So any books that show a thoughtful, responsive woman, even if she doesn't do exciting things, is good because it encourages women to listen to their own thinking, to say 'Yes, I have a mind and it's worth my while to explore my thoughts.'"

"Read books by women. The very fact that a woman's name is on the book will mean something to a girl, even if it is unspoken."

Ellen Silber

THE IMPORTANT THING ABOUT THE BOOK IS . . .

Whatever books you choose, you want them to be enjoyable and thought-provoking for discussion. We also wanted to broaden our horizons as readers, so we looked for books the girls might not choose on their own.

We found that the novels that held up best under discussion were those that invited closer inspection. By that, I mean that the characters had some substance. They weren't simply good or bad, clever or dull, pretty or ugly. Their thoughts and choices made them interesting, even if they weren't always likable. The plots were engaging and unfolded in ways that weren't completely predictable. The author's language or style added to the richness of the reading experience, perhaps using words or phrases that could be understood in more than one way. There is no single right kind of book that does all those things. That's the beauty of books. Look around. Read around. Share what you find.

READING THE BOOK: SHARING TIME AND FEELINGS

When I remember reading as a little girl, it isn't necessarily the books I remember. It's the smell of the park where my mother

On Reading with Your Child

Reading aloud to a child, a parent can foster an introduction into a wonderful world of imagination in a way that doesn't happen in school because you're so much more focused on your own child, and can follow her, and your own, interests together.

"It's rare that mothers and daughters feel they really have much to talk about, but the book club provides one central uniting topic: literature. I think that through book discussions, I've learned more about the way my mother thinks, and why she sometimes says the things she does."

JESSICA

One thing I think is important at the baseline of all of this is the intimacy somehow you can achieve by sharing literature; even before the question of discussion, the heightened experience you capture in literature makes it possible for people to get to a place closer to their heart, a place closer to the quick. Children feel this.

—ALICE LETVIN, FORMER PRESIDENT, *The Great Books Foundation*

READING THE CLASSICS
Debunking Myths, Giving Girls a Voice

If you like the idea of reading classics, but you're put off by insensitive stereotypes, maddening views of girls and women, unsavory characters and brutal behavior, you're not alone. Here are some thoughts on fairy tales and how to talk through the hidden issues, from Ellen Silber, Ph.D., Director of the Marymount Institute for the Education of Women and Girls:

"I don't think children should read fairy tales unless they've got someone—an enlightened parent—to deconstruct the stories and show what's wrong. Someone who will ask:

"'What do you think about Snow White doing all the housework for the dwarfs? What do you think about Snow White in a coma and the prince coming along, and their getting married without ever having talked to each other about what's important to them? What do you think about all the bad older women in the fairy tales? What did the authors have against older women that they are there only as wicked witches, or other mean characters who persecute young girls? Why is that? What about the fact that Cinderella and Snow White do work that isn't very interesting, but they're patient, and they wait, and they get "the prize"—the handsome prince? And why is it always so important that they're pretty? Why is it a goal to get a man instead of to get a job, to get a life? Why do these women need rescuing? Is that the only way they can make it? Why are all the fairy tales so similar?'

"There are so many things you can say. If you don't say them, you're reinforcing the worst things those stories teach: passivity, hatred for other women, especially older women who in real life are so inventive and creative—none of the women get along together in these tales. That's such a lethal message.

"So, I think it's important for girls to read them, but not without someone to ask the really good questions."

BOOKS TO GROW ON

I've focused on books for girls ages seven to twelve. Some of the books we've mentioned are serious; some are silly. Some are historical and some are contemporary. But what they have in common is that each is about a strong, smart girl who is a true hero in her own way. Naturally, we can't help mentioning the American Girls Collection stories, because Felicity, Kirsten, Addy, Samantha, and Molly are all heroes to us!

The Hundred Dresses
Eleanor Estes

Julie of the Wolves
Jean Craighead George

From the Mixed-up Files of Mrs. Basil E. Frankweiler
E. L. Konigsburg

Prairie Songs
Pam Conrad

The Puppy Sister
S. E. Hinton

—JUDITH WOODBURN,
FORMER DIRECTOR OF
EDITORIAL DEVELOPMENT,
Pleasant Company

would take us, picnic dinner in hand, for a luxurious evening stretched out on the grass, reading.

> "Through the Mother-Daughter Book Club I have read many kinds of books and I found that they are all interesting in their own way."
>
> Ashley S.

I've asked around, and everyone I know who enjoys reading as an adult—and even some who don't enjoy it all that much—has pleasant childhood memories of reading with someone special, or reading in a special place, or enjoying some special aspect of reading that often had nothing to do with the book. They remember parents or elderly aunts who read with them. They remember sitting under a tree in the backyard or in a quiet, out-of-the-way spot in their home. They remember flashlights and books under the covers. As much as we think of reading as a thing we *do*, I think that reading also is a thing we *feel*. It is an experience of the senses.

When we read with our children, we are more than narrators. We become partners in their experience of the book. We are their traveling companions as the story takes us 20,000 leagues under the sea, or through a terrifying escape from oppression to freedom through the underground railroad. Even more important, we're there for the moments of stories that reflect choices in life, choices that lead characters down one path or another.

Sometimes the stories inspire conversation about characters, their behavior or their choices, or perhaps about the places or people that are part of the landscape. But often, our reading just allows us to relax together. In those unhurried moments, Morgan sometimes tells me about something from her day or shares a thought she's been tending until the coast was clear for quiet reflection.

Morgan is pretty protective of this time as "our" time and tries to discourage her older brother and younger sister from listening in. It doesn't always work out that way, and that's okay, too. Sometimes we read the book together; sometimes she wants to move ahead and I need to lag behind at my own pace.

Any way you devise your home reading routine is the right way if it works for you and your daughter. The mothers in our group each have a slightly different approach, and they change the routine when it needs to change.

Joyce includes both her daughters—Maya and her six-year-old sister—in the reading at bedtime.

Alice has made the home reading a family affair. It seemed that every time she sat down to read aloud with her daughter in the family room, the others just quietly gravitated over. "It's amazing," she says, "but when I read aloud, all my children all come around. It's become a family thing—a time for all of us to come together."

Kathie and Jihan have a routine that includes a little bit of everything: "Sometimes I read to her, and sometimes she reads to me, and sometimes we read separately and come back and talk about it together," Kathie says. "It means we always have something in particular to talk about."

In addition to the pure pleasure of reading with our girls and talking with them as we progress through a story, we've also discovered that our involvement supports their growth as readers and critical thinkers. Each of our girls has her own strengths and challenges along those lines—all of us do, in fact. By reading together, each mother has been able to tailor the home reading approach to meet her own daughter's individual needs or wishes.

FICTIONAL CHARACTERS

Learning from the Best and the Worst

The learning experience in a book is in the discussion much more than in any message you or I think the books are sending. It's the conversation that turns out to be more important.

You can have a very negative character, but it can serve as a stimulus for girls or young women to make connections. A character we think is wonderful might look priggish to a girl today. I wouldn't want to censor the characters of the books we give to our girls, but I would want to stress the importance of a woman author.

There may be the feeling that old books aren't germane, but I think it's good to read old books. There's no guarantee the book will be the same book for the next generation. The mothers may learn as much as the daughters. I wouldn't say to teach every book you loved as a child, but some of them have a lot of staying power.

—NINA BAYM, AUTHOR,
Woman's Fiction: A Guide to Novels by and
about Women in America, 1820–70

For instance:

📖 When the girls read aloud, we're able to identify when they have trouble with pronunciation, which also may mean they aren't familiar with the word. Sometimes they'll stop and ask about a word. If they appear to be struggling with it, or skipping past it, we might guide them through sounding it out and add a quick explanation of the word.

📖 When the mothers read, the girls become engrossed as listeners and tend to comment or ask questions more often about the story.

📖 Before we read, we might ask our daughter to refresh our memory about where we were in the story. This retelling process develops her ability to organize her thoughts and focus on main ideas.

📖 A character's behavior or other action in the story may prompt one of us to bring up a similar moment or experience from our own lives. It really does happen, and it makes for some very special moments!

> ## BOOKS TO GROW ON
>
> Six books I'd really want my teenaged daughter to read (if I had one):
>
> *Shizuko's Daughter*
> Kyoko Mori
>
> *Celine*
> Brock Cole
>
> *Weetzie Bat*
> Francesca L. Block
>
> *Gift from the Sea*
> Anne Morrow Lindbergh
>
> *High Wind in Jamaica*
> Richard Hughes
>
> *Letters to a Young Poet*
> Rainer Maria Rilke
>
> *The Trials of Molly Sheldon*
> Julian F. Thompson
>
> —JULIAN F. THOMPSON, AUTHOR,
> *The Fling*

Even if you each read independently, you can compare notes on the story as you progress, encourage the retelling and reflection, and share each other's reactions to the story. In her comments, you can listen for any hints that your daughter might need some additional support from you in reading or understanding the story.

Pam at the Cheshire Cat Bookstore points out that sometimes the first few chapters of a book, or a chapter introducing a new character, may seem formidable to a young reader. They may need some help getting into the book.

"Certain chapters are like meeting somebody for the first time—you may be a little uncomfortable—and you've got to get beyond that," Pam says. "Especially if it's not very fast-paced, it's useful to sit and read that chapter together and help them get beyond that. Once they do, you'd be amazed at what starts happening."

"What starts happening" is really the essence of the Mother-Daughter Book Club. We read more, we share more, and we enjoy more.

ACTIVE READERS—DON'T JUST READ!

The Great Books Foundation, in its leader training materials, describes the "interpretive reader" as one who "reads actively, raising questions and striving for understanding. An interpretive reader wants to know why the characters in the story act as they do, what the meaning might be of unusual or surprising events—what an author is trying to communicate through his or her words."

Whatever you call it, active reading is rewarding.

Here are some fun tips to turn on the active reader in your life—*just don't use them all at once!*

📖 **EXPRESS SURPRISE OR** wonder at a character's actions and ask why the character might have done what she or he did.

📖 **WONDER ALOUD** about how things might have turned out if something had happened differently, if a character had made a different choice or if people had responded differently at a certain point in the story. Ask your daughter how the story might have unfolded differently or ended differently.

📖 **ASK YOUR DAUGHTER HOW** she would like the story to end, or how she might have made it end if she was the writer.

📖 **MARK WORDS, PHRASES, IDEAS** or anything you think might make a good question for discussion. Encourage your daughter to do the same.

📖 **PICK AT SOME DETAILS.** Why might the author have used certain words or images? What was she or he trying to convey? Did it work?

📖 **PLAY WITH WORDS.** Some words or phrases can be understood in more than one way. How does it change the story if the word or phrase is understood differently?

📖 **JUST FOR FUN:** Invite your daughter on a "scavenger hunt" for five new or unusual vocabulary words or phrases from the text to share with the group.

> "Don't make your books childish, because if you read babyish books, some of the older girls won't enjoy them."
>
> *Brittney*

📖 **COMPARE ART TO LIFE:** How do your real-life experiences or your observations compare to what you read in the book?

MOTHERS AS GATEKEEPERS: CALLING ALL IDEAS, INSPIRATION

I enjoy the search for "good books." I like hunting up authors and stories we may not have encountered before, I like reading the books to preview them for the group, and I enjoy the excitement of finding the gems to introduce to our club, books we would otherwise have overlooked. I also believe that any mother who is willing to help organize a book discussion group very likely wants to use it to expose her daughter to the shelves of fine literature that the girls might not get around to reading in school or on their own.

That said, I think it's important to add that it's hard to go very wrong with as many well-written books as there are today—from classics to modern fiction, biographies and poetry—and with a group of mothers and daughters who like to talk about stories, ideas, and feelings. Give yourselves some credit: If a book turns out to be a little thin, it won't sustain much discussion on its merits, but in discussion you can reflect on the quality of the story and the writing, what they give the reader and what they don't.

The fact is, even if you read a 1930s Nancy Drew mystery book, there are ways to talk about characters and plot, attitudes and expectations, that reflect the era in which they were written.

The girls are learning all the time; the mother-daughter dialogue thrives.

POETRY

Reading into the World of Emotions

Mothers have a gorgeous opportunity to introduce their daughters to poetry. Especially as girls grow older and outgrow the rhyme-scheme poetry so frequently used with younger children, they can enjoy free verse poetry—so flexible and full of images and ideas. Poems about nature, animals, people—these are wonderful for getting kids to respond. Poetry is the most immediate form of expression of feelings. Of all kinds of writing, it speaks most directly to the human heart. Poetry makes feelings very accessible—the perfect source for a mother-daughter discussion!

Some questions that will take a discussion into the heart of a poem might be:

- WHAT IS THE POEM ABOUT?

- WHAT IS THE POET SAYING; what are the words saying?

- CAN YOU SENSE ANY FEELINGS the poet might have about the topic? Look at words, lines, phrases.

- DO YOU FEEL there are any hidden meanings?

- WHERE MIGHT THE POET BE WRITING? Outside, under a tree? Inside, in a pleasant place, or from a lonely window seat?

- HAVE YOU EVER FELT LIKE THIS? Have you ever looked at a tree or a flower or an animal and said, "Yes, that's how I feel!"

- COULD YOU IDENTIFY the person writing?

- HAVE YOU EVER WRITTEN about this topic?

—JOAN FRANKLIN SMUTNY, EDUCATOR, AUTHOR

I've been reminded of the value of *all reading* as I've heard or read reflections by respected authors, scholars, and others who speak of it, and sometimes of their own memories of reading.

Virginia Hamilton, celebrated author of so many fine books, recalls her early reading with a laugh:

"When I was young I read a great deal—I had sisters and they brought books into the house—and I loved the Nancy Drew stories. Some librarians don't like it when I say that, but those books were very available and I found Nancy Drew very interesting. She had her own car and she solved mysteries!"

When we think about age and reading levels, we should try to be less concerned about matching numbers and screening out things we're "not sure they're ready for" and be more open to the challenge—and potential inspiration—of stretching ahead, notes Rita Dove, 1966 U.S. Poet Laureate:

"It's a real danger, you know, making children's books too easy, presenting lessons in them instantly and effortlessly. . . . It's such a danger, because nothing in life that is worth anything is presented instantly to us, and children are perfectly willing to be challenged by something."

Stretching to meet new ideas, to reflect upon them, and to discuss them is the work of life and the heart of what we want to share with our daughters.

Jane Addams, social activist and 1931 Nobel Peace Prize winner, said it clearly, nearly a hundred years ago in the book *Twenty Years at Hull House*:

"Perhaps I may record here my protest against the efforts, so often made, to shield children and young people from all that has to do with death and sorrow, to give them a good time at all hazards on the assumption that the ills of life will come soon enough. Young people themselves often resent this attitude on the part of their elders; they feel set aside and belittled as if they were denied the common human experiences."

And our bookstore friend Pam Sacks brings that thought to us as it relates to our mother-daughter discussions today and into the future. "You can't rewrite history, but you *can* discuss it," Pam says. "If you read a book where the moms feel girls are treated in an old-fashioned way, then discuss it. Ask them to compare it to how things are today—or how they would want them to be."

> "Now when I read a book I think it through, and sometimes I go back and read a page again and again."
>
> *Maya*

Whatever book you read with your daughter, whatever book you discuss within your club, it is transformed by the sharing. So are we all.

ENDNOTES

📖 Make sure someone you know and trust has read a book before you recommend it to the club.

📖 Be creative—novels aren't the only kinds of books.

> "Our book club selections were books that I would not necessarily have read or discussed if not for the club setting, so the book group broadened my literary experience in a major way. Book club introduced me to a wide range of ideas and interpretations that I would not have experienced reading books of my own choosing."
>
> *Ari*

Choose books that are both enjoyable and thought-provoking.

> "It's fun picking books you think the rest of the club will enjoy. If your club flows well, you will pick a book that the others in the club will find interesting; trust yourself."
>
> *Skylar*

> "If I like a book it is really fun to read."
>
> *Molly*

FIVE

How to Structure and Lead Groups

THE MOST IMPORTANT THING ABOUT BEING A LEADER IS TO HAVE GOOD QUESTIONS AND LET EVERYBODY GIVE THEIR ANSWERS.

—MORGAN

Celia & Amy Reingold

Hi! I am Ceila Reingold, I am sixteen years old, in the tenth grade at Georgetown Day School. My mother has passed down her passion for the arts to me, and one day I hope to be as knowledgeable as she is. I have always been interested in drawing, painting, designing and making clothes and jewelry. A few summers ago I took a fashion design course. Ever since that class I knew I wanted to become a fashion designer and have been working toward that goal.

In school I enjoy all of my classes and cannot say that I have a favorite. I am part of two clubs: Brenner, which is a women's rights and discussion group, and the Harvard Model Congress.

I have a job working at a local children's clothing store, Full of Beans, which has helped me learn about retail and designing. I see the changes made in cuts and colors of clothing from season to season. Learning how to deal with customers and companies, learning the basics of running and managing a store, will hopefully help me with my career.

My sister, Olivia, who is three years younger than I am, and I have had a company since 2001. We make bracelets, tie skirts, quilts and other gifts. Our company sells at many different types of functions as stores, but we are trying to become only an online store. My parents could not be more helpful, moving all of our products back and forth to and from shows. I am so lucky to have the amazing parents that I do. They are incredibly supportive. Our company *ba ba baubles* does sell some of our products at Full of Beans. Working at a store where our products are sold allowed me to see the challenges of selling our own products.

This past summer I discovered a passion for tennis. I signed up for a week of tennis camp and ended up staying a month. I now play on my school team and plan to keep playing.

My mom's name is Amy. Creativity is something that my mother has in excess, and I would love to be lucky enough to have just a little of her creativity as I get older. She has traveled the world, combining her creative passions in design and cooking. After receiving a BFA in textile design, she went off to cooking school. She graduated from the Cordon Bleu and stayed in London for a year to work at a highly regarded French restaurant. Back in the U.S. she worked as a pastry chef for another top French restaurant. Her career in food continued for years, not only cooking but developing recipes and traveling to the Far East to research the Fusion concept. After I was born, she started her own company, consulting to major food companies. We lived in Hong Kong for two years when I was too little to remember. My mom now has a company making beautiful one-of-a-kind long jackets. They are really "wearable art."

One of the best stories that has unfolded within our circle wasn't on our book list at all. It's been the story of our own daughters growing up and, one by one, meeting by meeting, showing maturing qualities of friendship, intelligence, and leadership, all in the space of a two-hour book club session. This doesn't happen by accident. But it's not something anyone can put on an agenda.

In fact, the philosophy that shapes our club's structure and leadership style reflects the reality of our lives as girls and women. All of us, whatever our ages, have a need for friendship and laughter, for the stimulation that reading and discussion bring to our lives, and for the opportunity to grow within this special and supportive circle. Just as we're making the time and space in our lives for the Mother-Daughter Book Club, the way we structure our time together makes it meaningful, comfortable, and rewarding. Our club creates a time and space for us to *be*.

Once you focus on the meeting structure as a reflection of your group—not a management device—the rest falls into place. For example, when we arrive for a meeting, the girls head off one way to socialize while the mothers meet separately to take care of any administrative details, to preview books and unwind a bit.

> "A woman might be prepared to give some complicated analysis, and a girl might simply say, 'I thought it was great.' Well, how do we talk from there? You can say—and it's better if you're not the one saying it to your own daughter—'I thought this scene was really strange' or 'I don't understand why a girl would do that, can we act it out . . .' and often that can be a fun way to ask those questions."
>
> *Elizabeth Debold*

We didn't set it up that way; it just happened the first time we met and it felt right. It worked for everybody. And it still does. That little socializing up-front gives the girls time to *play*, time to connect with one another before they widen their circle to connect with us.

TIPS FOR STRUCTURING MEETINGS AND LEADERSHIP

📖 **KEEP IT SIMPLE.**

📖 **AVOID WRITTEN AGENDAS,** assignment sheets, or anything that looks or sounds like school or homework.

📖 **ENCOURAGE THE GIRLS** to take charge of the club and let each one exercise her judgment in her own way. Encourage creativity *and* simplicity in hosting and planning any book-related activity. (See Chapter Ten: "Beyond the Books.")

📖 **WHEN IN DOUBT,** err on the side of respecting the girls' choices. If the selection process is open to any books the girls suggest, then be ready to start sleuthing if they choose a Nancy Drew mystery.

📖 **INSTEAD OF RIGID RULES,** express expectations: respect for each other during discussion, and commitment to the club in terms of reading the books, attending meetings, and contributing to discussion. If you're going to be absent for a meeting, let the host know.

📖 **DECIDE HOW YOU FEEL ABOUT ABSENCES** or attendance of girls without their moms. Although we all understand that a twosome is preferred, on the occasional afternoon when either mother or daughter simply can't come, we encourage the other to come alone. Sometimes it becomes clear that a mother and daughter simply can't attend dependably. Then give them a graceful way out. Most likely you'll continue to see them and value them as friends—so show that you respect their priorities and wish them well.

ENCOURAGE THE OPEN EXPRESSION OF IDEAS AND FEELINGS. Unlike most adult book discussion groups, where sharing related tales or feelings is discouraged, the Mother-Daughter Book Club is just the place for that kind of sharing, along with more objective responses in discussing stories or characters.

SET A GOOD EXAMPLE. When the girls hear us sharing thoughts—including different points of view—in a respectful, collaborative way, they're learning about the world of women in a way they won't see in many TV sitcoms, movies, or even books.

DON'T FEEL PRESSURED to demonstrate smart, witty, insightful, sophisticated, and sensitive literary analysis. Relax, listen, contribute when it's comfortable, and watch for ways to help the girls explore the questions they seem to find compelling.

IN ALL MATTERS, ask instead of tell, and facilitate only when the girls make it clear they need help.

The sound effects for those thirty minutes—giggles, squeals, easy laughter, and confident camaraderie—remind me each time that our girls are at a special age of in-between. They still have this wonderful, silly energy that they're quick to lavish all over one another. Then a few minutes later, they're debating fine points of character development in a novel. As a mother, you wonder: How can they seem so young one minute and so much older the next? The answer is, they are young, and everything they are is part of that. They still have a need to giggle and play. They also have a need to exercise their intellect and leadership abilities in an environment of support and good times.

Another aspect of the meeting that has become established over time is the uninterrupted forty-five minutes we reserve for our discussion period. Once everyone's had a chance to relax and socialize for that initial half hour or so, we call the girls back and gather around for the discussion.

Forty-five minutes might seem like a long time, but both the girls and the moms feel it's just right. It's long enough for some real back-and-forth among the girls and mothers, long enough to explore ideas, to follow up on comments that beg for it, long enough for us all to enjoy expressing our thoughts in an unhurried way.

"We have different perspectives," Alexis says, "and one person will interpret something differently from another. It's been fascinating to hear my daughter express herself and get a read on her in this way. The group dynamics are wonderful."

"Even though children may not show you they've changed their mind, once they savor the conversation—it may be weeks or years from now—they'll think about it and understand and maybe at some point say, 'Ah, I see what my mother was saying, now I understand.'"

Alexis Christian

We hold off on refreshments until *after* the discussion, enjoying that as another opportunity for relaxed socializing. If your mother-daughter book club meets after school, you may want to put refreshments out for the girls' arrival time. That gives them an energy boost for the discussion period and puts a comfortable distance between snack and dinnertime. Whether the food comes before or after, it's nice to not have it as a distraction *during* discussion. The ups and downs for refills and inevitable questions about who wants what can sidetrack discussion.

Over time, you'll find that different mothers and daughters will contribute their talents in special ways. For instance, Alice, in our group, volunteered to write a simple one-page "newsletter" or update for our members. It includes some highlights from our last meeting's discussion, and any other information or reminders we want to circulate. It's been especially helpful for those who miss a meeting. And even if you were there, it's fun to read!

Every mother-daughter book club is unique and needs a structure that reflects the group's personality and objectives. If you all agree on some basic principles from the beginning, including hosting duties and a hosting and meeting schedule, then the leader simply keeps the group on track by tending to the other "light housekeeping" of administrative detail.

TIPS FOR THE CLUB LEADER

If your group plans a few meetings at a time instead of a year's worth, let the mothers know when they'll need to be prepared to plan some dates at the next meeting. Be the calendar watchdog.

If an author appearance or community event is of special interest to your group, bring it up for discussion. Stay active in the book and author hunt and encourage the other mothers and daughters to do the same.

You may want to ask one mother each time to handle the book-buying task, and let the others pick up their books from her and reimburse her for the expense. Or it may be more practical for each mother and daughter to be

> "I like the fact that the girls are so invested in this. They do look forward to it; even with the workload they have at school and after school, they won't give it up."
> *Kathie Thompson*

responsible for getting their own copies of the selection. Consider asking a local bookstore to provide your mother-daughter book club with a discount in exchange for buying multiple copies of the book.

NEW FACES, NEW FRIENDS: NEW MEMBERS AND GUESTS

Don't forget to put out the welcome mat for guests to your mother-daughter book club from time to time. Invite the grandmothers or aunts to read a book with you and join you for discussion. The girls might like to invite a special teacher from school. Or you may want to invite a respected person in the community whose area of expertise or activism ties in to the theme of your book. Guests add another vibrant perspective to the mix, and the girls experience the benefits of meeting and discussing ideas with someone they might not otherwise hear.

New members are another consideration. It's hard to imagine any group going on for any length of time without losing members to job transfers or other schedule priorities. The Mother-Daughter Book Club is no different. While it might seem tempting to invite mother-daughter guests to attend as prospective members, our group has tried to avoid any situation that leads to talking about other mothers or daughters who are not present, or "judging" guests for an invitation to join the group.

I'd suggest that when you feel the membership of your group has dropped to the point of needing some new regulars, you review your group's focus and any other relevant considerations, then think the prospects through in the same way you did to start your group. Someone will need to take responsibility—"take the heat"—for choosing whom to invite. Poll the mothers for any suggestions—they can ask their daughters for suggestions at home—and invite your "new member."

BOOKS TO GROW ON

I naturally consulted my daughter, Molly, who at age sixteen is one of the wisest readers I know. We both made up lists, put them together, and agonized over paring our choices down to a few, but agreed that the six titles we came up with—all coming-of-age stories, set in different times and places—were books we cared passionately about, books we would read and reread always. Here they are in no particular order:

A Tree Grows in Brooklyn
Betty Smith

Rumors of Peace
Ella Leffland

Anne of Green Gables
Lucy M. Montgomery

The Country Girls Trilogy and Epilogue
Edna O'Brien

To Kill a Mockingbird
Harper Lee

Anne Frank: The Diary of a Young Girl
Anne Frank

—SUZANNE FREEMAN, AUTHOR,
The Cuckoo's Child

GUIDANCE VS. INDEPENDENCE
Structuring Togetherness for Growth

Bertha Waters, a parent-training consultant, licensed social worker, mother of seven (including five daughters!), also serves on the Federal Advisory Commission of the Mary McLeod Bethune Council House National Historic Site. Ms. Waters' daughters—all busy women now—sometimes join her as co-presenters in her programs on women's history, health, and life relationships.

Asked how mothers can strengthen the mother-daughter bond yet respect their need for independence, she shared this story from her own life, about a moment when reading and mothering came together for a special and lasting result:

> "Everything I know about my mother now I think I learned through book club. I never really knew my mother before the club and I do not know if we would be friends like we are now without that time together."
> —MORGAN

"Years ago, when I was a young mother, I read a magazine article about a very respected mother, and someone asked her her secret. She said: 'Don't nag them; let them be as much as possible.'

"I had three children at that time. In those days—this was in the 1950s—it was considered out of style to have more than two children, so when we'd ride the trolley I'd always be right on them for every move they made or word they said, trying to make them behave perfectly—better than perfect—so no one would give us those disapproving looks.

"Well, with that mother's words in mind, I decided that when I rode the trolley I would sit in one seat and read—which I loved to do and never had enough time for—and I'd let my children sit in the seat behind me and I wouldn't get involved in what they were doing or saying unless they got to a point where it interrupted my reading. Everything worked out fine! And I remember that as a turning point for me, when I chose to be a person, and stopped being a 'professional mother,' and let them *be*."

TIPS FOR THE HOSTING MOTHER AND DAUGHTER

It's helpful to send out reminders a week or so before you host the mother-daughter book club meeting. Include the date, time, and place of the next meeting and the name of the book.

Remember, discussion is the main course at the meetings. Don't feel pressured to put out fancy food. For fun, look to the book: Sometimes the story includes a recipe or description of foods that you might make for the group.

The hosting daughter usually serves as leader for the discussion. She prepares questions to get the discussion started and keep it going along lines that interested her as she read the book. (See Chapter Six: "Discussion.") The host mom also may plan to bring up points for discussion.

If you want to try a book-related activity, it may include something as simple as bringing out a globe to locate geographic points of interest in a story or making refreshments that reflect the ethnic cuisine, as Linda and Rebecca did when they hosted the dis-

> "Thou shalt not correct to the point of causing frustration. Thou shalt not show any negative reaction to anything that is said, or make fun of anything that is said.
> *Grace Speights*

cussion for *Charlie Pippin*, a story with a tie to Vietnam. Your daughter might devise a game format for the discussion period, or you might arrange to visit an exhibit or see a film that relates to the book, and have the discussion there or over dessert afterward. It's important to keep this optional, and remember that you really need no more than the book and the group to have a great discussion. (See Chapter Ten: "Beyond the Books.")

A PLACE TO SPEAK FREELY AND GROW

How do you both let go and stay connected to your daughter? No textbook can show you the way. You just have to live it, listen to others who have been through it, and on occasion, step back and understand what's really behind the issue of the moment.

Underneath the yelling and screaming about "Help me with homework," there's a more profound statement being made: "I want to do it on my own. I want you there, but I don't want you there."

> "Book clubs are an easy place to talk because you know that what is talked about in the book club stays in the book club."
>
> —SKYLAR

I think what happens during the middle school years is the struggle for identity: "Who am I? Who do I want to be? What is it about my mother I like? What is it I don't like?" That fuels a lot of the struggle that sometimes occurs between mothers and daughters.

Whether they know it or not, when our daughters look in the mirror they look at us. Perhaps they don't always like what they see when they see what they may become. But they can't escape it. They'll come to either embrace it or reject it at times, and therein lies part of the struggle at this stage of their lives. They don't have what I have at fifty—or even at twenty-seven—a larger experience base and a broader view of what this relationship really is all about.

So many women I talk to who have grown daughters say they struggled during certain phases of their daughters' adolescence, and the relationships emerged totally transformed as their daughters became young adults. But you are not a young adult when you're thirteen.

—WHITNEY RANSOME,
National Coalition of Girls' Schools

ONWARD AND ONWARD: THE CLUB'S STORY UNFOLDS

It's easy to get distracted by all the exciting possibilities when you get good books and enthusiastic girls and women together. I like to encourage creativity, using simplicity as a touchstone. The best investment any of us can make in preparing for a meeting is simply to *read the book* with our daughters, enjoy talking about it together some at home, plan some thought-provoking questions, and come ready to share our thoughts. That thoughtful time and sharing with our daughters is the best investment we can make, period.

ENDNOTES

📖 Keep it simple.

📖 Encourage the girls to be creative and take charge of hosting and planning group activities.

> "My best book club memories are the meetings where the hostesses were really creative when planning the discussion. For example, when we read Dorothy West's *Wedding*, each daughter wore her mother's wedding dress."
>
> *Brittney*

📖 Prepare questions in advance, but welcome impromptu digressions that interest the group.

> "Don't be afraid of the discussion going off topic, especially if most of the people present seem eager to discuss the new topic."
>
> *Jessica*

📖 Invite guests for special meetings or even new members to enliven the circle.

> "Sometimes it's good to invite someone new to spice up the conversation and to hear a new point of view."
>
> *Skylar*

SIX

Discussion

THE LEARNING EXPERIENCE IN A BOOK IS IN THE DISCUSSION MUCH MORE THAN IN ANY MESSAGE YOU OR I THINK THE BOOKS ARE SENDING.

IT'S THE CONVERSATION THAT TURNS OUT TO BE MORE IMPORTANT.

—NINA BAYM

Jesse Greenblatt & Linda Adams

Hello, my name is Jesse Greenblatt and I'm sixteen years old. I'm in tenth grade and I have two sisters: Liza, age ten, and Haile, age six.

Unlike my mother, I have not always loved to read. My most vivid memories are those of me sitting on the couch watching television and my mom begging me to read one of the hundreds of books she bought for me. I remember her always saying things like: "I used to love to read when I was your age" or "If I only had the time you have to read." Many times I would just respond with: "What is so special about reading anyway?" and "Mom, I don't like books, GOD!" It was not until the sixth grade when I overheard some friends talking about a new book called *The Secret Life of Bees* by Sue Monk Kidd that I decided I would give reading a real try. Of course, because my mother had bought me every book that had a good review in desperate hopes of me reading, this book was already one of many on our bookshelf. I fell in love with the book within the first chapter. Never before had I pictured myself actually engrossed in a story, so when my mom would walk in on me reading before bed she was just as surprised.

With all of the new experiences that came with "being a freshman" I could not imagine a mother-daughter book club in which there would be a candid exchange about some of the issues that come up in high school. These discussions do take place, but what continues to amaze me is how all the mothers are able to balance what is okay to talk about in a mother-daughter conversation and what is wait-for-coffee-alone-with-the-other-moms appropriate. By being a part of this book club I have gained not only a new appreciation for books I never would have imagined reading but also a reassuring feeling that my mom is not the only one with high school–related concerns.

I know I will never share the same passion for books as my mom does, but I hope that one day we will look back at all of the books we read together and realize that with these books came great discussions and with these great discussions came even greater memories.

Hi! I'm Linda Adams, Jesse's mom. I have always loved to read. My earliest memories are of a hot summer day on my stoop reading one book after the other until the characters and plots ran together. I often read myself into a stupor.

I learned to read very early, probably kindergarten, and was able to read what were considered to be adult books, although my parents did not allow me to read them. One day my father figured out that I could read upside down and that I had been reading his books at the same time he was.

My taste in books has changed over the years, although I am still strongly drawn to books with complex character development. I like a good story, but the evolution of the characters' personalities is what draws me to my current favorites. I am now reading books set in southern Asia, a part of the world that I know very little about. Some of my favorites have been *A Suitable Boy* by Vikram Seth and *A Fine Balance* by Rohinton Mistry.

While I was waiting for the results of my amniocentesis, pregnant with my oldest daughter Jesse, I said this prayer every night: "Please, God, let our baby be healthy, and let her love to read." One of the things that I like most about Jesse is that she is able to balance all of the priorities in her life. While she does not have the same passion for reading that I do, being together in the book club has given us an opportunity to share the common ground of having encountered the same characters from our own perspectives.

Recently I read *The Lovely Bones*, a book chosen by my daughter for our mother-daughter book club. It is the story of a murdered teenage girl as she looks down on the people in her life from heaven. In the book everyone has his or her own personal heaven. In my heaven there would be bookstores, comfy chairs, and chocolate.

I don't know whether it's a gender thing or just a sign of intelligent life, but when girls get together, they talk. They like to talk about things they like and about things they don't like. They'll debate about anything, *anything*, until they lose interest, and then they'll drop it so fast you can hear it thud.

When I overhear a conversation between girls at the museum or on a playground, or listen to Morgan relaxed and chatting with her friends, I am impressed by the passion they invest in expressing themselves. Whether they're negotiating turns on the swings or bemoaning a homework assignment, they do it with feeling and they do a thorough job. If you can get past the *sound* of it—the part we tend to call whining or complaining—and listen for the *structure*, you'll often hear all the makings of mature, intelligent discussion: A girl states her case, expresses her opinion, backs it up with some evidence, entertains other views, and eventually arrives at a conclusion that ends the conversation.

> "I like to use the sleight of hand: You think a character is one thing and then it turns out the character is more than you thought."
>
> *Virginia Hamilton*

So, how do you tap into that reservoir of conversational energy and funnel it into a satisfying group discussion of literature and life?

There are some time-honored approaches that are helpful, such as the "shared inquiry" method of the Great Books Foundation, and other guidelines put forth by book club experts such as the American Library Association. As helpful as the guidelines are, it's important to remember that they're written for groups that come together to focus on the literature—*not* on the personal lives of the readers.

The Mother-Daughter Book Club is unique in our desire to explore literature *and* strengthen our mother-daughter relationships through the shared experience of reading, discussion, and reflection that very much includes our personal lives. Not only that, but our goal is for the *girls to lead discussion*—not the mothers. The discussion simply won't sound like a college literature class or any book discussion group with an adult leader. But when, over the course of a few meetings, you start to see your daughter expressing herself confidently, asking thought-provoking questions, listening carefully to others and encouraging others to speak and be heard, the sound of that discussion is a joyful noise.

If we want our girls to learn about leadership, we have to step back from the role of expert more often and let them practice it. The Mother-Daughter Book Club is the perfect place for it. They are among caring friends and loving mothers. No family politics, no grades or evaluations, no fear of failure, no risk of shame. Just happy opportunity.

So, as you read advice here or anywhere on how to lead discussion, when it comes to "rules" of discussion, remember that the first rule—and maybe the only rule—of the Mother-Daughter Book Club is that you always do what's comfortable and what works for you and your particular group of girls and mothers. Structure dictates so much of life outside this special circle; let your daughters lead the way here. You'll like where they take you.

> "A big part of how I learned to be a woman was overhearing my mother talk with her women friends, watching how grown women talk to each other.
>
> *Elizabeth Wheeler, Associate Professor of English, University of Oregon*

DISCUSSION: SHINING A LIGHT INTO THE HEART OF THINGS

When I think of our Mother-Daughter Book Club's most enjoyable and satisfying discussions, the quality that best describes them is illuminating. A good book tells a story. A good book discussion illuminates that story with the light of experience each of us brings to it. Discussion also adds to our experience of the book and of one another. We see further, deeper, or from a different perspective. It can be transforming.

One example stands out in my mind:

Patty Ann was the girl everyone loved to hate. One of the key characters in the book *Cousins* by Virginia Hamilton, Patty Ann is beautiful, talented, always well dressed, and earns the best grades in school. She is also a snob and her mother is too. Did I leave anything out?

Patty Ann's disgruntled cousin Cammy echoes our own daughters' sentiments when she describes Patty Ann as so "good at everything . . . in school, at home, at her piano [that] everything she did was like chalk scraping on a blackboard." By the time the story plays out to its dramatic conclusion, Patty

---

BOOKS TO GROW ON

The King James Version of the Bible

The Catcher in the Rye
J. D. Salinger

Jane Eyre
Charlotte Brontë

Wuthering Heights
Emily Brontë

David Copperfield
Charles Dickens

— KAYE GIBBONS, AUTHOR,
Ellen Foster

Ann doesn't have any sympathizers—in the book or among the Mother-Daughter Book Club girls.

In our discussion of *Cousins*, the story's plot and action grabbed everyone's immediate attention. But as we began to question the details of one critical episode, our discussion moved back to Patty Ann and her attitude: that impervious diamondlike perfection that put everyone off.

One comment led to another, and scouring the text for clues, we talked our way back, *past* Patty Ann's façade of perfection, to a place where we could look more objectively at her. Once there, we discovered that in many ways her world reflected the real world we all know well, where pressures for perfection are all around, and where girls measure themselves constantly against one standard or another.

Comments from mothers and daughters showed a surprising difference in how we each perceived the Patty Ann character and her motives. And the perceptions weren't divided along generational lines. Some girls thought she shouldn't have been so stuck up. Others didn't like her but thought her attitude was understandable given the fact that she was, in fact, smart, pretty, and talented. Some mothers remembered a girl like Patty Ann from their childhoods; others remembered *being* Patty Ann, at least in some ways, as a bright, talented girl who didn't fit in or who felt a relentless pressure to excel at everything they did.

By the end of the discussion, Patty Ann wasn't the snooty stranger she had been an hour before. The story felt closer—as if we'd *been* there. And the feelings we had shared made each of us more *visible* to the others, more real as an individual with life experience and a point of view, no matter what our age.

"Discussing issues in the group is different than reading alone or discussing it just the two of us at home," Alexis says.

"There's an added benefit. Not only do I hear myself and my daughter talk, but she hears the other mothers, as do I, and where I might hold back saying something, some other mothers will go ahead and say it, and I can get my daughter's opinion— my daughter can agree or disagree and it's just part of the group discussion—not a personal issue with me. And it's wonderful because we come from such varied backgrounds that we all bring something different to the group."

The death of a baby in another story we read was heartfelt by the mothers in our group. When none of the girls picked up on that as a point for discussion, we asked them what they thought of it. The truth was, they didn't much. One of the girls volunteered that she'd feel sad about it. Another said she'd feel sad, but then she'd get on with things. There was, of course, no way they could imagine the loss in the way a mother would. Some of us described what we were feeling about it, and how the loss might have affected the characters within the context of the story.

> "In books, you're talking about experience and life a little removed, so you have a wonderful vehicle for people to talk about themselves, in addition to learning about someone else's vision. And you can try on other visions, the many different portraits of girls and women."
>
> *Ellen Silber*

And then—in the words of our young partners—we got on with things.

"If we get a reaction, that's wonderful," Grace says. "If we don't, then we just move on. We don't want the point to get ignored, but we don't harp on it."

BOOKS TO GROW ON

BOOKS

Aesop's Fables

Greek Myths, Geraldine McCaughrean

Grimms' Fairy Tales, Jacob and Wilhelm Grimm

Hans Christian Andersen's Fairy Tales, Hans Christian Andersen

Alice's Adventures in Wonderland, Lewis Carroll

Lord of the Flies, William Golding

POETRY

The Rime of the Ancient Mariner, Samuel Taylor Coleridge

Shakespeare's Sonnets, William Shakespeare

Sonnets from the Portuguese, Elizabeth Barrett Browning

Invictus, William Ernest Henley

"A Psalm of Life," Henry Wadsworth Longfellow

"In Memory of W. B. Yeats," W. H. Auden

Annabel Lee, Edgar Allan Poe

— DIANE RAVITCH,
HISTORIAN OF EDUCATION,
New York University

GIRLS REACT TO WHAT WE SAY—AND DON'T SAY

When a subject hits a dead end, it may signal a lack of interest or it may be because the girls are taking a detour because they sense a roadblock up ahead.

Elizabeth Debold, a developmental psychologist and co-author of *Mother Daughter Revolution: From Good Girls to Great Women,* suggests that the obstacle to discussion sometimes is an unspoken dialogue that often goes on between mothers and daughters:

"Girls are also incredibly sensitive to who we are and what we expect as mothers, and where our anxieties are. Sometimes if we are really prepared to talk about a 'big issue' and are nervous about it, girls have a profound instinct about wanting to stay away from that. They'll turn away from the discussion because they feel there's something bothering their mom."

If we can say what we feel—sad, confused, angry—instead of silencing ourselves about things that disturb us, it gives our daughters an opportunity to know us as people—which is what they want. Then we open the possibility for true dialogue and connection.

"If you listen to the kinds of comments girls make about these things, they don't say, 'the character development was really poor,' or, 'I had trouble believing the plot.' They may say it felt fake or tell you they thought one of the characters was dumb—developmentally they're at a very different place than you are," Elizabeth Debold says. "But if you listen to them speak, in their own terms, you can hear that they're seriously engaged."

DISCUSSIONS THAT WORK: STRATEGIES FOR SUCCESS

Not every book inspires soulful reflections. Some discussions are more memorable than others. Some are memorable more for their humor, unexpected reactions, or a sudden encounter of a generation or maturity gap. All of them can be satisfying in one way or another.

A lively discussion needs a sense of purpose or direction, good questions, enthusiastic participation, recognition of each person's contribution, and a satisfying conclusion. Most of that boils down to thoughtful reading, careful reflection, and a respectful leadership style by girls and mothers.

"Some girls talk more than others and it's good when the quiet ones talk, too," Jamexis says. "It's more fun for them because then they're not just sitting there. And then everybody gets to hear their ideas."

"Don't ask questions where the answer's too easy or right there in front of you," Brittney suggests. "It's more fun if it's an answer you have to look up or think about."

One of the most helpful guides to leading discussion is *An Introduction to Shared Inquiry,* a reader-friendly training manual by the Great Books Foundation. "Great Books," as most people call the foundation, has provided materials and training for book discussion groups across the United States for many years. The Great Books style, as described in the leader's manual, offers a carefully structured approach to group discussion that focuses intently upon "fundamental questions raised by the text."

"The search is inherently active," the Great Books manual notes, because "it involves taking what the author has given us and trying to grasp its full meaning, to interpret or reach an understanding of the text in light of our experience and using sound reasoning."

One mother in our group is a trained junior Great Books discussion leader, and we have all benefited from the wisdom she brings from Great Books and her experience with groups of children using the program. We've borrowed from that sense of structure, creating our own unique approach to combine active reading, critical thinking, and the relaxed interaction of mothers, daughters, and friends.

The results are worthwhile.

"In the school setting my daughter was becoming a little reserved, but in our club discussions, I can actually hear her thoughts, and she's much more expressive," says Alexis. "I watch her as she listens to others, and she has become much more in-depth in the way she asks questions and listens to the answers. I can see she's really trying to understand someone else's point of view."

BOOKS TO GROW ON

Fiction about women coming of age in hard times:

How the Garcia Girls Lost Their Accents
Julia Alvarez

Jane Eyre
Charlotte Brontë

The Grass Is Singing
Doris Lessing

The Joy Luck Club
Amy Tan

Jasmine
Bharati Mukherjee

The Beet Queen
Louise Erdrich

—KATHLEEN COURRIER,
VICE-PRESIDENT,
COMMUNICATIONS,
The Urban Institute

QUESTIONS

It Takes All Kinds

• QUESTIONS OF FACT help define the story. Use these to make sure the girls understand what happened factually. Questions of fact can lead us back to the text to see what the author said, compared to what we thought the author said.

• QUESTIONS OF INTERPRETATION have several different answers that can be supported with evidence from the text. Why *did* a character do it? Why *would* a character do it?

• QUESTIONS OF EVALUATION ask us to think about something in the work in light of our own knowledge, values, or life experience. To decide whether we agree or disagree with the author's idea or point of view. What does the author say? What does the author mean? Do I agree with it?

—*Adapted from* An Introduction to Shared Inquiry, *Third Edition,*
The Great Books Foundation

TO GET A GOOD ANSWER, ASK A GOOD QUESTION

Spirited discussions begin with strong questions. Strong questions come in a lot of shapes and sizes, but what they have in common is that they lead through a process of discovery.

In the early meetings of our Mother-Daughter Book Club, the girls often came up with questions like those you might imagine on a fill-in-the-blank test at school. "What game did Jimmy hate to play?" "How did the wolf mother feed her babies?" The questions went for facts but didn't ask for much in the way of reflection or analysis. The girls had fun with them, regardless, but the mothers felt obliged to toss out follow-up questions that probed a little more deeply: *"Why* did Jimmy hate to play baseball?" And if he hated it so much, *"Why did he continue to play it?"*

With each daughter's hosting experience and her questions to lead discussion, all the girls learned a little more about what kinds of questions seemed to spark discussion.

Then one day a reporter called and wanted to sit in on a meeting and write about our club. Our next meeting was weeks away and they wanted the story *now*. We weren't ready to discuss our next book, so we called a special meeting and came prepared with questions that had us compare characters, plots, and other aspects of the first three or four books we had read. It was a *wonderful* discussion. This single experience of comparing and contrasting from book to book gave the girls a model for using comparison as a way to think and talk about literature.

Since that time, the girls routinely bring in questions that include comparisons from book to book. And our discussions weave and reweave previous themes and characters into the

GOT A GOOD QUESTION? ACT IT OUT!

Play-acting is a great way to bring issues to life for girls of any age.

Abstract thinking is a developmental step and it may be difficult sometimes to have a discussion about an abstract idea—like self-esteem or relationships—with younger girls. Before they're ten or eleven most girls take people and situations very literally, and if it makes sense in the story and makes sense in terms of what they know about people in their lives, then they don't have many questions. But you can ask the girls to play-act a character or act out one of the scenes in the book, or have the mothers play the scene and have some fun with the story.

You might go to a point in the story where you have a concern and say: "I thought that was a really strange part of the book" or "That part really bothered me, why don't we play it? Who wants to be the girl? Who wants to be the mother? Let's see if we can understand it or try different ways the scene could go."

The girls—as characters—can explore the situation in their own words and thoughts, and you can listen to their responses and learn a lot about what they know and don't know, and what they think. It gives girls a chance to bring their knowledge and questions in without having to make that kind of intellectual leap to the abstract issue. By role-playing a scene you approach the issue one step away from firm reality, but a step closer than the girls might experience it just by talking about it.

It allows you to ask questions without putting the girls on the spot. It gives everybody a real feeling of collaboration—and it's fun!

—ELIZABETH DEBOLD

material of the moment. That frame of mind makes it even easier to involve personal feelings and experience in the discussion. If you can compare two characters' attitudes about an issue, adding your own view seems like a natural third perspective to include. The girls don't feel put on the spot to disclose, and the mothers, with a comfortable entry into the conversation, seem more able to relax and leave the lectures behind.

> "I'm not so sure that any one particular type of character in a book is good or bad. What is much more important is for the character to be talked about—to hear this opinion and that opinion and get different perspectives on the character."
>
> Nina Baym

You may want to spend a few minutes during one of your early meetings talking about how to develop questions that fuel a lively discussion. Or just talk about it and do it for fun with your daughter during home reading time.

A few other tips for developing good questions:

📖 Avoid questions that can be answered with a yes or no.

📖 When in doubt, ask "why?"

📖 Ask questions that pull you back to the text to find out how you "know" something. Is it because the author or a character said it right out, or have you assumed something? Could there be a different conclusion?

📖 Ask about motives. Why *did* a character do what she did? Or why would she?

📖 Ask about details. Why *did* the author make it storm that night—what did that allow to happen in the story? What did the character's clothing or choice of foods tell about him? Why would the author want us to know that?

Why did characters feel the way they did? Are their feelings spelled out, or do you sense them in some other way? How?

Explore language. Do the characters talk in a way that tells you something about them?

DISCUSSION: HOW TO KEEP IT SIMMERING

Our discussions usually begin as the host daughter introduces the book, gives a short synopsis of the story and then presents her first question to get things started. Sometimes girls will raise their hands and wait for her to call on them; sometimes they just spontaneously toss out a thought or comment. The hosting daughter is the only girl who needs to have questions ready, so the other girls really are eager to hear them and start talking. Usually the discussion moves quickly, but everyone who wants a say gets it. And if the leader notices that someone hasn't said much, she may ask that person to pitch in a thought.

Early on, the moms wondered if we'd need to establish some rules about interrupting and hand raising and the like, but we've discovered the same heartening thing over and over again. When the girls know they're in charge, they take charge quite effectively, working these things out in a most respectful and responsible way.

Once the mothers got used to the feeling of their daughters being in charge, we discovered how refreshing it was to sit back and enjoy the experience. We found that we listened more objectively, we reflected more calmly, and we enjoyed

THE ART OF DISCUSSION
Advice from the Girls

"If you talk about interesting things, then it keeps people wanting to talk. Ask questions like, 'Who was your favorite character,' or 'What part did you like the best?'"
    —ASHLEY B.

"If you're the discussion leader, don't keep choosing the same people to answer questions all the time."
    —BRITTNEY

"Sometimes the moms will get a little carried away. The host will ask one question and the moms will get into this huge discussion. But then somebody—one of the girls—will just say, 'Can we get back to the discussion?'"
    —MORGAN

"Moms should let girls answer the questions first, so the girls get a chance to talk."
    —BRITTNEY

"One question that can be interesting is 'What would you do if you found yourself in this situation?'"
    —MAYA

"The mothers should help make sure that everyone has a chance to answer questions and each person feels that she is an important part of the club."
    —REBECCA

being heard as equals within the group.

One way to help yourself step back from the coaching role and enhance the discussion and participation by the girls is to try what Bonnie Diamond, an elementary school language arts specialist, calls her "thirty-second rule." In her classroom discussions, when she poses a question, she pauses a full thirty seconds before calling on any student to answer. This gives everyone a few moments to collect her thoughts. It also slows the pace of the discussion—which otherwise can race at runaway speeds with young talkers—and makes it more inviting for the shy or reflective thinkers to join in.

> "In discussion, you want to open opportunities and don't want to foreclose on possibilities."
>
> Nina Baym

A relaxed version of that works well for a mother-daughter discussion group, too. If the mothers simply try to refrain from prompting, or otherwise stepping in, for about thirty seconds, it gives the girls time to think. If a question hits a dead end with no response after that generous pause, then it may help for a mom to rephrase or reframe a question to help the discussion along. If discussion stalls out, put everyone at ease by acknowledging it and suggesting another line of thought. Real-life discussions aren't scripted as they are on TV. It's good for us all to feel the pace of genuine reflection and thoughtful conversation.

It may take a little practice to pause—we're all so accustomed to responding to everything and everyone as quickly as possible. But it's worth the try.

"Silence can be uncomfortable for people—even just a few seconds of it," says Kathie. "But I like to wait it out and see where the girls take the discussion naturally, where it goes."

LESSONS FOR LIFE

Passing Them On

Family stories can be a way of handing lessons down from one generation to the other. My grandmother used to tell us different kinds of stories. When she was trying to make a point about determination, she'd tell us one story. When she was trying to make a point about virtue, she'd tell others.

My great-grandmother was a teenage slave girl, and as such she was forbidden to have books or any reading material. Later, as a free woman, she placed a great importance on education for her children. And she shared the stories of her life. Her daughter, my grandmother, used to tell us this story about her making the beds in the "big house." Because the beds were so high, they used to use a long broomstick to reach across and push that bedspread under that pillow to make the fold.

One day my great-grandmother was making the bed that way when the master's son came into the room and attempted to molest her. Well, she had been so conditioned to protect her virtue that she hit him with this stick! Her mistress complimented her for protecting her virtue but then gave her a whipping for being so audacious or bold as to hit the master's son.

My grandmother told us the story in order to point out the importance of being virtuous and of not letting anyone talk you out of your virtue no matter how important or powerful they might be. That experience, passed down in that story, has affected all of the girls and women in our family.

—BERTHA WATERS

SHARING LIVES AND
LEAVING LECTURES BEHIND

Excerpt from The Man in the Ceiling

Jimmy nodded in the same way he did when Mother took him forcibly by the hand to the Museum of Modern Art in New York and made him look. Jimmy didn't mind art if he could see it alone and decide for himself what he liked and what he didn't. But when it came to art, his mother was like his teachers. The questions she responded to were her own, not Jimmy's. And the more she lectured him about Picasso and Braque and Cézanne, the more the canvases on the wall began to remind him of math problems on Mrs. Minnafy's blackboard. . . .

"You don't have to lecture to 'speak from experience,' " says psychologist Elizabeth Debold. "For instance, if there's a girl in the story who is overly concerned about her appearance or her weight, could that be something that the girls or women have had to struggle with or are familiar with in their own lives? To engage in a discussion, the women present can ask themselves, 'Is there a place in my experience that I can speak from?' Think about sharing experience rather than lecturing or wanting to lecture about the perils of eating disorders or whatever."

—ELIZABETH DEBOLD

Don't feel questions have to be "hard" or complex to inspire good discussion. Simple questions have great discussion potential when they ask what the reader thinks or feels. Nina Baym shares her experience as a professor in the college classroom:

"I used *Little Women* as the basis for a discussion in a class of undergraduate women. I had assumed that Jo would be everybody's favorite character, but that wasn't the case," she says. "Some identified with Amy—she was ambitious and wanted to be an artist—and some identified with Meg. Nobody identified with Beth because she died, but what I assumed to be automatic wasn't the case at all. So you can ask: 'Who's the main character?' and you'd be surprised in some cases."

> ### BOOKS TO GROW ON
>
> These are books from my childhood that I still love to read:
>
> *The Bible*
>
> *Winnie the Pooh*
> A. A. Milne
>
> *The Secret Garden*
> Frances Hodgson Burnett
>
> *The Yearling*
> Marjorie Kinnan Rawlings
>
> *A Tale of Two Cities*
> Charles Dickens
>
> —MARY RODGERS, AUTHOR,
> *Freaky Friday*

BOOKS AND AUTHORS: LET THEM BE YOUR HELPERS

In group discussion, the books become your partners, your teachers, your tools. They give you the benefit of someone else's research, someone else's wisdom, to help you explore an issue.

Whenever you get mothers and daughters talking, the daughters don't all the time hear the mothers, and mothers don't all the time hear them, but they can hear each other through the book—it bridges the communication gap. You can step out of yourself as an individual and into your role as part of a group, which gives you the ability to deal openly with issues that might be difficult one-on-one.

The comfort level of discussion within our circle lets us take some of these touchy questions home to talk about there. And sometimes it works the other way—bringing conversations from home to the club—as Alice recalls about our time with the book *Julie of the Wolves*:

"There's a part in *Julie* where the little girl has been promised in marriage to a little boy, and at thirteen she goes to marry this little boy. One evening the little boy decides he needs to consummate the marriage. Nothing actually happens because the little girl runs away," Alice notes, "but I hadn't told Holly that this issue was in there. She came to me alarmed when she read it, and said, 'Is this sexual abuse? Is this right? Is this fair?' I had to stop and think: 'Now that I've introduced it, what do I do, where do I go with it?'

"We talked about the cultural aspects of it, how the marriage was an accepted part of that culture, and how it still goes on in some cultures," Alice says. "Of course, when it came up at book club discussion, Holly blurted out that it was sexual abuse. Some of the girls giggled. A lot of them didn't even want to discuss it. There was a shyness about it, but a sense that something was wrong about it. From that point on, when they needed to refer to that period of time in the story, they'd say 'that time.'"

We had been curious to see what the girls' perception of

this situation was, and how we could help them to better understand it as a cultural issue. Unable to make much of an impression with talk of cultures, finally one of the mothers asked the girls if they would like their parents to arrange their marriage. There was a resounding "No!" Once we were speaking their language, they knew just how to speak their minds.

The discussions always hold more surprises for us—more discovery—when we aren't directing them. Sometimes we expect a discussion of some issue to take off because we're *ready* for it, and the girls skip right past us and down some other avenue of thought. We may try to pursue the idea by asking a question or pulling their attention to it, and sometimes it brings about a good stretch of conversation. But you never know. The girls are just as likely to giggle, groan, or otherwise shrug it off. That's when it's important to stop and listen and hear what they're telling us—they're not interested, maybe *not ready*, and the topic is best just left for the moment.

It's not forgotten, though. Inevitably the idea resurfaces during conversations at home, or for no apparent reason when we're reading the next book. The candor and comfort level that we enjoy with each other at our Mother-Daughter Book Club meetings carry over to the unlimited horizons of daily life. As it turns out, the Mother-Daughter Book Club discussions aren't an end point in the study of a book. They're a starting point in our mother-daughter relationships for exploring and sharing our lives.

BOOKS TO GROW ON

My daughter and I had (and still have) a very special relationship. I never had any sisters and therefore never experienced as a child the wonderful children's books Elizabeth and I explored together. Nothing can ever take those hours away from either of us. She still remembers our reading *Caddie Woodlawn* while she was sick with the flu in fourth grade. And every once in a while, when she's sick, we'll be talking and she'll say, "I wish you were here to read a little *Caddie Woodlawn* to me, Dad." Those are the lifetime relationships that are built with family reading.

Here's my list of favorites:

PICTURE BOOKS

Madeline, Ludwig Bemelmans

Good Griselle, Jane Yolen

Monster Mama, Liz Rosenberg

NOVELS

The Bears' House, Marilyn Sachs

Bella Arabella, Liza Fosburgh

A Blue-Eyed Daisy, Cynthia Rylant

The Day It Rained Forever, Virginia T. Gross

Caddie Woodlawn, Carol Ryrie Brink

The Girl with the Silver Eyes, Willo Davis Roberts

Roll of Thunder, Hear My Cry, Mildred D. Taylor

Words by Heart, Ouida Sebestyen

— JIM TRELEASE, AUTHOR,
The Read-Aloud Handbook

ENDNOTES

📖 Encourage the girls to lead discussion—not the mothers.

> "Sometimes if the mothers speak too much it intimidates the girls. Make sure the discussion is evenly matched."
>
> *Skylar*

📖 A good question is the key to a good discussion. When in doubt, ask "Why?"

> "I love questions that make us look at an issue from different angles and that can be discussed for hours on end."
>
> *Brooke*

📖 Let the book and the author guide your discussion. Act out scenes from books to spark conversation

SEVEN

The Mother-Daughter Dialogue

IT IS THE RESPONSIBILITY OF EVERY ADULT—ESPECIALLY PARENTS, EDUCATORS, AND RELIGIOUS LEADERS—TO MAKE SURE THAT CHILDREN HEAR WHAT WE HAVE LEARNED FROM THE LESSONS OF LIFE, AND TO HEAR OVER AND OVER THAT WE LOVE THEM AND THAT THEY ARE NOT ALONE.

—MARIAN WRIGHT EDELMAN,
FOUNDER AND PRESIDENT, CHILDREN'S DEFENSE FUND

Joanna Rothkopf & Jane Prelinger

Hello, my name is Joanna and I'm sixteen and in tenth grade at Georgetown Day School. My sister, Laura, is a year younger and attends the same school. This is my first experience with a book club. I guess one of my defining characteristics is my abnormal preoccupation with the future. I have known exactly what I want to do the next twenty-five years, if not longer, since I could gurgle. Currently, I am planning on becoming a general surgeon, epidemiologist, or a working dancer . . . if not all three.

I have been dancing practically since I was walking; however, I think I've grown a bit technique-wise since my blue garbage bag tutu days at Periwinkle Dance Studio. I developed an interest in all types of performing arts a few years ago when I went to Long Lake Camp for the Arts in the Adirondacks. This interest may have been sparked because both of my parents have some history in theater. The past two summers I attended Stagedoor Manor in Loch Sheldrake, New York, for musical theater. While my main artistic passion is dance, after this experience the Broadway stage beckons.

I have also always had a deep interest in writing as well, which makes the book club especially interesting for me. It has exposed me to so many different writing styles and has taught me what types I like and what types I could live without.

Psychological aspects of life and people have also always appealed to me, and with this book club I have found that my mother and I uncannily get each other's thinking.

Hi! I'm Jane Prelinger, Joanna's mom. Being a mother of two girls is the most powerful, profound life experience I can imagine. I am also a clinical social worker, clinical director of a mental health agency, and have a private practice doing psychotherapy. I love being a mother and I love my work. Sometimes I feel as if I can't devote enough time to either, although I'm always trying.

Growing up, I was sandwiched between two sisters, so having two daughters sometimes re-creates old experiences. But it has also given me a new way of looking at the world. Reading has always been the thing I turn to in order to soothe me to sleep and provide escape. Now that Joanna is a teenager, I am finding the time we spend together at the book club to be a special gift. I get to look at her and listen to her from a different perspective. I find myself admiring this intelligent, sensitive, and sensible young woman, and thinking that I can't believe she's my daughter. We have a forum to talk about things as equals, which is sometimes hard to do in our everyday lives. I'm valuing this book club even more than I had anticipated.

The script for motherhood was written a long time ago. You'd think it would have improved over the years, but here we are, into the twenty-first century, and the dialogue still comes down to something like this:

MOTHER: Hurry up or you'll be late for class!

DAUGHTER: I can't find my shoes.

MOTHER: Where did you take them off?

DAUGHTER: They aren't there.

MOTHER: Nobody came along and took your shoes. Wherever you left them is where they are. If you put things where they belong, you can find them when you need them. The same thing goes for your homework, your clothes—I left your folded clothes on the bed a week ago and you haven't put them away yet—if you'd keep your room clean, you could find—

DAUGHTER: Mom, I found my shoes!

MOTHER: Where?

DAUGHTER: Where I left them. Hurry up, Mom, you're making me late for class!

It isn't the kind of dialogue that melts naturally into a thoughtful sharing of inner lives. In fact, from the sound of things around our house, it would be natural for my daughter to think my interests in life are laundry, meals, homework, and getting places on time. That and forcing other people to think my way about laundry, meals, homework, and getting places on time.

Maybe I'm a little oversensitive to patterns in history—it is, after all, something I work with a lot as a museum administrator. But from one busy day to the next, I hear the age-old pattern of mother-daughter dialogue playing out all around me.

As Morgan was turning nine, I could see that pattern of communication taking shape in our lives. There were days when most of our conversations—if you could call them that—fell into one of two categories: maintenance or compliance. I was on her case about everything. I didn't mean to be. I did it because I thought she needed the direction. She didn't see it that way at all, of course, and said so. We were both getting weary of the debate.

Other mothers were telling me similar stories about the mother-daughter dialogue in their own homes. We all had the same wistful conclusions: We could see adolescence looming for our daughters, and we wanted to strengthen our relationships with them while there was still time—before they became teenagers and completely lost interest in us.

I thought about how I only began to really get to know my own mother a few years ago when she came to live with us for a time after she suffered a stroke. One day during that time, I was astonished to hear her playing our piano. I had no idea she could play. Turns out she'd learned as a girl, and it had been a source of pleasure to her all these many years. How could I not know that? The truth was, we had a lot of unexplored territory between us, and that visit began our belated effort to step beyond our generational identities and get to know each other, one good woman to another.

When I thought about Morgan, and the kind of relationship I wanted to enjoy with her as the years press on, I knew I had to change the script somehow, and I wanted to do it *now*.

The quality of our relationship was nobody's priority but mine, and the demands of housework, homework, after-school activities, and family, community, and professional life weren't going to change. I knew that good intentions weren't enough; I'd had those for nine years.

When my thoughts turned to the idea of a mother-daughter book club, it felt promising. The experience of our first organizational meeting delivered on that promise of creating a space in our lives where we could talk about ideas, ourselves, and each other. Our Mother-Daughter Book Club experience has, in fact, changed the script of mother-daughter relationships, for all of us, in more ways than we ever imagined—all of them good.

SHARING: A CIRCLE OF TRUST AND TRUTH

You can sit by yourself and enjoy a good book. But something very different and special happens when you get together and talk about a book with other people. You experience the book differently. Discussion becomes a prism, breaking the book's events, characters, and themes into a rainbow of ideas that lead the way to still more discussion. Things we thought were obvious can become intriguing; the ordinary can become interesting. The assumptions that so often define our attitudes toward each other as mothers and daughters, and which limit our experience of each other, can fall away.

With their friends, the girls feel the strength and security to say things that, alone, they just wouldn't say to your face. They feel fortified. The respect for their mothers is still there, but the veil is lifted.

"We don't always see things from the same perspective, but we encourage them, " Cheryl says. "There's a lot of respect between the mothers and daughters. Part of this is about helping them learn to think independently and not be overly influenced by another's opinion—even when the 'other' is your mother."

Sometimes the moments of discovery have nothing to do with the books at all, but the fact that we're all together just relaxed and talking about things, speaking what's on our minds.

For instance, one of our mothers mentioned to the group that she was facing a potential promotion at work with some mixed feelings because it would require that she work year-round instead of the nine-month school year. "I hope you don't get it," her daughter declared. "I like the time we get to spend together in the summers." She hadn't told her mother how she felt about the situation before, but the comfort level in our circle made it easier for her to say something difficult. It gave them a bridge for talking more about it later, just the two of them.

> "When I look at my daughter, I can see that in many ways we're the same and in many ways we're different. My job as a mother is to help her become what she wants and needs to become, rather than what I may wish. Her dreams will become her life."
>
> *Harriet Mosatche,*
> *Director of Program*
> *Development,*
> *Girl Scouts of the U.S.A.*

There's a certain level of trust built into the group, too. We're here as pairs of mothers and daughters, but the understanding is that we're all individuals and this is a place where we speak for ourselves and listen respectfully to each other. We don't interrupt or correct the girls as they speak. We don't try to make over their answers to please ourselves or to fit an image we wish they would project. And we don't feel responsible for what our "partner" says. We're all there to explore. We really

AN AUTHOR'S FAMILY HISTORY
Strong Women and Storytelling

In the first year of our Mother-Daughter Book Club, we read four books by Virginia Hamilton: *Cousins, Her Stories, The House of Dies Drear,* and *The Mystery of Drear House.* Mothers and daughters alike were swept into these powerful stories; the characters and events come up time and time again in our discussions of new selections and life themes. In this interview, Ms. Hamilton shares with us a bit of *her story:*

"I came from a storytelling family. My parents were great storytellers—my mother particularly. My mother *told stories.* It's something she did all the time. The first one I ever heard was of my grandfather's escape from slavery to this part of Ohio. So often the subtexts of my stories are from that period of time and that place.

"One of the books that particularly impressed me when I was younger was by Shirley Graham, who became the wife of black scholar W. E. B. DuBois. She wrote a book called *There Was Once a Slave*—the biography of Frederick Douglass—and for me it made him come to life. I read that and said, 'I'd like to do that.'

"Storytelling was the way my family passed along cultural learning—the family's lineage, for instance. My family had been in Ohio for six or seven generations, so it gave you a sense of history because everyone talked and nobody told the story the same way twice. It was a wonderful way of being together, talking and spending time together.

"My father was a classical mandolinist and traveled widely, setting up these mandolin clubs all over the country. He met my mother in Canada—she said that when she met him she knew that was the man for her, and they were married some time later. She told stories about it all. My father told me about the last great camps of the High Plains Indians because he saw all that. I came by dialogue at an early age, knowing that talking had a beginning, a middle, and an ending. As soon as I could write, I could write dialogue.

"My mom and dad let us grow and learn. There were only three things I had to do: Be home before dark. I had to be on the honor roll. And I had to not play too hard—I used to get nightmares if I did that. That was about all. We had a twelve-acre farm. My uncles all had farms, and you could play all day and never leave family land. It was a very secure place; the outside world didn't often get into ours.

"My mother was very strong; all the women in my family were. She had her circle. The women were very vital in my life. I write my books for everyone to read—*girls and boys*—but I do write books that are often female-oriented. In my books, the female characters are always searching for something and they often find it, and what they find is themselves and their own strength. I want girls to understand there has been a long history of strong women and women doing their own kinds of work for a very long time. Women have always been oppressed but managed to see their own way, and there is a long tradition of females doing what they want to do, and that's what *girls* can do. They can have selves of their own, a definition of themselves.

"Me? What I do is write and I really enjoy it. That's what I do. That's the important thing."

don't know what the girls are going to say about some subjects as they arise. At times the things they say may make us squirm a little, but the feeling is: We're among friends.

Here's a snippet of the discussion that arose one day when talk turned from the characters in the book to the characters at home:

MOTHER: This is maybe a dangerous question: Do your moms get depressed?

GIRL: Yes. *(laughter)*

MOTHER: Do you all do anything to help us when we're depressed? What do you do?

GIRL: I try to get my momma to come back.

GIRL: When she goes in the library, I talk with Daddy.

GIRL: I usually try to leave my mom alone because she just gets stressed.

One afternoon's discussion took an unexpected turn when the girls picked up on a scene in the book in which the character retreats to the bathroom when she wants to be alone. Her family's apartment is so cramped and crowded that she has nowhere else to go. One mom asked the girls if they had a special place at home where they went when they wanted to be alone. Instead of answering the question, one daughter mentioned that when her mom and dad have an argument, her mom goes to the study to be alone.

From there, we moved back to the book to answer the next question, and the discussion forged ahead to new material.

When I play that scene back in my mind, I see points at which we could have squelched the discussion with a motherly quip—"Let's talk about something else." We could have sweetly shamed them into dropping the topic by saying something like "Let's move on—we don't want to embarrass anybody."

Believe me, it was tempting. But we kept to our good intentions and they worked! The girls were able to share their experiences, we learned more about how they see things, and we were able to contribute a few thoughts before they turned back to reflect on their own feelings and the universal need, at times, for a place to be alone with one's thoughts.

I couldn't have planned it better myself.

READING BOOKS, SHARING STORIES, SHARING LIVES

I am a daughter, too, after all. I was young once. Think about who you were at age nine or ten, and where you were in your thinking and your understanding of the world. When I think about life as I knew it at ten, I'm not sure what's memory—memory of real things—and what's images of stories I heard over and over as a child. Even more than the facts, I recall impressions I had of the people and events going on around me. I remember feelings—feelings of comfort, delight, pride, or disappointment. The fact is, all of it counts; all of it shapes the life of a girl.

Clearly, no matter what we say as mothers, our daughters hear us through their own experience. And they "hear" that mother-daughter dialogue through our actions even more than our words.

I can tell Morgan that I respect her intelligence, that I like to hear what she thinks about things, and that I want our relationship to include a feeling of friendship as we both grow older.

BOOKS TO GROW ON

Here is a booklist my sixteen-year-old twin daughters (Mavis Gruver and Nia Kelly) and I came up with:

Moon Over Crete, Jyotsna Sreenivasan

A Wrinkle in Time, Madeleine L'Engle

Pride and Prejudice, Jane Austen

The Secret Garden, Frances Hodgson Burnett

To Kill a Mockingbird, Harper Lee

Up the Down Staircase, Bel Kaufman

An Outbreak of Peace, Sarah Pirtle

Finding My Voice, Marie G. Lee

Women Who Run with the Wolves, Clarissa Pinkola Estes

Sula, Toni Morrison

Twelfth Night, William Shakespeare

New Moon: The Magazine for Girls and Their Dreams

— NANCY GRUVER, PUBLISHER,
New Moon magazine

The words tell her what I think, but our Mother-Daughter Book Club discussions give me a place to show her what I mean.

We've also noticed that the girls respond differently to our comments when we make them at group. We all respond differently, in fact. When someone expresses disagreement over a point, it's taken as a springboard for more talk—not a personal complaint that has to be remedied. When a mother shares a life story or view, it isn't told or heard as a lecture, as it so often seems to be at home. The girls listen. Sometimes they'll pick the thought up for discussion. Other times, they want to move on.

"In discussion, you hear it from your point of view and your mom's point of view, and sometimes they're different and sometimes they're the same," Jihan says. "It's definitely more interesting."

Jamexis adds: "When the mothers start talking, it's different than when the children are talking. The mothers talk deeply about things, with different insights."

An observation from Holly offers a slightly different perspective on the same scene: "One thing I've found out is girls really like to read, and mothers can really talk," Holly says. "We answer questions and it's in like five sentences at the most. The moms talk in paragraphs."

These old moms' tales don't go totally unappreciated, however. Says Brittney: "It's okay when the mothers talk about things. You can learn about what happened to other people when they were little."

And Ashley B. offers this definitive piece of sage advice: "I would tell moms not to go on and on about what happens to them. That just makes the discussion longer and boring. We like hearing their stories some, but if they think it's going to

MOTHERS AND DAUGHTERS IN THE CLASSICS

Seeing the mothers and daughters in classic literature interact is so enlightening because the girls all related to their mothers in very different ways than children relate to their mothers today. And mothers interacted with their children quite differently.

The thing that fascinated me most was I found there are so many wonderful parenting techniques modeled—wonderful things to do with children and how to talk with children, even how to effectively discipline or motivate them to do certain things. In *Little Women, Anne of Green Gables,* and the *Little House* books, all these girls interact with their mothers or a mother figure in very real ways.

All the mothers—including the mother figure in *Anne of Green Gables*—were very sensitive, but they were strict and had a definite plan as to how their children should behave, how they should develop as people, about their moral development. And it wasn't preachy. In *Little House,* when Laura was about to do something a little naughty, all Ma had to do was say, "Laura," and Laura knew she had better shape up. The mothers had very definite expectations about behavior and yet they weren't unreasonable.

What this did was it gave children a measure of confidence that they could connect with the adult world, they could be in the adult world, and yet be accepted as children.

—CAROLYN STROM COLLINS, AUTHOR
The World of Little House,
The Anne of Green Gables Treasury,
The Little Women Treasury

be a long, boring one, they shouldn't start it. If it's short and interesting, that's okay."

Okay. So we do sometimes get a little carried away with expressing our views. But we never gang up on the girls with motherly advice. In fact, the mothers often have different perspectives on a discussion point. But the presence of several mothers in the discussion seems to lend some credibility to each mother when she makes a point of her own.

"It's been very good to talk to other moms with girls the same age, " Grace says. "It shows you that what you're going through—the developmental stuff—you're not going through alone. You learn how others have dealt with these issues. We can talk about issues that otherwise we wouldn't take the time to do. We've developed wonderful relationships with the moms."

Our reading selections, and our group discussions, give all of us—girls and women alike—a feeling of shared lives. Sometimes we find company in the characters or authors we meet through our books. I'm not the only woman struggling to balance responsibilities and desires in my life, as well as in the lives of those I love. Sometimes we find support or encouragement as we compare our lives or thoughts with those we're reading, or share our own tales from the front. Whose fact, whose fiction? It doesn't matter. We're all on the same field trip, taking in some views. It's all part of the landscape.

LEARNING HOW TO LISTEN TO GIRLS

How is it that a child can get high marks for "listening skills" on a school report card and seem so totally oblivious to the spoken word at home? Am I the only mother who has to repeat

MOTHERS AND DAUGHTERS
Celebrating Our Individuality

We look at our daughters and we think: "They're our daughters and we should have this immediate connection and bond." Yet that's not always the case. We have to listen and listen to them and to ourselves.

We all carry our childhood selves with us. As mothers, we think we can empathize relatively easily with what it's like to be nine or thirteen or seventeen, but what we're remembering is what it was like for us to be nine or thirteen or seventeen, and the social context isn't the same.

Times change and people are different. People are individuals, and our daughters are individuals. We need to make sure we value our own individual selves. Then we can value our daughters' individuality and not expect to relive our lives through our daughters—thinking of things we didn't do quite right and trying to make sure they "do it right." A lot of the difficulty comes from that: seeing them in terms of what we hope they might be, rather than seeing them for themselves.

I'm not sure we need to see things through their eyes. Rather, we need to understand they have their eyes and we have ours, and not expect them to see things as we do or us to see things as they do—we mothers have a much longer and different experience. They don't have the experience to know what we know, or even to know that we know it. We can't expect them to know. We didn't used to know it either.

It's better for all of us if our daughters can understand that we see things a little differently. Then there's a basis for dialogue. It's always illuminating to be in any discussion of what our daughters read because it gets to what they think and like, and getting daughters to talk about what they like and read is the important thing.

Whether it's mothers and mothers, or mothers and daughters, or daughters and daughters, the more the opportunity we have to have those discussions, the more we learn about other people and ourselves.

—SUSAN MCGEE BAILEY, EXECUTIVE DIRECTOR,
Wellesley Centers for Women

requests for children to clean up rooms, put the milk in the refrigerator, or get started on homework?

Listening means different things in different places. On a nature walk, it means to silence yourself and pay attention to the sounds around you. At school and at home it usually means to follow directions. Sometimes it means to learn a fact or a concept. Listening is something you almost always hear adults asking children to do. You just don't often hear children ask adults to listen, but that doesn't mean we shouldn't try it more often.

You might think of listening as a passive thing to do, but in our Mother-Daughter Book Club discussions, we put our listening skills through a real workout. We listen for opportunities to recognize every girl's contribution as important to the group, to encourage the quiet one to speak and the rushing one to reflect. We listen for the sound of their lives: for hints of courage or confidence that we can bolster, for misinformation or confusion we can clarify. As the discussion moves along, our girls are expressing themselves about issues and in ways that we may not often see at home, so the payoff for listening is that we learn more about them.

For all of us, but especially for the girls, the experience of being *listened to* is exciting.

They show obvious pride in leading discussion when it is their hosting day. And they've become more intent upon listening to others' comments and weaving the thoughts into the ongoing discussion. Being *listened to*, they have become better *listeners*.

We've discovered some pleasant side effects at home, too. Morgan, for instance, credits the Mother-Daughter Book Club with all manner of improvements in my attitude. In the past, we argued about her choice of clothes. Lately she likes my suggestions about clothes, explaining that "now that you know me better, you pick out things I like." I honestly don't know whether I'm picking clothes differently, or if Morgan is simply more open to my suggestions. It doesn't matter. We've also noticed a definite drop in the decibel levels around the house—Morgan and I are communicating in quieter, calmer ways. We even complain more considerately.

Whatever it is, something has changed and we like it.

MOTHERS: SHARING OUR WISDOM AND WONDER

I was at a long, sort of lonely business dinner one evening and during the cocktail hour I noticed a copy of the Smithsonian's Engagement Calendar, "Black Women Achieving Against the Odds, " on a table. I hadn't seen it before, and as I glanced through it I came to a page entitled "Women in Politics." And there, in this panel of pictures, was a picture I remembered from a wall in my *grandmother's* house. *It was my great-aunt: Charlotta Spears Bass.* She was in the Smithsonian's book because she ran for vice president of the United States on the Progressive Party ticket in 1952. My vague memory was that it was some sort of family joke. *But it was true.* She had lived in California and had been the editor of the *California Eagle* newspaper. I remembered this tall, stately woman, my great-aunt, coming from California; I saw her about twice in my life.

I think about her, and about my own mother, about the women whose pictures you see in other historic photographs, and the women whose lives and life's work have gone unrecognized— even in their own homes at times—and I feel that I'm here on the backs of so many women's shoulders, so many who have come before. We all are. If we want our girls to benefit from the courage and wisdom of the women before them, we have to share the stories.

I want Morgan to know who her mother is: that I'm human and I go through trials and tribulations. I want her to know that I struggle to satisfy my twin desires to nurture a strong, loving family and at the same time help make a strong, caring community through my professional work and volunteer efforts. I want her to have the sense that it's important not only to develop your talents for your own health and happiness, but also to give back to your community and help bring somebody else along.

There are things you'll see in reading a book together that you don't come across every day with your daughter, and this is your opportunity to explore those things. You can say, "Oh, I've been there," or "I've done that," or "I've wondered about that," or "I've felt that way." "What do you think about it? How do you feel?"

That is the most exciting part of the Mother-Daughter Book Club. The group discussions become a unique combination of intellectual and personal sharing. That's what brings mothers and daughters closer, and that's what gives all of us a special appreciation of each other as individuals.

COMPARING LIVES: MOTHERS, DAUGHTERS, FACT AND FICTION

None of us ever planned this as a continuing lecture in women's studies. For the mothers, that sounds too much like work. For the daughters, it sounds too much like school. But the girls enjoy the comparison aspect of discussion, so we use comparison as a framework for discussing the way girls and women are portrayed in our books and in life.

We look at the mother-daughter relationships in the stories—how authors portray them or how a relationship contributes to a story. We look at how the culture of the time and place treats them, and how girls and women treat one another in the stories. Of course, we share our own experiences when it feels right.

Sometimes we're startled to hear what the girls think about the mother characters in a particular book. In the following discussion, the girls were comparing some mother figures, most of whom they had identified as "wimps" in one way or another. Then they picked out the mother in *The Man in the Ceiling* to give some pretty harsh judgment. Most of us mothers saw her as an intelligent woman, a caring mother, and an artist trying to balance the demands and desires of work and family. Here's how it unfolded:

MOM: I don't understand what you mean when you say they're "wimpy." I take a little offense to it. And I'd like to have, at some point, some more discussion about that. The mothers make a difference in the lives of these children. And everyone's oblivious to the way these parents in the book function. They aren't loud and they aren't going out to the meetings and they aren't going to exciting things, but they make those families work.

GIRL: But they don't really do that much.

GIRL: In *The Man in the Ceiling*, the mom didn't do anything. She was very forgetful. She just went upstairs most of the time and would sit in that little room and paint.

MOM: She worked at home. She was an artist who worked out of her home.

GIRL: But she really didn't listen to anybody and nobody could bother her when she was up there.

MOM: Do you think that her children would be the people they are but for that mother? She provided an enormous amount of support . . .

GIRL: But she was also very forgetful.

MOM: But—it wasn't that you couldn't come, that she was trying to keep people out. She was making a clear separation between when she was working and when she was doing things in the house. So she was saying you couldn't just come up into her special place—disrespect the fact that she was working—come into her studio at just any time.

GIRL: But also, what if they needed something? Their dad usually wasn't there. He overworked.

MOM: That makes you think. When they thought they needed to interrupt her, did they really need her? Was it really an emergency? Or were they just taking advantage of the fact that she's in the house?

MOM: Do you think that the father's work was more important than the mother's work?

GIRL: Before . . . it didn't say anything about the mother working ever.

MOM: You just told me she went to her room and she painted.

GIRL: Yeah, but it didn't say anything about the mother ever *selling* her pictures.

MOM: So the only value is if she actually made money as an artist.

GIRL: Noooo, not necessarily. But if the dad was overworked, why couldn't she make a little bit of money, too?

MOM: Well, I am not a "working" mother and I love it. I would not trade this for anything in the world. And in fact, because I'm not working right now, with kids at this age, I'm able to do more of the kinds of things I think they need. But they don't seem to appreciate that. . . .

The discussion went on to touch on the roles mothers play in the books we read, and the roles they play in real life. Our group includes mothers who balance demanding professional careers and family, those who have stepped back from their successful professional careers to devote more time to family and those who devote full-time attention to family and community. The diversity of our roles, and our attitudes, adds to the depth of possibilities our girls see for motherhood, careers, and individual pursuits.

The result is that without making this the "purpose" of the club or discussion, and without putting it on a written agenda, we explore the lives of girls and women. We identify the influences of history, culture, and family on the lives we read about and the lives we live. We examine characters in full to discover the ways in which challenges strengthen or defeat them, and how individual courage or fear comes into play. It may be hard to imagine that such weighty topics could be fun, but the group makes it so.

MOTHERS: LEARNING FROM DAUGHTERS

The more we see of mothers and daughters in literature, the more we find to talk about and the closer to home the discussion drifts. Eventually the conversation and reflection settle on our own lives, and our own relationships as mothers and daughters. When we lay down the books and speak candidly about our own lives, our own stories, the characters glisten like teardrops; the plots unfold, surprising in some ways and shamelessly predictable in others. We are girls growing up—still—even as we speak. We are the mothers of whom our daughters speak. How can we fail to see the themes played out in these lives of ours?

"I was the brainy kid on the sideline, " Leslye says. "My father was a chemist and my mother was a teacher and a guidance counselor—education and doing well in school were always stressed in my home because my parents believed that was the key to opportunities for blacks in the United States. I felt that pressure to be perfect and was the first black valedictorian in my high school. I had a few good friends, but most of my classmates probably viewed me as a Miss Goody Two-Shoes, and I *was* different. I don't have fond memories of high school. It was nothing bad, but it wasn't an enjoyable time.

"Sometimes, when Brittney is having trouble finding close friends at school, " Leslye says, "it's hard for me to know whether it's just normal for her age, or am I seeing too much of myself? We talk about it in terms of how it feels—that's something we both know and we can share our feelings."

When Linda's daughter Rebecca introduced her at our first club meeting, and someone asked what Linda "did," Rebecca made the now infamous remark—infamous in our circle, anyway—that "she lives." The fact was, Rebecca really didn't know what her mother did anymore since Linda had stepped off the fast track on Capitol Hill to devote more time to her family at home. After some initial consternation, Linda reflected more thoughtfully on her daughter's words: "Rebecca has taught me a lot about life—what's important and what's not—and about

BOOKS TO GROW ON

These are books I've shared with children in urban neighborhoods whom I've known as a teacher or a friend. All of these, although in diverse ways, strike me as spiritual or religious books. Even Pooh has his transcendent days. . . .

The House at Pooh Corner
A. A. Milne

Selected Poems
Gwendolyn Brooks

Night
Elie Wiesel

St. Francis of Assisi
Johannes Jergensen

Selected Poems
W. H. Auden

All Creatures Great and Small
James Herriot

Selected Poems of Langston Hughes
Langston Hughes

The Long Loneliness
Dorothy Day

—JONATHAN KOZOL, AUTHOR,
*Amazing Grace: The Lives of Children
and the Conscience of a Nation*

living—focusing on what's important," Linda says now. "Before the Mother-Daughter Book Club, Rebecca never knew that I learn from her as much as she learns from me. I guess she had just never taken the time to think about it. It sort of hadn't occurred to me either."

Grace had been out of town on high-pressure work for days when she caught a flight that landed her at home in time to tuck her daughter, Ashley, into bed with some book club reading.

"It was two days before Ashley was supposed to go on this camping trip with some others," Grace says, "and she was packed and everything, and during our reading time that night she said, 'Mom—you know that camping trip? I want to talk with you about it, but I don't want you to be upset about it.' Then she told me she hates camping, she doesn't want to go and hopes I won't get angry. We talked a lot about my past experiences camping, and hers, and finally I said, 'It's up to you.' You know, I don't think we ever would have had that talk if it hadn't been for our reading time and the fact that we've grown more comfortable talking about our feelings. That's what I want out of it. She'll grow up saying, 'My mom and I were in this book club. . . .'"

Sometimes it is a simple theme of love and caring that we enjoy and want to perpetuate in our daughters' lives. Says Winnie: "The journey from childhood to adulthood to motherhood is an ongoing learning experience that recycles from generation to generation. Right now, I'm enjoying my second childhood through experiences with Tiffany. We love to travel together. And we discuss lots of things together. Tiffany is kind and gentle. I like being a mother; I like children. I wish I had a house full of children so we could sit in a circle at night, share our day, and read books."

Even in lives where there is time enough for special moments, the Mother-Daughter Book Club remains a time-out of the nicest kind.

"We cook, we read, we do a lot together, but the club gives us a special place where Holly and I can be equals," Alice says. "As equals, we go to a book we haven't read before, and we analyze the book as equals. There are no right or wrong answers at the meeting and discussion; nobody's there to perform—just to share what we've gotten out of the book."

THE DAUGHTERS: LIVING AND LEARNING

The gap we feared would widen between our daughters and ourselves doesn't loom as large or as threatening in our thoughts anymore. As girls once, and mothers now, we know the distance will impose itself during the teen years ahead; it's only natural. But we know, as well, that the bridge of sharing we have established through our Mother-Daughter Book Club can span those years and beyond. The bridge is strong from both sides. The girls' views of us as individuals and their expressions of our role in their lives tell us that love can bridge the gap if you give it a way to get across.

Their comments make sweet background music for our literary and motherly endeavors:

"I can talk to my mom about anything and I like talking to her," says Ashley B. "She's smart. She has a sense of humor, and I think she's a little playful. My mom is a really good friend. I love my mom very much."

"My mom encourages me," says Maya. "She helps me with my schoolwork but doesn't do it for me. Sometimes we disagree

Mothers' Wisdom
Reaching Out for Peace

I was influenced by my mother's philosophy. She grew up in the apartheid of the South and the opportunities were nothing like we have now. Even so, my mom often said that hatred serves no purpose. I may be angry or mad about what happened, but you know, everyone who participated in this is dead now. We can be angry and sad about these things, but we need to have a chance to talk about them without going into corners and hating. You have to find a place for forgiveness.

If you're a mother, then the focus should be on your child, and if you focus on loving and caring and protecting that child, how much time do you really have to rail at the world? If you obsess about what's wrong in the world, you can spend your entire life focused on the stuff that's wrong. Fighting every day just wears you down, burns you out.

—CONNIE PORTER, AUTHOR,
The American Girls Collection, Addy series

about clothes. She picks out dresses I don't really like or shoes I don't like. What I like best about her is she helps me; she likes my ideas and stuff like that. She loves me."

"My mom and I can talk to each other a lot more now," says Ashley S. "Like if there's something going on in school that's bothering me, I can talk about it with her and not worry."

"My mother is a kind of happy person—she likes to interact with other people," says Jamexis. "I've learned from her that you should always approach a person with an open mind and not judge them by what other people say about them. Think for yourself."

"My mom knows about me—somehow she knows what I'm going to do before I do it," Morgan told a friend who asked if the book club *really* made things better between us. "Some things we do the same—like save things and collect stuff. But we have different ideas about some other things. Like clothes. And now that she's getting to know me better, she's picking out clothes better, too."

MOTHERS AND DAUGHTERS: MOVING AHEAD TOGETHER

I can't remember any other place or time in my life when I experienced this kind of talk among mothers and daughters. Every month our Mother-Daughter Book Club meets, we share more of literature and our lives, and it continues at home.

We're still grappling with laundry, meals, homework, and getting places on time. But in larger, more meaningful ways, the mother-daughter dialogue is getting broader and better. The script is changing and it doesn't stop here.

MOTHERS AND DAUGHTERS
Talking from the Heart

The essence of a close relationship between mother and daughter is truthfulness, a capacity to be able to talk about the whole range of our experience and to be able to understand that—to put into context the kinds of forces and pressures that affect both of us.

I know of a mother and a daughter who went shopping to buy the girl a formal dress for a dance. The daughter was kind of chunky, and none of the gowns looked right because she was bigger than the kind of body the designers had in mind when they designed these dresses. The mother and daughter began getting very upset, both of them, and then they began to get upset at each other.

The mother finally pulled herself up short and said: "You know, I'm getting really, really angry and I'm really angry that they make clothes only for anorexic girls." She stopped herself before getting furious at her daughter for being overweight and when she realized that—wait a minute—her daughter was not really overweight, her build was different, and this was a whole cultural, society thing that is done to women about our looks and weight.

When she put it that way, her daughter said, "Yeah, that makes me really mad and makes me feel bad." They began to have a conversation that was really different—the girl wasn't the problem, at all—and one that allowed them to stay connected.

Part of what is important about staying connected is being able to understand there are a lot of forces and pressures in our culture that are easy to get caught up in and not recognize. When we have some understanding of how that works, we can share a different and deeper kind of truthfulness between mother and daughter, a truthfulness that takes the blame away, allows us to keep perspective and be able to speak about these things.

—ELIZABETH DEBOLD

ENDNOTES

📖 The Mother-Daughter Book Club expands the range of mother-daughter dialogue.

> "The material from book club gives us a lot to talk about, and meetings are a chance to sit down and focus and not worry about school or the next meal."
>
> *Sylvie*

📖 Girls speak (and listen) freely in the club setting—even when the conversation is not about books.

> "As I think back on my mother-daughter book club experience, the thing that comes to mind the most are the discussions that we had about touchy subjects, mostly things that mothers and daughters blatantly disagree on, such as teen dating."
>
> *Rachel*

📖 Club discussions provide a springboard for mothers and daughters to talk more about an issue later, one-on-one.

> "I love the spirited discussions we had as a group, but I also remember the discussions my daughter and I had on the way to and from club meetings. These were very good talks—a true bonding experience."
>
> *Monice*

Mothers have as much to learn from their daughters as their daughters do from them—once they learn to listen.

> "I have learned to appreciate my mother as her own person, instead of just as a mother figure."
>
> *Joanna*

> "I've learned that my mom has very strong opinions on issues that I thought she was completely oblivious to, like the nature of teenage life."
>
> *Sylvie*

> "The discusison will be a lot more interesting if everyone is willing to listen without prejudgments."
>
> *Skylar*

EIGHT

Girls Will Be Girls: Age and Attitudes

TO EVERYTHING THERE IS A SEASON, AND A TIME TO EVERY
PURPOSE UNDER HEAVEN.

—ECCLESIASTES

Molly & Irene Klores

My name is Molly Klores. I'm sixteen and have a twin brother, Steven. Some of my hobbies include playing lacrosse for my school's team, ballet, surfing, playing the piano, and being with friends. My favorite subjects in school are probably science and French.

I consider myself a "people person" and loved working at an ice cream store. It was very satisfying and fun. My family spends the entire summer at the beach without any television or computers.

I love fashion and unique styles and am a big fan of second-hand stores. My favorite color is royal blue, especially paired with greens. *The Lovely Bones* and *The Catcher in the Rye* are two of my favorite books.

My mom, Irene, is very youthful and an overall sweetheart. She is a former elementary school teacher. She left teaching to become a professional ballet dancer and then opened her own ballet school, The Ballet Center of Washington, from 1984 through 1998. Ballet music is her passion and she still occasionally takes ballet classes. She enjoys listening to me play classical music on the piano; she says it puts her in a calming mood.

We enjoy a lot of the same things: horses, art, and the beach.

My mom is the most considerate person I know and she knows how to have a great time. The thing that I love most about my mom is how understanding she is, and her ability to be my friend.

A couple of times a year, when the clutter in Morgan's room grew so thick and loomed so large that I could no longer overlook it, I staged an ambush. She was never there, of course. She couldn't imagine parting with the cardboard backing pieces from packages of decorative stickers, or the scraps of notes, or the valentine cards from last year's school party. I could.

I was often moved to action around her birthday in the fall, and again at the end of the school year. I think perhaps both calendar moments carried a special sense of time passing, of Morgan growing, and reasonably *outgrowing*, some of the trappings of the year past. As I sifted through the layers of clutter, tossing into a trash bag that which was rightly trash and trying to decide which other things to pass on to Morgan's younger sister, I was reminded that a child's age alone is not always a useful measure. It was not Morgan's *age* that I was thinking of as I searched for the toys and things she has "outgrown" and could pass on to others. It was *Morgan:* her likes and dislikes, her interests, skills and talents, her emotional maturity and life experience.

"She's ten now, so she doesn't talk as much to me anymore. The Mother-Daughter Book Club has been great for helping to keep the communication going. It gives us a special time together. And it gives us a lot to talk about."

Linda Chastang

Certainly, age was a consideration as we selected books for our Mother-Daughter Book Club, and in our expectations about discussion and socializing. It played a role at the organizational stage of our club, too. We aimed for girlfriends basically the same age or a grade level. But the exception—the friend who was a full year younger and a grade lower than the others—has been no more giggly than her older friends, and no less insightful in her contributions to discussion. Rather than focus strictly on a girl's age as you organize your group or scout books for them to read, it may be more useful to think about a girl's interests, maturity, her reading skills and confidence level in group discussion. If a book, or club, provides a comfort zone for a girl in each of those areas, then it's likely to be a good fit.

MAKING AGE-APPROPRIATE SELECTIONS: THE PLOT THICKENS

The mothers were ready. Our secret agendas were in place: In the book *Cousins*, that annoyingly perfect and reed-thin Patty Ann character had a problem she thought no one knew about: an eating disorder. Secretly, she would make herself throw up after meals. It was mentioned only in passing, in a scene where her teenage cousin—belittled, angry, and looking for some way to shatter that flawless composure—taunts her about "upchucking" and idly threatens to tell her mother. The issue presents itself and is gone in a less than a page; the story moves on.

In the reality of life for adolescent girls these days, eating disorders are no idle threat. They are among the many self-destructive responses experts say are growing more common among girls and women who are struggling with issues of self-image, self-esteem, and lack of power in their lives. Among the mothers in our group, the feeling was unanimous: *Here* was something that needed *talking* about. When does the conversation at home just naturally turn to eating disorders? This was our moment.

So when the discussion began with a comparison of girl

characters from different books the group had read, one mother asked if all of these characters were happy. Here's the dialogue that unfolded among the moms and girls:

> BOOKS TO GROW ON
>
> *Sophie's World*
> Jostein Gaarder
>
> *Go Tell It on the Mountain*
> James Baldwin
>
> *Another Country*
> James Baldwin
>
> *Selected Poems of Emily Dickinson*
> Emily Dickinson
>
> *Raisin in the Sun*
> Lorraine Hansbury
>
> *The Bluest Eye*
> Toni Morrison
>
> —RITA DOVE

GIRL: Yeah, they had good grades and everything else.

MOM: Were they happy?

GIRL: No. Well, Patty Ann was happy.

GIRL: No . . .

MOM: You think Patty Ann was happy?

GIRL: Well, she wasn't happy because she didn't have a lot of friends, but she was happy because she was pretty and because she got good grades.

GIRL: I say no, she wasn't.

MOM: What about—why did she make herself throw up?

GIRL: Because she thought she was fat.

GIRL: And she also didn't like her food. . . .

MOM: She thought she was pretty, and she was always very good at things and she knew that. She believed she was better than the others. . . .

GIRL: But she wasn't really happy, because she got good grades so that her mother wouldn't get mad at her—

SENSITIVE SUBJECTS

When Mothers Care Enough to Talk

There are difficult issues you need to talk about. But who wants to talk about race and sex discrimination? Look at the book *Amazing Grace* by Mary Hoffman. I really love the way she writes about both of those issues and does it with such sensitivity.

The story is about a little girl who wants to be Peter Pan in the school play. There are kids who say she can't possibly do it because Peter Pan wasn't black, and she is. And because Peter Pan wasn't a girl. But there is a grandmother figure in the story, and she tells Grace, "You can be anything you want, if you put your mind to it." There are so many aspects of the book that I appreciate: There is the figure of the grandmother, and the idea of the extended family. My mother is seventy-three years old, and every time she comes to my house she wants to read *Amazing Grace*.

People will ask me about the Addy books, "Why do you want to write about slavery? There's so much else to write about."

I can understand their concern. But this is our history and if we sidestep it, it's because we're uncomfortable and not because our children are uncomfortable. These are our great-great-grandfathers and grandmothers I'm writing about. Their voices need to be heard, and nobody heard them for so very long and very few people cared about what they thought. I feel I've been blessed to talk about someone's life.

—CONNIE PORTER

GIRL: Yeah, but she had some happiness, like playing the piano and rehearsing.

GIRL: That's true.

MOM: Was it her decision to take piano, to rehearse?

GIRL: I think it was her decision to play piano and practice some.

MOM: Did anyone feel differently? Did anyone think it was someone else's decision?

MOM: How many people take piano? How many people love to practice?

MOM: I think Patty Ann took real pleasure in her talents.

MOM: I think Patty Ann was thrilled to be the best that she could be. Some of the things, certainly, she was pushed into being, but I think she was happy also.

MOM: My sense is that she was very unhappy. When young ladies have eating disorders, it usually suggests they are unhappy. Maybe not about something specific, but they're generally not happy people. It's something that's eating at them from the inside that shows up as an eating disorder.

GIRL: They think they're fat.

MOM: Then appearance is very important to them. . . .

MOM: And an eating disorder is also a manifestation of her not having any control of anything else but what goes in her and so she is getting rid of that. That is the only thing she has control of. Her mom is controlling everything else.

MOM: I really am curious about why the mothers are so divided about whether she was happy or not. What do you girls feel?

GIRL: I know she's happy at some things that she chooses. But she's unhappy to think she's going to be fat.

GIRL: I think she's half and half.

GIRL: I think she's happy about her hair and her piano and everything.

The discussion went on to explore how different characters showed they were happy or unhappy.

MOM: When I read the book, at first I thought that Patty Ann was happy wearing beautiful clothes, having very long hair, being adored—she loved being adored. And the reason she had the eating disorder and the reason she was mean to some people, was that she was afraid that people wouldn't like her if she changed. She was afraid if she gained weight people wouldn't like her. She was afraid that if she didn't have pretty clothes people wouldn't like her. So, now, after thinking about it, I come out thinking that Patty Ann was really kind of sad.

MOM: Happiness is really generated from feeling good about yourself, and having friends and a supportive family. She thought she had to have long hair and play the piano and get straight A's to get that. But what she really wanted was the love and warmth you get from friends and family.

MOM: I tend to disagree with that because I don't think you should rely on others for your happiness. My happiness never comes from just friends. I'm real happy just by myself.

MOM: But a child . . .

MOM: Even for a child. I think some children are just loners.

MOM: I think it's okay to be a loner, but there's something about being loved that makes you able to be alone and be comfortable. And I think—in fact, I hope the girls think in terms of love being what really matters. The long hair is not going to give you the happiness and satisfaction that I think we all want. Even Patty Ann wanted that more than anything. But she thought the way to have it was to be attractive physically. But it didn't work.

MOM: I think that was my concern. That's why I wanted to press the issue a little bit. . . .

At this point one of the girls introduced a new question, and the discussion moved on to the subject of the grandmother characters in the books. They discussed how those characters were similar and how they were different. And how their cooking had been a part of the characters. Then one of the girls asked again: "Why do you think Patty Ann had an eating disorder?"

GIRL: I don't know.

GIRL: Because she wanted to be Ms. Perfect and so she thought that if she ate all this food and stuff, she would get fat, so she just wanted to make herself stay thin so she wouldn't get fat.

GIRL: I agree—Patty Ann didn't want to be fat. She would put her finger in her mouth and throw up her food because she didn't want to be fat.

GIRL: I think it was partly that. But I also think she didn't really like the food and she didn't want to upset her mother.

GIRL: You can eat something you don't like so much and just forget about it—you don't have to throw up.

GIRL: She didn't want to be fat and also she might not have liked the food. It could have been both.

That discussion forged ahead into many other aspects of the characters and the stories, none of them getting back to Patty Ann's troubled state of mind.

ON AGE AND ATTITUDE

"Books can't damage people, but they can be inappropriate. The reader's emotional development has to be taken into account. An eight-year-old who is a very good reader might have no trouble reading a particular book, but it might not be appropriate for her in terms of her development."

— PAM SACKS

"It's a mistake to create set patterns—that this happens at this stage and another—because it's not necessarily true. These things don't happen for everybody on the same time line and in the same sequence. We're always trying to measure ourselves: Are we doing what's right at this point? Well, it may be right for another mother and daughter at another point."

— SUSAN MCGEE BAILEY

"During those nine-to-twelve-year-old years, mothers really need to be open and listen to what daughters have to say, and not get upset if the daughters don't seem to be as devoted to them as they would like them to be. Listen to their goals and their dreams. Because if a mother has some goal set in her mind, and it isn't the daughter's goal, that's when the daughters rebel. That can escalate and damage the relationship. I like to tell mothers to just keep an open mind, allow your children to express themselves, and talk with them."

— BERTHA WATERS

"It's wonderful sharing books and sharing a real love of reading. I have a daughter who's eight and a son, eleven, and I started reading to them when they were two days old. It was a wonderful way to share a wonderful experience from my own childhood, and to know that my children have that."
— HARRIET MOSATCHE, PH.D.

"Sex discrimination, race discrimination — I'd rather let them know it's out there, and sit down and talk about it."
— CONNIE PORTER

Taken as a whole, the discussion touched on lots of issues—friendship, happiness, peer pressure, self-esteem—that brought out thoughtful responses from the girls. But their attitude toward that eating disorder was rather matter-of-fact. It was clear from their comments that most of them dismissed it as an extreme act of dieting by a girl who simply "didn't want to be fat." Or didn't like the food. Neither response suggested they had any understanding of eating disorders or the kinds of issues that foster that kind of self-destructive behavior. And they didn't pick up on our explanations and pursue those thoughts.

Later, when I thought about their comments, I realized that the girls actually were making a very strong statement; it just wasn't about the subject we had in mind. It was about themselves, their level of experience in the world, and their readiness to discuss the subject. They were ready to talk about happiness, motivation, and the ups and downs of grades, looks, friendships and grandmothers—things they understood well from experience. But they weren't ready to talk about the psychology of eating disorders.

The mothers might have

"We don't always agree on things. There was a book where people were feeling like one character was a mean little girl—the girls saw her as someone who thought she was better than everyone else because she got good grades and wasn't 'part of the crowd.' But I compared her to myself at that age and I could relate her situation to things that had happened to me. I asked the girls if she reminded them of anyone they knew, maybe someone from school."

Leslye Fraser

wished the girls had reached a moment of clarity and insight about the subject—some one-line moral to the story to carry through adolescence. They didn't, but that didn't mean the discussion fell short of any mark. In fact, the girls had talked candidly about their ideas. Without lecturing, the moms had woven in a few pieces of information about eating disorders, including that they are a sign of something else that needs attention. And the conversation included discussion about other normal, but sometimes stressful, aspects of everyday life. That was, perhaps, the most important message our girls needed to hear that day: Life can get complicated, self-destructive behavior needs attention, and it's okay to talk with their mothers about any and all of it.

A collection of folktales brought us to a discussion of marriage, and then to another question involving men and women and the division of power and strength in the world. The girls said they felt women had power, but when the talk turned to specifics, they got giggly.

GIRL: Okay. The questions are: Pretend you're old enough to get married. What are some qualities you think would make a perfect man?

MOM: Whoa! *(laughing)*

MOM: Anyone want to go first?

MOM: Is it that you all don't know what qualities would make a perfect man, or is it the thought of getting married—why are you all hiding your faces?

GIRL: He'll be nice and kind of sweet. . . .

GIRL: And thoughtful.

GIRL: And patient.

AGE AND ATTITUDE
Readers and Writers

Two books we think of now as classic children's literature raised a few questions when they were new. *Charlotte's Web* told the story of a pig saved from slaughter by a kind and literary spider. In *Stuart Little*, a caring, intellectual mouse sets out in search of a missing friend. Author E. B. White's letters share some thoughts he had about his young readers:

Letters from E. B. White, author of Charlotte's Web *and* Stuart Little

October 22, 1952

. . . So far, *Charlotte's Web* seems to have been read largely by adults with a literary turn of mind. I have had only a sprinkling of childhood reaction to the book . . . and will not know for a little while how it sits with the young. I have a step-grandchild named Caroline Angell who is a quiet little girl of about five. She listened attentively to the reading of the book by her father, and said: "I think there was an easier way to save Wilbur, without all that trouble. Charlotte should have told him not to eat, then he wouldn't have been killed because he would have been too thin."

Trust an author to go to a lot of unnecessary trouble.

April 18, 1961

Dear Mrs. Sanborn:
The ending of *Stuart Little* has plagued me, not because I think there is anything wrong with it but because children seem to insist on having life neatly packaged. The final chapters were

written many years after the early chapters and I think this did affect the narrative to some extent. I was sick and was under the impression that I had only a short time to live, and so I may have brought the story to a more abrupt close than I would have under different circumstances. My reason (if indeed I had any) for leaving Stuart in the midst of his quest was to indicate that questing is more important than finding, and a journey is more important than the mere arrival at a destination. This is too large an idea for young children to grasp, but I threw it to them anyway. They'll catch up with it eventually. Margolo, I suppose, represents what we all search for, all our days, and never quite find.

RAISING COMPETENT GIRLS
One Size Does Not Fit All

Age isn't the only dividing line for maturity and perspective among girls. The standards for self-worth by which our girls measure themselves often are different from girl to girl, depending on a lot of issues including racial or cultural influences, according to the study "Raising Competent Girls: One Size Does Not Fit All."

Sumru Erkut, at the Wellesley Centers for Women, and her colleagues—Fern Marx, Jackie Fields, and Rachel Sing—evaluated information from 161 adolescent girls about what qualities they felt were important for a girl to like herself.

Most of the girls put a lot of stock in "physical appearance, behavioral conduct, and scholastic competence"—good looks, good behavior, and good grades. In one particular category called "global self-worth"—meaning how a girl measured her overall personal worth—African American girls measured their worth more by grades; Caucasian girls measured it by physical appearance and behavioral conduct; Chinese-American girls measured by behavioral conduct and close friendship; and Latina girls measured their global self-worth by physical appearance and behavioral conduct.

LISTENING

Hearing the Growing Girl

As girls get older, as they leave those preschool years and hit the six-to-eight-year-old range, what becomes more and more important is being able to listen to them and give them the space to be people— to be themselves. Girls, up to the age of twelve, are extremely clear about who they are and what they want.

As they go into adolescence, they become more sophisticated in how they express those feelings, and it's important for us to listen. Sometimes it's hard for mothers. In some ways we feel we know them so well, but their minds are developing and they're getting older, and sometimes we forget to give them the room they need to be able to question and change. We keep assuming they're the same little person they were when they were younger. It doesn't mean there aren't ways they are the same. There's just much more going on for them that's different, and it helps to be able to approach who they are with curiosity and not with certainty.

—ELIZABETH DEBOLD

MOM: What else? Anybody?

GIRL: Well, I'd probably want the person to have a job. But not a garbage collector.

GIRL: A big house . . . *(all laughing)*

MOM: Handsome?

GIRL: Yeah.

MOM: Well, wait a minute, now. Let's talk about this. What is "personality"? Why do you say you don't want a garbage collector?

GIRL: He'll come home smelly.

MOM: Not necessarily. He probably showers and changes at the plant.

BOOKS TO GROW ON

My favorite reading list recommendations for preteen and teenage girls:

The Secret Garden
Frances Hodgson Burnett

A Tree Grows in Brooklyn
Betty Smith

Little Women
Louisa May Alcott

Heidi
Johanna Spyri

Helen Keller: The Story of My Life
Helen Keller

Pride and Prejudice
Jane Austen

—MARY ROSE MAIN, NATIONAL EXECUTIVE DIRECTOR, Girl Scouts of the U.S.A.

MOM: What if he owns the company? You know, you have to work your way up through the ranks. Maybe he started out as a garbage guy and moved up to own the company. What about that?

GIRL: *(groaning)* Mo-o-o-o-om. *(all laughing)*

MOM: Do you all want to get married? This is just fun—do you want to get married?

GIRL: No.

GIRL: Yeah.

MOM: Why?

GIRL: I don't know.

MOM: Well, why did you say yes?

GIRL: 'Cause I like kids. No, I'm not going to get married. I'm going to adopt them.

MOM: And you—you don't want to get married either?

GIRL: Nope.

MOM: Why?

GIRL: I want to have a profession.

The discussion moved on to other aspects of the books under discussion. In one folktale, a man and a woman have to choose between their desire for power and their desire for strength. The woman chooses power, while the man chooses strength, a decision he later regrets.

MOM: Which would you rather have—power or strength?

GIRL: I would rather have power because then you'd be smarter.

GIRL: I'd rather have power because then you can be strong and do other things.

MOM: Do you think that women are more powerful than men?

MOM: Why are you all acting so embarrassed when you talk about men having power? I know you have strong opinions. Can't you share them?

MOM: Let me ask it in a different way. If you believe women have more power, why haven't we ever had a woman president of the United States?

GIRL: Because it's too much work. You have to work all the time. And you don't have time for yourself.

MOM: Anybody else?

GIRL: Maybe it's because women think they can't do it. So they don't want to bother with it.

MOM: But you all believe you have the power. So, therefore, you might try . . . . *(no response)* Is it individual power you think you have? And does that translate into collective power for women as a group? Or do you think women individually are powerful within their own homes?

GIRL: Huh?

MOM: Do you think that you're powerful by yourselves, or do you know how to put that power together and do something as a whole group?

GIRL: If you set your mind to it, you can do both.

SENSITIVE SUBJECTS AT ANY AGE

Is there an "appropriate" age for reading the language of hate or violence? Should we draw our girls' attention to books that portray pain, sadness, and grief when there seems to be too much of it already on the pages of the newspapers and the TV screens in our homes?

Every mother has to reach her own conclusions. Some books you'll simply pass by, maybe for now, maybe forever. Other books may have important stories to tell—stories you'd like to share with your daughter—but they include words or images with which you are uncomfortable or which you find inappropriate. Some of the "classics" present this problem: They have powerful stories to tell but sometimes include insensitive or derogatory references to people. Some modern fiction—just like the movies—includes language or scenes we may not feel our daughters are ready to encounter without explanation.

> "Our Mother-Daughter Book Club has been everything I thought it might be, and maybe a little more. I didn't imagine in the beginning that the girls would bring about the depth of discussion that they have."
>
> *Alice Thomas*

Life itself is more painful than fiction at times, deserving of explanations, yet still unimaginable for some children growing up today.

"When we drive back to see our family in South Carolina, where I grew up, I talk to my daughters as we pass landmarks and I take them back to see the houses we lived in," says Joyce. "When we go to the Rexall drugstore there, I explain how on Saturday afternoons black people like us didn't go 'uptown' because that's when the Ku Klux Klan was there soliciting and passing out literature. It wasn't a safe place for us. I can tell they regard it as fictional. They hear me, but they don't. You want to share with them, but you don't want to scare them."

The Mother-Daughter Book Club provides a comfort zone for meeting the troubling fictions, as well as the facts, of life. Shared reading at home and group discussion provide an excellent opportunity to explore *what* the author wrote and *why*. We can talk about the influence of culture and how it sets the scene for the story—whether in books or life. We can talk about cultural pressures on the individual—that's peer pressure in our daughters' lives—and the qualities an individual can

Lafayette Bookworms Mother-Daughter Book Club

The Bookworms began in January 2000, with ten fourth-graders from Lafayette Elementary School and their moms. Our first book was *Anastasia Krupnik* by Lois Lowry. Now the girls are all turning sixteen and are in tenth grade, and we are reading *Memoirs of a Geisha* by Arthur Golden. Of the original ten girls, eight are still members; one was added in fifth grade and one has moved away. In 2001, one of the mothers died of cervical cancer. That was our saddest moment. Her daughter stayed with the group for another year, until she went to a new school. After sixth grade, other girls left for private schools but stayed with the group. Right now, four of the girls are away on a school program for four months. We have arranged the schedule so that they will only miss two meetings. If we can, we hope to keep it going until the girls leave for college.

We meet monthly, setting the schedule in the beginning of the year. We used to decide the next book at the end of each meeting, but we have evolved into a system of choosing all our books in one mega-meeting at the beginning of the year. Every family recommends three to four books, and we all vote. The top vote-getters are put into the schedule. Somehow, we always end up with a good variety of books, including contemporary fiction, classics, and nonfiction.

We meet in the late afternoon on Sundays and have an unstructured social time at the beginning before we discuss the book. We have made an effort at times to go around and let each person in the group respond to the same question so we're sure all are included in the discussion. Sometimes the discussions have branched off into totally different directions, from politics to racism. Once, I remember the discussion turned to what made up an ideal man, and interracial relationships that the mothers had had and how their parents reacted.

One thing we incorporated early on was a poetry month. One of our members is a poet, and she compiles a packet of poems, either that we have all recommended or by one particular poet. Then we take turns reading them out loud. We have timed this meeting to coincide with a time of year that is particularly busy for the girls in terms of school requirements, so no one has to prepare. It is a wonderful meeting that everyone enjoys because it is unique. Last year we also incorporated the idea of a documentary film meeting, along with a potluck dinner.

Last year we got together to discuss sex and sexuality, outside of a book discussion. We wanted to discuss values and share information in an open and honest way. We went down a checklist of questions that girls and boys ask about sex that one of the girls had brought home from a weekend-long sexuality retreat she participated in through her synagogue. It was illuminating to explore this topic as a group and helped ease the embarrassment that can arise when the topic is discussed one on one.

Over the years, we have held together through many life changes as the girls have grown and matured. I think one thing that is so special about our group is the way the moms and girls have been such a positive stabilizing influence for each other. We all know that no matter what is happening in our lives (during years that can be difficult for girls socially and for family relationships), once a month we will spend time with a group which includes peers and adults who enjoy each other's company and respect individual opinions. The moms and daughters vary a great deal in terms of their strengths, interests, and communication styles, but all are strong and capable, which provides another great life lesson.

— Wendie Lubic, Founding Mom,
Lafayette Bookworm Mother-Daughter Book Club,
Washington, D.C.

bring to life that enable her to survive and thrive whether it is a character in a book or the reader herself.

The moms in our Mother-Daughter Book Club dropped some books from consideration after we previewed them within our mothers' group. Other books had passages or scenes that we felt were stretching our comfort zone, but for a good cause. Reading the story with our daughters at home, we were able to put mature or troubling aspects of a story into a context, and identify historical or cultural influences at work in the plot or dialogue.

> "In the beginning, after we'd read our books, we were surprised at how many people answered the questions and really got into the questions. I thought it was fun."
>
> *Morgan*

We talked about the reasons an author might write about painful or disturbing things in a book for a young reader. We talked about the author's choice of words or events used in the story. By the time we got together for our group discussion, both mothers and daughters had defused these issues and were ready to share these thoughts and others in stimulating discussion.

WHEN TO START A MOTHER-DAUGHTER BOOK CLUB

It took me nine years with Morgan to reach a point where I felt the need and the inspiration to organize a Mother-Daughter Book Club. You don't have to wait that long. Nor should you feel that you've missed your chance if your daughter is older.

Any age is a good age to read with our daughters. When is the best time to start a Mother-Daughter Book Club? That depends upon your interests, your daughter's interests, and the kind of club you envision.

For us, that nine-to-twelve age group seemed like such a perfect fit for a number of reasons. By this age, the girls have developed solid reading and listening skills, and are developing critical thinking skills and the confidence to contribute to group discussion. They're able to discuss abstract ideas to some extent and enjoy expressing their opinion as a way of communicating. They're thinking deeper than they let on sometimes, but then they're willing to share those thoughts if you give them a little nudge. The discussion is always lively!

A group of first-graders isn't going to pursue the same kinds of books and discussion you could reasonably expect to share with a group of fourth-graders. That doesn't mean you can't have a Mother-Daughter Book Club when your daughter is in first grade. You just need to organize one that provides an age-appropriate response to her little-girl reading skills and interests and seems appealing to the mothers involved.

> "It's helped me at school, too. When I read to the class, I recognize and understand words that I did not know before we started the club. Reading at home has allowed my mom to work with me to help me pronounce and recognize words better."
>
> *Ashley S.*

For instance, you might plan to have mothers and daughters read short novels together—with mom doing a lot of the reading aloud. Or you might decide to make the club meeting into a read-aloud storytime followed by twenty minutes of discussion. You couldn't expect a six- or seven-year-old child to lead a group discussion by herself. But she could enjoy other

SIMPLE STORIES
Universal Themes for Any Age

Some books are good for discussion at any age because they have a quality that produces interest—something that lends itself to looking at the story from the character's perspective.

Appelemando's Dreams by Patricia Polacco, is a wonderful example. It's about a sleepy, drab little village where there lives a young boy who dreams incredible and colorful dreams. The adults in the town think he's a "slow, " do-nothing kind of kid, but his four friends see his dreams. His dreams come right out of the top of his head—they're very colorful—and at one point cover the town, buildings and everything. The townspeople think the kids have painted the town and are very upset with them. The children, feeling very dejected, run off to a dangerous forest. When they become afraid they're lost, they ask Appelemando to dream. At the urging of his friends, the boy starts to dream, and his dream fills the sky. The townspeople, who really do love the children, are able to find them by following the dream. At the end of the story, the townsfolk acknowledge the importance of dreams, and the village becomes a vibrant place—a changed place because of a young boy's dreams.

You can ask some of the same questions of any readers, any age, and you'll hear a different discussion depending on where they are developmentally and in life experience:

• WHY DO THE ADULTS SEE THE DREAMER AS A DO-NOTHING? Do you agree or disagree with them?

• WHY DO HIS FRIENDS APPRECIATE HIM?

- WHAT DOES IT MEAN TO BE A FRIEND?

- THE DREAMER IS DIFFERENT FROM HIS FRIENDS. How are you different from your friends?

- HOW DID THE DREAMER FEEL when his friends loved him but the adults didn't understand him? How did he feel about himself?

- HOW WOULD YOU FEEL in a situation in which you agreed with your friends, or they supported you, and your parents didn't?

- HOW DO YOUR FRIENDS INFLUENCE YOU? How do you influence them? What can you do if your friends are doing something you don't agree with?

- THINK ABOUT SOLUTIONS. How could you deal with the problem to avoid a crisis or confrontation?

- WHY DID THE CHILDREN RUN AWAY? How could a problem like this be solved without running away?

- WHAT DO WE MEAN WHEN WE SAY "DREAM"? What makes a sleeping dream different from a daydream? How can dreams become expectations? What are your dreams or expectations for the future? What can you do to make those dreams real?

—BONNIE DIAMOND, LANGUAGE ARTS SPECIALIST

aspects of hosting the meeting, help come up with discussion questions, or select the read-aloud story for that meeting. With sensitivity to younger children's patterns of thought and activity, you might start the meetings with a story and discussion, shifting the playtime to afterward.

As you consider adaptations to make for the younger and younger child, when the idea starts sounding more like a mother-daughter play group than a book discussion group, do your play group. Simply include a read-aloud story as part of it. Have some silly fun, talking about the characters in the story or what they did. Whether you call it a Mother-Daughter Book Club or just an age-appropriate good time, our daughters are never too young to enjoy books, stories, and us.

Some books, too, are good for nearly any age, or good reading again and again as we age. Sometimes it's because the themes are so beautifully simple and beautifully told that they can be appreciated by readers of any age. Other times it's because the story is so rich, and the author so gifted a writer, that we experience the book differently as we come to it at different times in life.

"I've read *The Thorn Birds* every year for fifteen years," says Alice. "I never tire of it; it's like going back home again. There are characters I saw in a certain way when I was younger, and now that I'm where I am in my life I see them in a different light. Every time I read it I see more, different things. I look forward to reading it each year."

When Joyce was in second grade, her teacher read *Charlotte's Web* to the class. "That year I checked it out and read it again and again

> "Sometimes I read after dinner, or if I get up early, I just take a flashlight and read in bed."
>
> *Maya*

and again, " Joyce says. "It's still one of my favorite books of all time. It introduces the life cycle and it introduces death to kids, but shows how people can approach that calmly and with dignity. As a child, I was sad when Charlotte, the spider, died. But I was delighted that Charlotte lived on in her children, and I wondered what life was like for them."

What about older daughters? There's no doubt in my mind that mothers and their teenage daughters can enjoy a Mother-Daughter Book Club tremendously, and that there's a real need for the kind of sharing and communication that goes on in the circle.

However, as they move along into their teen years, the girls get busier and absorbed more completely in their own lives and blossoming independence. Their interests change—sometimes by the hour. And pretty predictably, I'm told, their interest in socializing with mothers fades fast. Still, I'm an optimist. And a realist—I do have a teenage son and know many teens and their mothers through church and other community activities.

I believe it can be done.

The two biggest challenges to developing the club with teenagers are the issues of time and "cool."

Time is a flexible thing in terms of Mother-Daughter Book Club meetings. Make them quarterly, or plan them for vacation breaks.

Cool is another thing. Cool is what the Mother-Daughter Book Club needs to be in the eyes of your teenage daughter, and anything organized by moms is not likely to qualify. I'd suggest asking for outside help. Look to the youth group coordinator at your church or synagogue, or the local community center, for advice or involvement as a facilitator. These or other individuals who enjoy a special rapport with teens can make *anything fun*—even a book club discussion with *mothers*!

MOTHER-DAUGHTER BOOK CLUBS AT ANY AGE

Within the context of age, interests, skills, experience, and maturity, the steps for organizing a mother-daughter book club remain the same:

• THINK ABOUT THE KIND OF GROUP you'd like to see develop. Identify any special objectives you have in mind. Avoid anything that feels like school, from kindergarten to college.

• KEEP IN MIND ANY AGE-RELATED ASPECTS of the mother-daughter relationship that are likely to influence how daughters or mothers experience the reading, the discussion, or the social aspects of the mother-daughter book club.

• DISCUSS YOUR IDEA with your community or school librarian, bookstore adviser, or others who have special experience that might help you adapt ideas to fit the needs of the daughters and mothers in your group—whatever their age.

• TALK TO PROSPECTIVE MEMBERS about the idea. Find a core group. Select some books to get started. Give it a try!

• ESTABLISH REALISTIC EXPECTATIONS for the group and stay flexible about details.

Remember, the point of a mother-daughter book club is to share books, ideas, and fun. If it doesn't feel right, change it.

There is life after the teen years, and I know for a fact that some adult daughters and mothers pass books back and forth between them—often by mail if they don't live close by—and they enjoy chatting about them on the phone.

I don't think there's a bad time to start a mother-daughter book club. There's no age limit on our desire to have strong, loving relationships, and there's no age limit on the fun of doing it through shared reading and discussion.

GROWING TOGETHER: ACROSS MILES AND YEARS

Change is a natural part of growth, so anticipate change in your mother-daughter book club as time goes by. You may change the focus of your reading selections to reflect new group interests. You may change the time you meet to accommodate other commitments. Even the group itself is bound to change over time, as this family moves away or that person can no longer fit the reading or meeting time into her schedule. But you invite new members to join the group. You explore new territory on the bookshelf. You continue to share your reading list with the one who leaves, and share conversation through phone calls, letters, or e-mail. And through it all, mothers and daughters keep reading and talking together.

When we talk about our group, we talk about it as a group that will go through life. I believe it will. I believe, too, that every time we meet and talk, the embrace we give to ideas is felt in a way that will stay with each of us through life. The experience shapes us at any age. We're never too young or too old to enjoy the benefits.

BOOKS TO GROW ON

Coming-of-age stories for girls and their moms (that might inspire you to write your own):

A Thousand Pieces of Gold, Ruthanne Lum McCunn

A Tree Grows in Brooklyn, Betty Smith

Anne Frank: The Diary of a Young Girl, Anne Frank

Catherine, Called Birdy, Karen Cushman

A Wrinkle in Time, Madeleine L'Engle

Diary of Latoya Hunter: My First Year in Junior High, Latoya Hunter

The House on Mango Street, Sandra Cisneros

—PEGGY ORENSTEIN, AUTHOR
SchoolGirls

Here are four of my favorites:

Oh, The Places You'll Go!, Dr. Seuss

The Story of Ruby Bridges, Robert Coles

Ella Baker: A Leader Behind the Scenes, Shyrlee Dallard

Thank You, Dr. Martin Luther King, Jr., Eleanora E. Tate

—MARIAN WRIGHT EDELMAN, FOUNDER AND PRESIDENT, Children's Defense Fund

ENDNOTES

▨ Think about a girl's interests, maturity, her reading skills, and confidence level rather than just her chronological age when determining your book selections.

▨ The mother-daughter book club provides a comfort zone for talking about all kinds of subjects—even sensitive ones.

▨ Any age can be a good age to read with our daughters or to start a club.

▨ Think about asking an outside discussion leader to help organize a mother-daughter book club for teen daughters.

NINE

Using Themes to Guide Choices

A PEOPLE'S LITERATURE IS THE GREAT TEXTBOOK FOR REAL
KNOWLEDGE OF THEM. THE WRITINGS OF THE DAY SHOW THE
QUALITY OF THE PEOPLE AS NO HISTORICAL RECONSTRUCTION
CAN.

—EDITH HAMILTON, *Preface to* The Roman Way

Riley Collins & Pam Riley

My name is Riley. I am fifteen years old. Besides reading, I love being with my friends and playing basketball. My favorite place to go on vacation is to the beach. Because we moved around a lot when I was younger, I have learned to make friends pretty easily, but I usually have a smaller group of really close friends. Most of my friends would probably describe me as easy to talk to, sometimes a little too private, but also loyal and good at keeping secrets. I can be bossy when I am in a group, but I am tuned in to others' emotions.

The types of books that I like most usually involve younger characters around my age who go through problems dealing with the same type of things that I deal with: family, friends, boys, and so on. My favorite book, *Extremely Loud and Incredibly Close,* was written by Jonathan Safran Foer, a graduate of my high school, Georgetown Day. I liked the book for many reasons, but mostly because the main character, a nine-year-old boy, was so believable. His emotions dealing with his father's death were intensely real, and it definitely did not describe his pain in a clichéd way.

My mother's name is Pam Riley. My mom and I have always been close, partly because of how similar we are. We both love analyzing people and we hate being in fights with people. We decided to join the book club because we love to read, and our interests in books are pretty similar. My mom was also a childhood reader. Reading hour, on mom's bed at night, began when I was an infant and my older brother, Dylan (now a senior in high school), would nestle in the pillows to hear about the exploits of *Good Dog Carl.* Reading hour continued throughout the years, well past when my brother and I could read on our own. It was my mom's way of insuring one uninterrupted hour with us after a long workday. When I was in grade school, our family traveled a great deal, and mom and dad always seemed to have a stash of kid-friendly paperbacks ready to hand out when the airplane was delayed or they wanted more time in the restaurant. My mom still enjoys going to the library once a month and checking out twenty or more novels that she thinks I will like, even though I only read three or four of them.

Every mother-daughter book club is a "special interest group" in the best sense of the word. Each mother and daughter there has a special interest in sharing quality time together and exploring the world of ideas through books and group discussion with other mothers and daughters.

There are other ways to use special interests, or themes, to open up new opportunities for learning and experience through your mother-daughter book club. You might use a theme as the basis for selecting books to read for a period of time—focusing on historical fiction, biography, or poetry, for instance. Or you might use a theme as the cornerstone in organizing your mother-daughter book club—inviting friends with whom you share a particular interest or life experience.

The mother-daughter book club can round out our daughters' education without sending them to another classroom. Schools tend to educate in general; they don't educate to the specifics. They can't fill some of the voids or instill your values and the things you care about. One way to do that is through reading. There are so many books that reach any interest area that it's fun picking and choosing. And the search is ever-evolving. The theme you pick initially may not be the theme you stay with indefinitely.

Themes allow us to make special connections, fill a void, or bring a balance to our life experience through the books we choose or the people with whom we read and discuss our books.

THE THEME-BASED CLUB: BRINGING A BALANCE TO LIVES

Two particular themes first motivated me to organize our Mother-Daughter Book Club. One was the mother-daughter relationship and my desire to find ways to expand the common ground for friendship between Morgan and myself. I thought of the other mothers I knew who felt the same need. We all agreed that a mother-daughter book club might help strengthen our relationships by providing some connections through literature, discussion, and the sharing of our own stories. And the special time together could bring some balance to our lives, which felt increasingly pressured by outside commitments and expectations.

My other objective was to bring together a group of mothers and daughters who shared our African American heritage and the desire to explore the diversity of African American literature and lives in a full way. That couldn't happen in school or in most of the girls' after-school activities, where the composition of the group and the curriculum or activities reflected other, generalized cultural perspectives.

Many parents today, regardless of their particular ethnic or religious identity, are looking for ways to help their children preserve their cultural roots as they grow and establish themselves in a multicultural society. That can be quite a challenge. Our homes are in one place, our work in another. Grandparents and other extended family may be scattered around the globe. We're all so busy with demands of the day, within the culture of the present tense, that there aren't many opportunities to casually reflect on the experience of generations past. Our children don't learn enough about their own family's heritage through the school system, and this is another way to bring in that history and culture without making it burdensome on top of their academic load. A mother-daughter book club gives you a special circle of affirmation, a place and a "family" of partners with whom you explore and celebrate these cultural connections.

GETTING IDEAS FOR STUDY THEMES AND BOOKS

Whether your group wants to focus on a special interest for a few meetings or as an ongoing exploration, you'll find many sources of great ideas and materials in your community. Pick a topic and ask for suggested reading, book-related activities, author information, or theme-related activities. Use some networking skills to build your list of resources. Always ask contacts if they can suggest any other people, organizations, or resources for you to try. For starters:

- ASK BOOKSTORE CONTACTS

- ASK LIBRARIANS

- ASK TEACHERS

- ASK INSIDERS—clergy, scholars, professionals, counselors or social workers, athletes, etc.

- CALL MUSEUMS OR OTHER CULTURAL CENTERS in your area or elsewhere. Many have education departments or staff members who would be glad to help you on your way.

Keep all contact names and suggestions in your club notebook or filed away. You may want to turn to them again or help someone else on the same quest!

Others may find those connections easy or close enough, and wish instead for a group that includes a more diverse collection of friends. Or friends-to-be: A community-based mother-daughter book club could expand your circle of friends among mothers and daughters who simply share a love of books, discussion, and friendship.

> "I read for fun. I like to read a lot of Native American folklore, tales and things. I like how they have a free and perfect world there, and I like the descriptions of the places in the woods."
>
> *Jamexis*

EXPLORING SPECIAL INTERESTS THROUGH LITERATURE

Whatever brings your group together, theme-based reading selections can add a special dimension to your literary explorations and discussions. The key is to stay flexible and use themes to broaden your reach—not limit it.

When our group organized, we thought we'd focus completely on African American authors and literature. There's such a wealth of it, and historically it wasn't included in school programs or even on the shelves at most bookstores. Our first year was exciting with our discovery of the rich array of voices from the black community. In addition to vibrant historical fiction, we discovered wonderfully written stories depicting more modern times. Universal themes played out in the context of the lives of girls who were of African American, Puerto Rican, Jamaican, and other cultures of color.

African American titles from which the girls chose the books we read.

Arilla Sun Down, Virginia Hamilton
Come a Stranger, Cynthia Voigt
Down in the Piney Woods, Ethel F. Smothers
Edith Jackson, Rosa Guy
Fall Secrets, Candy D. Boyd
Freedom Songs, Yvette Moore
Gifted Hands: The Ben Carson Story, Ben Carson and Cecil
  Murphey
A Girl Named Disaster, Nancy Farmer
The Glory Field, Walter D. Myers
*Grand Mothers: Poems, Reminiscences, and Short Stories About
  the Keepers of Our Traditions*, Nikki Giovanni
Growin', Nikki Grimes
Letters from a Slave Girl: The Story of Harriet Jacobs, Mary E.
  Lyons
Maizon at Blue Hill, Jacqueline Woodson
M. C. Higgins, the Great, Virginia Hamilton
Plain City, Virginia Hamilton
The Road to Memphis, Mildred D. Taylor
Roll of Thunder, Hear My Cry, Mildred D. Taylor
Ruby, Rosa Guy
The Secret of Gumbo Grove, Eleanora E. Tate
*Shimmy Shimmy Shimmy Like My Sister Kate: Looking at the
  Harlem Renaissance Through Poems*, edited by Nikki
  Giovanni
Sweet Whispers, Brother Rush, Virginia Hamilton
When the Nightingale Sings, Joyce C. Thomas
Zeely, Virginia Hamilton

Then we branched out. The girls elected to read about girls from other cultures. The selections we read included *Homesick: My Own Story* by Jean Fritz, about an American girl who was born in China and came to the United States at age twelve; *Julie of the Wolves* by Jean Craighead George, the story of a native Alaskan girl; and *The Friends* by Rosa Guy, a story set in Harlem, which touches on class issues confronting two Jamaican sisters when their family relocates there.

Regardless of the composition of your group, themes are a fun way to add a little structure to your reading plans and enjoy the three-dimensional framework it provides for discussion as you read and compare the books. There's so much good literature, it's a treat to look at the ways you can track a theme through fiction, poetry, biography, and nonfiction.

The process of picking a theme and selecting books within that theme provides more opportunities for mothers and daughters to talk about ideas. When our girls pick the subject, they enjoy the feeling of having chosen the direction for the club's

---

BOOKS TO GROW ON

Anne of Green Gables
Lucy M. Montgomery

The Secret Garden
Frances Hodgson Burnett

Harriet the Spy
Louise Fitzhugh

Dragonflight
Anne McCaffrey

*The Autobiography of
Miss Jane Pittman*
Ernest Gaines

When Hitler Stole Pink Rabbit
Judith Kerr

—PAMELA WOOD,
HEAD OF MIDDLE SCHOOL,
Friends Seminary, New York,
New York

MIX AND MATCH
Exploring Themes Through Books and More

Pull from the full world of literature to explore a theme topic! Consider novels, nonfiction books or essays, short stories, poetry and plays. Enrich your reading experience with related activities such as movies, video documentaries, author contact or field trips to historic and other sites of interest.

Sample Special Interest Theme: ANIMALS/NATURE

BOOKS
Black Beauty by Anna Sewell
Charlotte's Web by E. B. White
The Secret Garden by Frances Hodgson Burnett
Venus Among the Fishers by Elizabeth Hal and Scott O'Dell
Rachel Carson's biography

POETRY
The Earth Is Painted Green: A Garden of Poems About Our Planet, edited by Barbara Brenner

BOOK-RELATED ACTIVITIES
Refreshment, fresh fruits, vegetables, grains, and edible flowers.

Centerpiece: "Season's Greetings" any time of year with a table centerpiece made of recycled sticks, bark, stones, leaves, moss, etc., from yard or park.

Nature Scavenger Hunt: Compile list of words from book describing things in nature, and find as many as possible in the backyard or neighborhood park.

Field Trip: Go to a nature preserve, zoo, or animal shelter or talk with a naturalist, ranger, or community educator.

reading. The mothers then can scout out books that satisfy both the girls' interest in a subject and the mothers' interests in subjects we'd like to bring into discussion with them.

I think most mothers want to raise their daughters to become strong, responsible women. We want to teach them the values we hold dear—self-reliance, faith, compassion, and generosity—without hitting them over the head with it all. Selecting books by theme provides the basis for a balanced mother-daughter partnership: The girls' interests can provide the direction; the mothers can provide the books.

Think of themes as a visit to a big museum. It's a wonderful way to explore the unknown, satisfy your curiosity, expand your knowledge, and enlighten your perspective. But you don't have to stay in one place until everyone's begging to leave. Visit, go elsewhere, come back another time.

There's no limit to the themes you can identify and explore. For example, a group with a particular interest in the arts might start with a biography of an artist's life, discussing the personal qualities the artist brought to life's challenges and opportunities. Another book might be chosen as a way to explore a particular era or culture and the contribution it made to the world of visual or performing arts. A third selection might be one that had been made into a movie. The group could read the book, see the movie, and discuss how the story was translated from one form to another.

There are so many views from which to explore the world, and so many views of the world to explore. Some perspectives for creating either a theme-based group or list might include:

📖 **CULTURAL**—Multicultural, African American, Hispanic, Asian, Jewish, or other ethnic identities.

BOOKS TO GROW ON

Literature of Science

ASTRONOMY
Coming of Age in the Milky Way, Timothy Ferris

BIOLOGY
The Double Helix, James Watson

CHEMISTRY
The Periodic Table, Primo Levi

GEOLOGY
Rising from the Plains, John McPhee

PHYSICS
Surely You're Joking Mr. Feynman!, Richard Feynman

MEDICINE
The Youngest Science, Lewis Thomas

PSYCHOLOGY
The Man Who Mistook His Wife for a Hat, Oliver Sacks

NATURE
The Immense Journey, Loren Eiseley

AND FOR GOOD MEASURE
A Natural History of the Senses, Diane Ackerman

—ROBERT HAZEN, AUTHOR,
Science Matters

THEMES FOR ALL SEASONS, ALL PEOPLE

One of my favorite books, especially good for the nine-to-twelve age group, is *In the Year of the Boar and Jackie Robinson* by Bette Bao Lord. In the story, it's 1947 and a Chinese girl moves from China to Brooklyn, renaming herself "Shirley" after Shirley Temple. In Brooklyn she finds a true melting pot of people from every ethnic and racial group. She grows to love baseball, and Jackie Robinson is her hero.

The way the author handles the aspects of tradition, cultures, and ethnicity is extraordinary, and it models for our children the theme of diversity as something to celebrate.

The chapters are named by month, so I often tie that in to the start of the new calendar year and read it with children in January. That, in turn, ties in to Martin Luther King Jr.'s birthday, which gives the discussion a good starting point on the theme of prejudice, whether it's about race, religion, or the clothes kids wear to school. The book also introduces Jackie Robinson, a world-renowned figure "bigger than life" but having some of the same problems that ordinary people have. Some questions with which to explore prejudice:

• What do you think when you see someone dressed in a way that you see as unusual or different?

• In what ways do you form opinions about people? By their looks or language? By their age or grade? How do you form opinions about people when you don't know them?

• When you know someone, what are the qualities about them that make them special to you?

Change, and how we cope with it, is another theme in *In the Year of the Boar and Jackie Robinson,* and a very important part of life today. Our children can learn skills for coping from watching us and reading about others' struggle with change. Some discussion questions:

• What do you think about change? What kinds of changes do you like? What kinds of changes do you dislike? Can a change that's hard become one that's good? How?

• How do you cope with change, and how do your parents help you cope with change? How important is it to have help and support during change?

• What kinds of changes have you experienced and how did you cope with them? This might be changing schools, moving, family changes, events or illness that change our lives.

—BONNIE DIAMOND,
LANGUAGE ARTS SPECIALIST

📖 **RELIGIOUS**—explore your own or the diversity of religions in the world.

📖 **LIFE CHALLENGES**—divorce, illness, disability, loss, grief and recovery.

Brainstorm for ideas within your group. Take the "I wish" list of subjects or styles or authors your group would like to read, and consider the many options, including book-related activities. Here are a few for starters:

📖 **AN AUTHOR:** Read several books for opportunities to mix novels, nonfiction, poetry, if possible. Always check for a biography. Quite a few authors write for young adults and young children—read and compare the styles and themes.

> **BOOKS TO GROW ON**
>
> I've focused on secret adventurers:
>
> *The Egypt Game*
> Zilpha K. Snyder
>
> *Calamity Jane's Letters to Her Daughter/Martha Jane Cannary Hickok*
> Calamity Jane
>
> *From the Mixed-Up Files of Mrs. Basil E. Frankweiler*
> E. L. Konigsburg
>
> *Annie on My Mind*
> Nancy Garden
>
> *Gone-Away Lake*
> Elizabeth Enright
>
> *The Borrowers*
> Mary Norton
>
> —ELIZABETH WHEELER

Ask local bookstore or library advisers about any authors who might live in the area and be available to talk with your group, or about planned author visits to your community.

📖 **DIARIES:** Look under historical fiction for these treasures.

📖 **PLAYS:** There are many plays written for young people. Some are in paperback-style booklet collections and include adaptations of classics as well as newer plays. The Pleasant Company also publishes packets of plays featuring its American Girl characters. Check with a librarian for help in finding plays.

📖 **HISTORY:** Pick an era and read a couple of historical fiction books and a biography of a notable woman of the time. Consider a trip to a local museum, a movie depicting the era or a documentary video.

📖 **LEADERSHIP:** Ask a helpful librarian to suggest a few novels in which girls' leadership qualities are portrayed in a real-life setting. Add a biography of a woman leader in history. Consider inviting a local community leader to talk with your group about her life and personal history.

EXPERIMENTING WITH THEMES: BIRDS, BEES, AND BLUNDERS

Whenever you pick a book with a particular theme in mind, be ready for a lesson of another kind—always inspired by the reality of girls' thinking. We learned our lesson with an ill-fated motherly scheme to address "coming of age" issues within the comfort of the book club circle.

During our mother-time talks we had shared our feelings of trepidation at the looming need to discuss issues of sexuality with our soon-to-be-teen girls. Frankly, we felt like wimps. We thought that we—and the girls—might find courage and comfort in having the conversation within our circle, using a book as the focus of attention. We made two mistakes and one inspired decision.

The mistakes came first. First, over muttered protest by the girls, the mothers picked the book. It was a good book, a highly respected nonfiction volume written to introduce girls and women to their bodies and issues of sexuality in a clear and positive way. Second, over a background noise of quietly desperate objections by the girls, we assigned the book, and one of the mothers cheerfully volunteered to host the meeting. It was put on our roster for a meeting a few months off.

Within about a week, the mothers were on the phone to each other. It wasn't working. At home, individually, the girls' desperation had turned to defiance. They'd read it, but no way were they going to talk about it in a group. Even the girls who had read it before wouldn't admit it to the other girls.

Then came the inspired decision. We mothers agreed among ourselves to just drop it as a group activity. At the next meeting, when we turned to picking books for the future, I simply mentioned in passing that we all were reading

---

BOOKS TO GROW ON

Books I have enjoyed as a child and lower school librarian:

The Secret Garden
Frances Hodgson Burnett

King of the Wind
Marguerite Henry

Where the Lilies Bloom
Vera Cleaver and Bill Cleaver

A Begonia for Miss Appelbaum
Paul Zindel

Yolanda's Genius
Carol Fenner

Homecoming
Cynthia Voigt

The Little Fishes
Erik Haugaard

A Wizard of Earthsea
Ursula K. Le Guin

— PHOEBE BACON,
SCHOOL LIBRARIAN,
National Cathedral School,
Washington, D.C.

the book, and talking about it at home, but that we wouldn't plan to use it for group discussion after all. We didn't criticize or tease the girls for feeling the way they did. We treated the change in a matter-of-fact way, leaving it with a note of encouragement to mothers and daughters to read and chat about the book together. And then we moved on.

The lesson? I count four, at least: Don't be afraid to try new ideas. Listen to your girls and respect their feelings. Speak up when something isn't working. And be willing to change your mind.

SUPPORT GROUPS: MOTHERS, DAUGHTERS, AND SPECIAL NEEDS

No life is ordinary. But some lives contain particular events or circumstances—divorce, death, chronic illness, or other stressful conditions—that add an extraordinary measure of challenge for mothers and daughters. That challenge can bring them together or push them apart, and sometimes both. Quite often, mother and daughter are in need of emotional support from outside the family as well as from within their relationship.

For those who have challenges in common, a mother-daughter book club provides the emotional equivalent of a room with a view. The group offers a "safe haven" of acceptance and understanding, while the books and discussion can add new perspective to stimulate fresh thinking.

For instance, a group of single moms and daughters might find a special comfort zone in their own mother-daughter book club. Typically, the single mother and her daughter face so many challenges—emotional, practical, financial. In a group setting, there is affirmation and encouragement from others

Embracing the World Through Books and Discussion

Parents—black, white, Latino—need to talk about differences, about what makes this country what it is today. We may not all agree on the interpretations, but we all need to talk about what's happened. You can't talk about the meaning of a voters' proposition about affirmative action if you don't understand the history of what was done to black people.

I've always liked to read historical fiction, even as a girl. History is a continuous story of people. I wanted that to come through in the Addy books. The people were slaves, but you're talking about somebody's mother and father. There were moments of heroism and humor and joy. They didn't just sit around wringing their hands. Every day was not spent gnashing teeth. To portray them that way is to reduce people's lives to that.

A mother's love or a father's love is what life always has been about, and it doesn't change in slavery. In Addy I wanted to make sure that there is something in their lives that is joyous. Something that speaks of hope.

Historical fiction can really teach a young person, who has no way of contacting the past, to know about the past. When I go to schools and bring things, it gives the children a way of entering another time period and using their imaginations. It gives them a chance to go back and compare their lives with the lives of people a long time ago.

And I hope it gives them a sense of perspective on how life has changed in this country and how much they take for granted. And there should be a sense of pride, no matter whom you're reading about—a little Jewish girl emigrating, a black child coming out of slavery, a white farm girl on the prairie—they're getting a hope and appreciation for what it took to build a nation. It wasn't one person's story or one group's story.

I have to think that if there's any way for this country to survive, it will be in finding a common ground we can share. All around the globe, all around, there are many thousand examples of what happens when you separate and hate.

—CONNIE PORTER

Karen Lindstrom Mother-Daughter Book Club

We were inspired to form a group when we read about your book in the *Washington Post*. We started our group shortly thereafter and, of course, used your book to get started. The oldest daughters in our book club graduated from high school in June 2006 (one of these girls is my older daughter). We also have high school juniors in our group as well as one sophomore, my younger daughter.

Over the years, so many things have taken place within our group, from the most joyous to the most sorrowful. We've had some mother-daughters drop out due to lack of interest or time—and we've added wonderful new members along the way. We've had one of our mothers die of breast cancer—and we subsequently named the book club after her—we have also kept her daughter in the club with us since her death. Over the years, her grandmother (from Seattle) has joined us—and even her father on occasion. We feel that it's been a wonderful way that we could honor her memory and help "take care" of her daughter. Karen Lindstrom was an avid reader and a dedicated member of our book club. Another of our moms lost her young husband to a brain tumor about a year and a half ago. Our book club has been a haven for her and for her daughter as well.

We began our group by reading many of the books you recommended in your book when the girls were young. We enjoyed so many of your recommendations. We then branched out according to the tastes of individual members and we've taken off in many different directions. One of our traditions is an annual Christmas holiday event . . . sometimes we have a simple holiday tea complete with a book exchange for the daughters . . . on other occasions, we've gone to Hershey, Pennsylvania, to see the *Nutcracker* ballet and shared our favorite *Nutcracker* storybooks. We've had guest speakers at our meetings, including authors and/or "survivors" . . . and the geographically-inspired culinary spreads that our hostesses prepare each month (tied to the setting of the book) have given us a taste of many parts of the world previously unknown to us.

For me personally, your wonderful idea to create a mother-daughter book club has been such a special part of my life with my two daughters—I cannot thank you enough for inspiring us to create this group. Interestingly, this group of mothers and daughters were not the closest of friends to begin with—we were just a group of moms who felt the same way you did and we pulled a group together. Over the years, it has been a joy to watch all of the daughters share their love of reading with each other and to blossom into amazingly bright and articulate young women before our very eyes.

> *—Jeanne R. Wolfson, Founder, Karen Lindstrom*
> *Mother-Daughter Book Club,*
> *Rockville, Maryland*

facing similar challenges. When brought into a circle of caring others, that experience can translate into a wealth of insight and understanding.

The group might look for books that portray nontraditional families and individuals with challenges in common. Or it might shift the focus away from the familiar and look to biographies for compelling life stories or to poetry for powerful emotional expression.

The club concept can easily be adapted to groups in which any "significant other" adult in a girl's life is her partner for reading and discussion. Those possibilities are endless and offer a structure for sharing and strengthening a special relationship.

READING: A CONSTANT THEME IN MOTHERS' LIVES

When I was school age, the word *theme* meant term papers, essay questions on tests, and longwinded lectures from classroom teachers—bless them all. Today when I hear the word, I think about books and lives, and the threads that run strong through them, giving texture and definition.

Among the women and girls in our Mother-Daughter Book Club, reading itself is a theme that has shaped and inspired our lives as far back as most of us can remember.

My mother has always been a constant reader. I can't imagine her without a book in her hand, her travel bag, or on the table, or—if nowhere in sight—on her mind! That mental picture has turned out to be worth a thousand words—or books, to be more precise. When my brothers and I went to help her declutter the basement, we were overwhelmed by the number of paperback books we found! We packed up dozens of bags of books to give to charities, and, of course, my mother kept dozens more she wasn't ready to part with.

My bond with books goes way back, my mother tells me. She named me Shireen, inspired by what she thought was a beautiful name of a character in one of those paperback novels. What a lasting gift from a reading mother to a loved daughter.

Our Mother-Daughter Book Club is full of reading moms who are rich with happy memories of their own mothers and of reading. We took some time to reflect on that theme in our lives, and the memories made a wonderful sharing experience.

"My earliest memories of my mother are of her reading, always," Kathie says. "Books, magazines, articles. We could be going on a trip in the car and we'd ask a question and she'd always know the answer—and she could tell you where she'd read it, too. She still reads all the time."

Alexis remembers being a "voracious reader" as a child. "I would read under this walnut tree at my grandmother's house. Other times I would read in my room. I would close the door, and I would get so engrossed in my book I wouldn't even come down for food," Alexis says. "I would read for pleasure. Books took me so many places. I always felt I would see the places when I got older, but reading about them ensured that at least I saw them in my mind."

Reading was and remains important in her parents' lives, too, she says. "My mother and I are very close, and when I was young, I watched her—she was always there with the family. Most of her reading was recipes and the newspaper. I would watch her read, and being the inquisitive one, I would ask what she was reading. She would always put the book in front of my face and say, 'Here, you read it to me.' I think she enjoyed hearing my voice. When I go visit them at home even now, I read to them.

My father and mother both love *National Geographic,* so I'll read that to them and we talk about it."

Reading together in a home with busy mothers comes up again and again.

"I come from a family of seven children and we lived with my mother and father in a three-bedroom, one-bath home, " says Alice. "I would use books to escape. I remember sitting out under our apple tree and reading every single Laura Ingalls Wilder book. Then and now, when I find an author I really like, I read all the books that author has written, and then I move on.

"When I was young, I read a lot. I read the autobiographies, like Helen Keller's. I read a lot of the Bible—I read the Bible from cover to cover one year when I was about ten. I read a lot of Nancy Drew. It was more recreational than anything. I used to imagine myself as the characters in some of the books, and I would use those books to get ideas about writing and I'd write little stories about those characters, putting myself and my family into the book.

"My mother always loved, and still loves, reading, but she just didn't have much time, " Alice says. "With seven children, her hands were always busy, but I would sit down and read with her. And that's how we would read together."

MOTHERS AND DAUGHTERS: THEMES FOREVER

No matter what the general theme of our book selections, our interest in the theme of mothers and daughters remains a constant. We always take note of the ways girls and women are portrayed in the stories, the way the author uses them in a book's cast of characters, the qualities that the author assigns them. We compare their book life with our own life experiences to explore points of difference or common experience.

That exploration of the world and our own lives together—through books, discussion, and sharing—is the one theme that stays the same in a mother-daughter book club. It's one interest none of us will ever outgrow!

ENDNOTES

📖 Use special interests, or themes, as a fun way to add a bit of structure to your reading.

📖 Use themes to broaden your reading and discussion experience.

📖 Brainstorm theme ideas such as cultures, religions, or life situations within your group.

📖 Whatever your special interests, keep the theme of mothers and daughters a constant in your club's readings and discussions.

TEN

Beyond the Books

WHEN YOU THINK ABOUT IT, WE DON'T REALLY LEARN BY JUST
LISTENING. WE LEARN BY THINKING AND BY DOING.

—ELLEN SILBER

Sylvie Stein & Kris Heinz

Hi, my name is Sylvie Stein. I'm fifteen years old. I am in my sophomore year at Georgetown Day School, the school that I have attended for the last ten years. I love everything about my school—the sports, the classes, the teachers, and my friends. Despite the large workload, GDS offers many things to inspire and motivate me. My favorite sports are softball and soccer, both of which I have been playing since I learned to walk, and my favorite classes are English and history. I also love writing for the school newspaper.

I have an older sister who is a freshman at Tufts University, and along with my mother, she is my ultimate role model. I have two dogs, who are adorable, and two cats, who are extremely overfed.

I live with my dad in Cleveland Park and with my mom in Chevy Chase. I have lived in D.C. all my life and I think it is the greatest city ever. What I love most is hanging out with family and friends. Whether going to restaurants and concerts, playing sports, exploring around town, or going to book club, I just enjoy being with the people I love.

My mom's name is Kris, and she has the perfect mixture of goofiness and intelligence; for example, she is an avid belly dancer yet a successful consultant. I love learning from her and taking after her, although I am completely unable to belly dance.

When my mom was little, she would go to the library every other Saturday to check out as many books as the librarian would allow. Although a single working mom, she still reads a few books most months, primarily modern fiction. She says that she loves having her eyes opened to experiences through the characters in books that she herself would never have the time, nerve, or opportunity to have.

My mom likes to hike with our dog and she enjoys Rollerblading as well.

It was a dark and stormy night. The girls crept through the dim, secret passageway, looking for an escape. They checked their tattered map and located the wall panel that was supposed to fall open and let them run out to safety. Together, they pressed the panel.

"It won't budge! We're trapped!"

They pushed harder. The panel seemed to push back! They pushed again. And again. Suddenly, the panel gave way and the girls tumbled out—laughing and squealing and scrambling to catch the jokester on the other side—one of the girls' older brothers!

He had stationed himself on the outside of the cardboard box tunnel as they'd crept through it and had held the escape panel firm for that extra moment to add a genuine element of surprise to the great escape.

Our Mother-Daughter Book Club would never forget its

BOOKS TO GROW ON

Annie John
Jamaica Kincaid

To Kill a Mockingbird
Harper Lee

Having Our Say
Sarah and Elizabeth Delany

Member of the Wedding
Carson McCullers

Jacob Have I Loved
Katherine Paterson

Night
Elie Wiesel

The Good Earth
Pearl Buck

Bless Me, Ultima
Rudolfo Anaya

The Hundred Dresses
Eleanor Estes

—AMY SCHROTH, HEAD OF ENGLISH DEPARTMENT, The Madeira School, McLean, Virginia adventure of escape through the "underground railroad" the hosting daughter had created in her family's basement. Nor would we forget the book that took us there, *The House of Dies Drear* by Virginia Hamilton, the story of a family and a house haunted by its past as a Civil War–era safe house for those fleeing slavery.

Good books are a treasure chest of ideas. The stories themselves are the gems we enjoy first through reading and discussion. But when we look more closely within the stories, they sparkle with detail about history, foods, and the events and accessories of everyday life. Every facet of the book—the story, the author, the era in which it was written—as well as any creative descendants of the book, such as movies, plays, museum exhibits, visual art, or other stories—offers shining opportunities for fun and learning.

BOOK ACTIVITIES: REACH FOR YOUR SENSES!

There are enough lessons in life that we learn the hard way. When there's a choice, I think learning should be as much fun as possible.

The Girl Scouts have known that for a long time, and used that belief to shape their programs for success. "Not surprisingly, we have learned that girls' perspective is that Girl Scouts is, first and foremost, a place to have fun and share friendships," says a survey report by the Girls Scouts of the U.S.A. "The more they enjoy their experience, the more likely they are to remain in Girl Scouting. Achievement—through badge, patch, and award programs—is also important to many girls. But it is important to remember that learning and development can only take place in an environment that girls truly enjoy."

When children are very young, they learn primarily by playing. When they get a little older, they learn by doing, which includes playing, acting, planning, building, cooking, designing, sewing—you name it—and still aims for a good time.

At this preteen age, a book becomes meaningful in one way when it connects with their intellect. It becomes memorable in a dramatically different way when it connects with their senses and feelings. In the Mother-Daughter Book Club, our shared reading and wide-open discussion of each book help us connect with the characters, the setting, the history, and the author.

Book-related activities also can bridge a gap between individual learning styles. Some children learn best by reading, some by listening, some by discussing. And for some, "hands-on activity," as it's called in the schools, is the way they take an experience in.

Whatever our individual learning style may be, book-related activities are another wonderful way to enlarge our experience of the books. Book-related activities offer the girls an opportunity to be creative, each in her own way. The activity is planned by the host daughter and mother, and adds to the feeling of leadership each girl enjoys when it's her turn.

When the group read *The House of Dies Drear*, Holly took to her basement and put together cardboard boxes to make a segment of an "underground railroad" escape hideout like that depicted in the book.

"Anything that brings people together to discuss a common experience, whether it's a book or movie or having been to the same play or event, offers an opportunity to understand the same thing but know it differently, to take different things away from the same experience."

Susan Mcgee Bailey

BOOKS TO GROW ON

Little Women
Louisa May Alcott

The Hobbit
J. R. R. Tolkien

The Nancy Drew series
Carolyn Keene

A Wrinkle in Time
Madeleine L'Engle

A Tree Grows in Brooklyn
Betty Smith

Chronicles of Narnia
C. S. Lewis

All Creatures Great and Small
James Herriott

I Capture the Castle
Dodie Smith

Bridge to Terabithia
Katherine Paterson

Zlateh the Goat, and Other Stories
Isaac B. Singer

—ROBIN ROBERTSON,
FORMER HEAD MISTRESS,
Emma Willard School,
Troy, New York

"I thought hosting would be burdensome and that it would be difficult to find interesting things for them to discuss and do," Alice says. "Then when it was our turn, Holly and I discussed what we could do to make our discussion interesting and make the book come alive. She chose the topic; she chose the menu for that day. She turned our basement storage room into an underground railroad. She made maps, and for food we made what she thought slaves might have packed to travel: fried chicken and biscuits, raw vegetables, chocolate cake. She set the agenda, made all the questions. She did an incredible job. I was very proud of her."

Long after the meeting was over and her basement was straightened up, that underground railroad lives on in our memories.

Later we read Hamilton's sequel, *The Mystery of Drear House,* and hosts Maya and Joyce chose to put us all in Jeopardy!—the game, that is. Mothers and daughters squared off in this rapid-fire question-and-answer game based on details in the book. It was a tie-breaker, and the girls beat us to that last answer. They reveled in their victory. So did we!

"It was really fun," Maya says. "And then we were thinking about what the prizes could be and we got some bookmarks from the Smithsonian."

Trivia or mother-daughter Jeopardy!-style games can be used again and again for a good time. They help us celebrate the details of the books we read, and no matter how fierce it becomes, the competition is the best kind.

When we read *The Friends* by Rosa Guy, we contacted the author to see if she might accept an invitation to be our special guest at our book club meeting. She accepted, along with her goddaughter, Kathe Sandler, who had made a film of part of the *Friends* story, and we made arrangements to have our meeting in a room at the Smithsonian's Center for African American History and Culture. The girls were able to see the film and discuss aspects of the story with Rosa Guy.

"It was really, really interesting to get to meet Rosa Guy," says Brittney. "We got to ask her questions and see the movie—it was great!"

IDEAS FOR ACTIVITIES: THE BOOK'S THE THING

Every story offers images we can use to taste, touch, see, smell, or hear the story in a special way. Other aspects to explore include the author and the historical context for the book. Even

DO-IT-YOURSELF ACTIVITIES
BRING STORIES ALIVE

Books are a wonderful way to learn about so many things. You don't have to stop with reading the story. Whether it's about how laundry was done, or about crop rotation, or other aspects of life for characters in the book, once you start thinking, you start learning.

That's part of the value of any book. The experience of the research and activity takes on a life of its own.

In *The World of Little House* we explore the world of Laura Ingalls Wilder's Little House books, and one of the points we wanted to make comes through in thinking about how people lived. People did things differently then. For instance, today, when you see craft demonstrations, the focus is always on how to make things that are quick and easy.

The characters from the Little House books—and they are very true to life, all based on real people—did things in a very deliberate and caring way. They didn't mind that it took time. It was part of their entertainment and a way that they spent time.

When you see Ma giving the girls work to do in the dugout house, they're stringing buttons. Laura and Mary would string and restring those buttons, arranging them in different ways. How many children would do that now? But it's very appealing to think about it, how they spent time, concentrated, had fine motor skills. Laura was making a sampler with a needle and thread when she was four; Mary was making a quilt at five. They were doing some pretty sophisticated things as children.

Sometimes people romanticize the "old days" or fantasize about living in a simpler era past, when life was easier. We don't want to burst anybody's balloon, but we want them to know that life was pretty hard for these people, and it shows a portion of their character that they were able to persevere through a lot of hardship.

Doing an activity to bring the stories home really helps children. It gets them involved in the story a little bit more, and it becomes an experience to remember. Children sometimes need a little bit of a hook to start their learning experience, especially with history. Cooking something they've read about and remember, or making something, or growing something, is always a helpful connection. Our goal is to help them relate to the classic books and want to know more.

—CAROLYN STROM COLLINS, COAUTHOR,
The World of Little House

MAKING THE CONNECTION TO BOOKS — BY HAND

Tips for Planning Book-Related Activities

- Pick ideas that interest the girls.

- Think about ways to adapt them to make them age-appropriate for interest and skill.

- Aim for simplicity. Good projects don't have to be complicated.

- Aim for authenticity. Try to use materials that the character would have used at that time and place.

- Involve your daughter in collecting the materials.

- Reread a portion of the book where the activity is described.

- Organize all materials; get enough to allow for mistakes.

- Encourage girls to express their own creativity in any project.

- Be patient. Small motor skills improve with practice, not pressure.

- Acknowledge the effort each girl puts into her work, regardless of her skill level.

—CAROLYN STROM COLLINS

the story itself—the language or details about characters, plot, and setting—make good material for games.

THINK ABOUT FIELD TRIPS. A museum, movie, community exhibit, or other site may offer a special perspective on a book. Take your urban children to the countryside to experience a rural story setting. Take your suburban children to the city to see the rows of brownstones or skyscrapers that frame a character's life. A bus or train ride, or even a nature walk around your neighborhood, can be a special experience if it relates to the book.

THINK ABOUT AUTHORS. Ask a librarian for help in locating information about the author—biographies or magazine articles, for instance. Call or write to the publisher to find out whether the author plans to visit your area on a promotional tour or lives in your area and might be willing to talk with your group. If not, consider writing to the author.

THINK ABOUT HISTORY. Explore the historical setting for the story or the author's life. Museums are wonderful, but they're just one way to access history. Closer to home, books of historical photographs can add to the enjoyment of a story. Invite the mothers and daughters to come "dressed for the occasion"—in clothing reminiscent of the era. Or a simple activity from the book—the "old-fashioned way"—can be eye-opening.

THINK ABOUT BOOKS. Have some fun with simple art or craft activities. Invite the girls to illustrate their favorite scenes and see if your community or school library would welcome a display. Make bookmarks or decorate canvas tote sacks or T-shirts to reflect your mother-daughter book club interests.

📖 **THINK ABOUT READING.** Keep a running list of "wonderful words" or "phavorite phrases" from the books. Play games that make the most of recall—words, facts, descriptions, characters, and quotes.

📖 **THINK ABOUT FOOD!** Look in the book for descriptions of foods or mealtimes for refreshment menu ideas. Order takeout from an ethnic restaurant that captures the cultural flavor of the story. I made a tasty chicken dish from a recipe mentioned by a character in one of our books. And when another book took us into the Chinese culture, we asked a local baker if he could duplicate a Chinese "castle cake" mentioned in the book as an elaborate construction decorated in pink icing with little silver sparkles. The cake delivered to our house on meeting day was magnificent. It was, figuratively and literally, like something out of a book.

Girls often enjoy socializing over the kitchen table with a cooking or craft activity, their minds and hands busy with something fun to make. Activities like these are another opportunity for sharing stories and laughter between mothers and daughters. The important thing about book-related activities is that they be enjoyable and that they always leave plenty of time for book discussion. That might sound obvious, but it's important to keep it in mind, especially with a group of creative, enthusiastic daughters and mothers. If the book-related craft or activity becomes so time-consuming or complex that it overshadows discussion time, it may be best to think of a different idea. And an activity *isn't* enjoyable for a mother or daughter who feel pressured to do it, or if it strains the budget.

I am a believer in enrichment activities—the experience

of seeing, hearing, tasting, and touching pieces of the stories we read. The interesting thing about mother-daughter book discussion is that the discussion itself *is* an enrichment activity, an experience no museum or field trip can deliver. When we give our book discussions the right time and attention, we go beyond the books and into the stories of our *own* lives: our history, our feelings, our dreams and concerns.

That's what makes our Mother-Daughter Book Club different from every other class, program, or activity we do. That's what keeps it special. That's what keeps us coming back, despite our crowded lives and calendars.

> ## BOOKS TO GROW ON
>
> *Nina Bonita*
> Ana M. Machado
> (younger girls)
>
> *Sarah Phillips*
> Andrea Lee
> (junior high, high school)
>
> *Strawberry Girl*
> Lois Lenski
>
> *I Know Why the Caged Bird Sings*
> Maya Angelou
>
> *The Bluest Eye*
> Toni Morrison
>
> *Amazing Grace*
> Mary Hoffman
>
> *Boundless Grace*
> Mary Hoffman
>
> —CONNIE PORTER

"The club started out just reading and discussing the books, then some of the mothers became real creative with ideas for fixing food to match the books—anything to create, open up, and hopefully get that stick-to-it-ness, " Alexis says. "When you expand outward, it makes it a living book."

Whether we simply look to the book for refreshment ideas or plan a field trip, when it comes to book-related activities, if

A SPECIAL MEETING, A SPECIAL AUTHOR: ROSA GUY

Rosa Guy is the award-winning author of *The Friends*, a trilogy, and other works, including the recently published *The Sun, the Sea, a Touch of the Wind*, a book she describes as "vaguely autobiographical." Mothers and daughters had read *The Friends* and were delighted to learn that Ms. Guy's goddaughter, professional filmmaker Kathe Sandler, had produced a segment of her aunt's award-winning novel for film.

Ms. Guy and Ms. Sandler joined us for a special meeting, where we viewed the film segment together and enjoyed a relaxed round of discussion afterward.

Her thoughts after her visit:

"I was delighted with it, delighted with the fact that the young people knew the book and had wonderful questions to ask. One often has to read books more than once to come up with good questions. I was delighted. Here was a roomful of all of them having read the book, and it wasn't school, it wasn't required reading."

Her thoughts about her work, about literature, girls, and mothers?

"I just write from my experiences and my belief in people. Whether I write about girls or boys, I write with the belief that people, if they get to understand each other, there can be love for each other whoever they are.

"I grew up mostly in Trinidad; then I have lived in Harlem and the Bronx, Africa, England, Switzerland, and Haiti.

"I didn't have a mother. I was orphaned. My mother died when I was very young, and of course I always missed her and always projected what I would expect from a mother through my work, you know. So there is a sensibility there that comes from my being orphaned. All these things must have a particular effect; it comes through somehow.

"I was sort of a loner, part of a very small family, and didn't have a lot of friends. I read extensively. All the books I read have left impressions on me because, number one, around that time they didn't have books segregated into categories—adult, adolescent, children. Fairy tales were for the very young, and then there was the rest. I did read the fairy tales, and when I got to a certain age, I read adult literature. Certainly some of it stayed with me—the Brontë sisters did, in English literature, and in French, the wonderful *Jean-Christophe*—all of these left a fantastic impression on me and they are books I cannot forget ever.

"When I was in England, in 1995, *The Friends* was considered a modern classic. I was impressed; you see, when it came out—that was more than twenty years ago—it was the first book by a black author that was put on the syllabus in Great Britain's school system.

"A thing that people have told me about my work is that I never talk down to children, I just talk to them.

"To mothers and daughters, to everyone, I would just say read. Get the books that are considered good literature and read. In our libraries we have Russian literature, French literature, some of the best books in the world. *Les Misérables, Madame Bovary,* without preaching they give you the feeling of the lives these people lived. That doesn't mean you have to ignore the realities of today.

"All of it is important. The more you read, the more you know."

TIPS ON SUSTAINING
A MOTHER-DAUGHTER BOOK CLUB

"Keep discussion questions at meetings pretty broad, and make sure that any specific questions can always lead into discussions of larger topics."

—JESSICA

"It is important not only to consistently pick books that are fun to read and fun to discuss but to also have a group of women who enjoy one another's company so that the meetings themselves are enjoyable for everyone."

—BRITTNEY

"Try to invite a variety of people—rather than a group where everyone tends to think alike."

—MONICE

"Mutual respect, a belief that everyone has the right to express their own opinion."

—ALICE

"Have a willingness to be unguarded in your critique and comments. Plus a willingness to listen to others' points of view."

—MARILYN

BOOK LOVERS BRAINSTORM
To the Books and Beyond!

- GO GLOBETROTTING! Use a globe to locate the story's setting.

- SEE THE SITES! Check with the local librarian or historical society to find out if any book-related sites might be within traveling distance for your group. Consider having your meeting at the site or planning the field trip for a day of its own.

- WRITE TO AN AUTHOR—Ask your neighborhood librarian for help in locating an address for the author of a book the club has enjoyed. Ask for a volunteer from among the girls to write the club's letter to the author, sharing the group's thoughts about the book and inviting the author to write back if possible.

- COOK OR SERVE FOOD that reflects the era or ethnic flavor of the story, or use a recipe from the book.

- MAKE A STORY-RELATED CRAFT—Try to use materials and tools they would have used at the time in the story.

- LIGHTS! ACTION! READER'S THEATER! No need to memorize—just act out a few favorite scenes using the book as your script. Take turns being the audience and the actors.

- DRESS UP! Come dressed in clothing reminiscent of the era.

- PAPER DOLLS—Make story-related paper dolls from poster board and draw your own outfits to cut out from plain paper.

- STORY SHEETS—Use 3M's poster-sized Post-it sheets to jot down the group's ideas or invite girls to draw characters or scenes to display temporarily on a wall.

- ADJECTIVE AMBUSH—Divide into two teams to see who can find the largest number of descriptive words first to reach a target number. Write down words and page numbers on which they appear in case the challengers call a bluff!

- VERB VENDETTA—Go after the action words now—remember each word has to be found in the book!

- WONDERFUL WORDS—Keep an ongoing collection of great words or phrases the girls circle during home reading and contribute at meeting. Under a heading of the book's title and discussion date, invite each contributor to write her words in the club's book herself.

- PERSONALITY PARADE—Examine characters' personalities—list and discuss their positive and negative qualities.

- TABLETOP THEMES—Create a centerpiece or table decoration that goes along with the story. The host daughter might like to use toys or items she has—dolls, miniature figurines, action figures—to set up a scene from the book.

- BOOKMARKS—Make bookmarks as a memento of a story. Invite each girl to draw a picture of a character or scene from the story on one side of the paper, and on the other side write the name of the book and month and year she read it. Laminate it or use clear adhesive-backed shelf paper to cover the bookmark.

- BOOKLIST BOOKMARK—To celebrate the conclusion of your first year of reading together, create the bookmarks, listing the title, author, and date you read each book.

- HALL OF FAME—As you read more books, continue to compare and contrast characters from different books. Enjoy an ongoing nomination process for characters, such as the most inventive, the

most thoughtful, the most creative, and other categories that encourage the girls to think of qualities that make people special or
memorable.

• CRITICS' CHOICE—Ask for a volunteer daughter to write up the
group's comments about a book that was considered particularly
good, and check with the school or neighborhood library about
posting the book review for others to enjoy. Create an annual list to
share the same way.

• BOOK CLUB SCRAPBOOK—Create a scrapbook for the club, inviting
girls to jot down their thoughts or draw illustrations about the books
or the club to fill a page or two at each meeting.

• LET PICTURES TELL THE STORY—Contact local library, school, community hall, or nursing home to see about displaying art the girls might
make illustrating a story or idea from a story.

• PLAY DETECTIVE—A hosting daughter might compile a list of rid-
dles about characters or events in the story and begin discussion by
asking the group to identify who or what she's describing.

• X MARKS THE SPOT—Enjoy a scavenger hunt without moving from
your seat! Invite the girls to mark in the book or on a separate sheet
of paper several words from the story that describe people, places,
things, or feelings. If they jot the words on paper, be sure to tell
them to mark where they found them. Then ask each girl in turn to
name one of her words for the others to find.

we keep mother-daughter discussion first on our list, everything else we choose to do supports it, and every meeting becomes memorable.

ENDNOTES

📖 Good books are a treasure chest of ideas for activities.

📖 Book-related activities can bridge a gap between individual learning styles.

📖 Discussion—along with seeing, hearing, tasting, and touching stories—is an enrichment activity.

📖 Use the club to move beyond discussion of the books to the stories of your own lives: your history and dreams.

> "A lot of times books will lead to personal stories, don't be afraid to share openly."
>
> *Skylar*

THE END
Where New Stories Begin

This story of our Mother-Daughter Book Club, like any story in a book, has to end a page before the back cover. But a very special and exciting part of the story only begins here. It's not a subplot or a sequel. It's the story that begins in another mother's heart, in another home, in another town, where the idea of a mother-daughter book discussion group takes root. Mother-daughter book clubs can flower anywhere and anytime the desire is there.

When one of Grace's friends moved to Swaziland, Grace suggested that she and her daughter start a mother-daughter book club there. They did, adopting our club's reading list as a starting point. Now we trade comments and opinions about books electronically by e-mail!

In Chicago, my writing partner Teresa Barker and her daughter, Rachel, nine, both insatiable readers, organized a mother-daughter book club with friends. After a move put forty-five minutes between them and their longtime friends, the club became a way of getting together at least once a month, along with a new friend Rachel introduced to the group from her new community.

Many of Rachel's ideas, and the experience of her club, have enriched this book and given our Mother-Daughter Book Club new ideas for book-related activities. Lynae Turner, one of the friends in Rachel's club, shares our group's African American heritage and has found a special delight in becoming a pen pal with Morgan and our club.

In reflecting on the needs of our girls, all of us have become more vocal advocates for them, and more eager to strengthen and celebrate the mother-daughter relationship. Progress comes in small steps and big ones. Any step you take toward shared reading and discussion with your daughter is a step in the right direction. Whatever you do, the rewards far outweigh the effort.

Maybe you'll organize a mother-daughter book club that meets monthly or quarterly. Maybe you'll bring up the idea within your neighborhood or religious community and encourage someone else to organize. Maybe you'll find just one other mother and daughter with whom to share reading and book chat over hot chocolate and cookies. Maybe for now, you'll simply find the time to read with your daughter, one book at a time, and at tuck-in time, ask: "What did you think of that story?"

Whatever you do, when you do, I'd love to hear about it. I see our group as an evolving circle of experience. If there's a better way to do something, or an interesting way to do something, we're eager to hear about it. Please visit our Web site www.themotherdaughterbookclub.com.

This circle of mothers and daughters can reach around the globe and into so many hearts and lives!

Where does it all end? It doesn't.

Let *your* Mother-Daughter Book Club story begin!

MOTHER-DAUGHTER BOOK CLUB
SIMPLE START-UPS

Need a boost to get started? These simple steps will get you on your way. Keeping your club going is even easier—a mother-daughter book club generates its own energy!

Remember that the important things about your mother-daughter book club are that you enjoy reading the books, show up for meetings, and take time to let discussion flow. This doesn't have to be a costly venture. It doesn't require a professional to lead discussion. And the meetings can be arranged to accommodate any schedule.

You can do this. It's this simple:

📖 Share your idea with a few friends you know well and a few you'd like to see more often.

📖 As the first hosting mother and daughter, select a book for the group to read and discuss at your first meeting. Start with a favorite of your own, or consider one of the titles and discussion guides suggested here.

📖 Set the date and time for the first meeting.

📖 At home, help your daughter plan discussion questions about the book.

📖 At your first meeting, use an icebreaker game to get started (see Chapter Three: "The Organizational Meeting: Prelude to a Great Year"), have fun with discussion, and set aside time to talk about the kinds of books that interest the girls and mothers in your group. Select books as a group or invite each girl and her mother to pick a book and a date to host a meeting.

📖 Set a date and a book for the next meeting. You're on your way!

PART TWO

One of the best-kept secrets of Mother-Daughter Book Clubs is that young adult literature is so good, we mothers really enjoy reading the books as much as the girls do. In fact, so many wonderful books have been published since I wrote *100 Book for Girls to Grow On* in 1998, that choosing only fifteen books to include here was unbelievably daunting. My main criterion is that a book be a springboard to a fabulous discussion on a particular life issue. In some cases, the books had already passed this test: Four picks are books that Skylar's Mother-Daughter Book Club has read with great success.

First and foremost is *Whirligig* by Paul Fleischman. Since first reading it with the original Mother-Daughter Book Club, I have used *Whirligig* countless times when working with teens. It is my all-time favorite book for dealing with a myriad of adolescent issues, from teen drinking to girls accepting that it is okay to be smart. The discussions that have ensued are always insightful and varied and never cease to amaze me. I think it's telling that this was also the book Skylar chose to launch our new Mother-Daughter Book Club—it got us off to a great start!

Another no-brainer was Mark Haddon's *Curious Incident of the Dog in the Night-Time*—who doesn't like a good mystery? This one is a real category winner with a big twist. Christopher, the main character, is an autistic boy and the story is told through his eyes. The book does an outstanding job of letting you in to Christopher's world so you can appreciate it. Everyone in Skylar's book club loved this book.

Several of the books deal with more global themes that reflect today's world—a very changed world, as we all know, since 9/11. When I looked through *100 Books for Girls to Grow On*, I noticed plenty of books on war but absolutely none on terrorism. That's why I was thrilled to find Jonathan Safran Foer's

Extremely Loud and Incredibly Close. We seem to talk constantly about fighting terrorism, but what about the effect on our children's emotional well-being? Foer addresses the 9/11 tragedy through the eyes of a nine-year-old boy. His story made the tragedy seem much more real to those of us who were not directly affected.

Bel Canto by Ann Patchett also deals with terrorism but with multiple characters' perspectives and with viewpoints from both sides. I am eagerly awaiting the chance to discuss this book with Skylar's Mother-Daughter Book Club and to find out how much they, at fifteen and sixteen years of age, are willing to fight for what they believe in.

An ongoing problem in this country and around the world is racism. I believe it underlies a multitude of challenges we all face. By looking at skin color bias, Sharon Flake's *The Skin I'm In* provides a perfect entry point into a broader discussion of conflict. Although racism is often framed in terms of blacks and whites, *The Bean Trees* by Barbara Kingsolver deals with prejudice against Native Americans. Another much newer concern to reach global ears is female circumcision. *No Laughter Here* by Rita Williams-Garcia does an excellent job of presenting this very delicate subject. Where else but in the trusting, loving mother-daughter book club circle can young women discuss such horrific topics?

Coming-of-age stories abound and I selected several that I felt were particularly well done, with fully developed characters and enough plot twists and turns to keep the reader engaged: *Big Mouth & Ugly Girl* by Joyce Carol Oates; *Chu Ju's House* by Gloria Whelan; *Crystal* by Walter Dean Myers; *Hush* by Jacqueline Woodson; and *Speak* by Laurie Halse Anderson, which Morgan's club read when they were all in tenth grade.

Skylar's club chose Anderson's *Prom* instead of *Speak* and liked it equally well.

As in the case of Laurie Halse Anderson, often I discover a good book because I keep following a particular author's career and output. The original Mother-Daughter Book Club became particularly fond of Sharon Creech, for example. I read several of her more recent books for this new edition, and she did not disappoint. In the end I chose to include *Replay*, which is a great book for younger readers and stands out because it deals with the theme of how to get enough attention when you're part of a big family—and from a male perspective. It is always valuable yet rare for girls to view their lives through a new lens.

In addition to checking out other titles by an author you like, a good way to narrow your choices for a book club is by using the "If You Like This Book, Try . . ." feature. Each of the fifteen new discussion guides includes suggestions for further reading, just as I provided in the original edition and in *100 Books for Girls to Grow On*. I've indicated with an asterisk whenever these complementary titles are in *100 Books for Girls to Grow On*, where you will find detailed descriptions and discussion questions.

Another source for discovering excellent book club reads are bookstores. I highly recommend establishing a relationship with your local independent bookstore. You will find the staff extremely knowledgeable and always willing to help. My own private guide for more than a decade has been Jewell, who heads the children's department at my favorite bookstore, Politics and Prose. Several of the many books she suggested made my list. *A Northern Light* by Jennifer Donnelly and *True Believer* by Virginia Euwer Wolff are both great reads. When Skylar's Mother-Daughter Book Club discussed *A Northern*

Light, we talked about whether the mother's dying wish that her daughter take care of the family was fair. Most of us felt it was not fair, and the girls said they would never make any kind of dying wish.

I hope you enjoy sharing these selections with your daughters as much as I have enjoyed my hours with all the mothers and daughters in my book clubs.

Shireen Dodson,
2006

SELECTED BOOK DISCUSSION GUIDES

1. *The Bean Trees*, Barbara Kingsolver

2. *Bel Canto*, Ann Patchett

3. *Big Mouth & Ugly Girl*, Joyce Carol Oates

4. *Chu Ju's House*, Gloria Whelan

5. *Crystal*, Walter Dean Myers

6. *The Curious Incident of the Dog in the Night-Time*, Mark Haddon

7. *Extremely Loud and Incredibly Close*, Jonathan Safran Foer

8. *Hush*, Jacqueline Woodson

9. *No Laughter Here*, Rita Williams-Garcia

10. *A Northern Light*, Jennifer Donnelly

11. *Replay*, Sharon Creech

12. *The Skin I'm In*, Sharon Flake

13. *Speak*, Laurie Halse Anderson

14. *True Believer*, Virginia Euwer Wolff

15. *Whirligig*, Paul Fleischman

The Bean Trees
Barbara Kingsolver

Taylor Greer doesn't want to get pregnant and doesn't want to stay in Kentucky. So she heads as far west as her barely drivable car will take her. Along the way she is saddled with a neglected and abused child. Taylor decides to take care of the abandoned American Indian girl and names her Turtle. *The Bean Trees* is a story of abandonment, belonging, and loving friendship as Taylor and Turtle make their life in Tucson, Arizona.

READING TIME: 4 hours, about 336 pages

THEMES: family, gender/society roles, identity, race

Discussion Questions

📖 Why would the story open with the tractor tire explosion that threw Newt Hardbine over the top of the Standard Oil sign? What kind of tone does this set?

📖 Do we know if Taylor has been through a great deal before leaving Kentucky? How does she carry herself? How does she later think of herself during this time?

📖 Do you think Taylor handled being given Turtle well? What would you have done differently in that position?

📖 Though not overtly religious, *The Bean Trees* does refer to God a few times, like in Taylor's embellished Cherokee tree myth, as well as the 1–800-THE LORD toll-free hotline, and Jesus Is Lord Used Tires. What, if any, role does God play in this story?

📖 Throughout the book, Taylor describes strange plants native to the American Southwest. Can you name a few of these plants and come up with some explanations as to how they relate to the story?

📖 Soon after leaving Kentucky, Taylor meets Turtle, a child who was molested at least once before and perhaps once after being in Taylor's custody. Also, Taylor's best friend, Lou Ann, has been left by her husband, Angel, and the only man Taylor expresses interest in is already married. What is going on with men in this story? And how does it compare to your experiences, if at all?

📖 Jesus Is Lord Used Tires serves as a sanctuary for illegal aliens sneaking into the country. Of course, one could also say it serves as a haven for less fortunate people in a time of desperate need, including Taylor. How do you reconcile these seemingly contradictory facets? What does this novel say about displacement? How is it possible to be displaced in your own country?

📖 Would you call the adoption scene the climax of the story? Why or why not?

📖 According to Taylor, her mother always referred to their one-eighth Cherokee headrights as a kind of ace in the hole. Nonetheless, on her return trip to Oklahoma, Taylor discovers a Cherokee Nation quite different from the one she imagined. She goes on to think that perhaps it would be impossible for her to claim her headrights at this late stage, even as she begins the process to legally adopt Turtle. Does there seem to be an unconventional attitude toward race throughout this story? How would you describe it?

📖 Money is tight for Taylor and her friends. But nowhere does Taylor, or anyone else, seem to complain. Why do you think this is?

📖 What is meant by the description of the symbiotic cycle of wisteria at the end of the novel? Why would the book be titled *The Bean Trees*?

Beyond the Book

SOUP: Make a vibrant and zesty "Bean-Tree soup." Use what you have in the kitchen as well as your imagination. Let yourself experiment with the ingredients and, like Taylor traveling west with nowhere in particular to go, let the journey lead you to your destination. Serve with crusty bread and a salad.

NAME GAME: Jesus is Lord Used Tires has a pretty distinctive name that likely wouldn't exist at all anywhere outside of America. Can you think of a similarly distinctive name for a store or shop and write a very short story around that location? Don't limit yourself to Arizona; try any place in the world.

SPEAK IN FOODS: Adorable as she is, Turtle tends to speak in terms of food—even when the topic is decidedly unrelated to food. Some people in Tucson think it means she is slow, but Taylor knows it simply as Turtle being herself. Make up your own food language. Try to rhyme normal words with foods where you can, and where you can't, simplify the sounds. Don't forget for everyone who is female and older than you, add Ma to the front of their names.

If You Like This Book, Try . . .

Animal Dreams or *Pigs in Heaven* by Barbara Kingsolver
The Secret Life of Bees by Sue Monk Kidd
Where the Heart Is by Billie Letts
Seventh Heaven by Alice Hoffman
The Great Gilly Hopkins by Katherine Paterson (for
    younger readers)

About the Author

Barbara Kingsolver is the author of numerous other novels, including *Animal Dreams, Pigs in Heaven,* and *The Poisonwood Bible.* She grew up in rural Kentucky and now lives in Tucson, Arizona, and on a farm in southern Appalachia with her husband and two children.

Bel Canto
Ann Patchett

On a gala evening in a small South American country, honored guests from the world over gather to celebrate the birthday of a powerful Japanese businessman and to listen to the dulcet voice of the world-famous soprano Roxane Coss. When she finishes her signature aria, the lights go out, and the evening heads for disaster as terrorists take the revelers hostage. At first, as would be expected, the terrorists are harsh and abusive, the guests horrified and shocked. But as the hostage situation unfolds, the months go by and even the seasons change, the two vastly different groups learn to coexist and even to love each other. But the artificial balance of their isolated and utopian world is fragile: It started with violence, and it is doomed to end with much more.

READING TIME: 5 hours; 336 pages

THEMES: courage, political conflict, aesthetics, love, identity, transcending cultural boundaries

Discussion Questions

Mr. Hosokawa goes to the party on false pretenses: He allows the government of the country to believe that his company will help them, but he doesn't intend to follow through. Is this deception better or worse than an outright lie? When Mr. Hosokawa blames his action for everything that resulted from the party, do you think he is right? Can blame be given in this situation, or is it oversimplifying to pin the blame on only one of the participants?

📖 Music takes on a tremendous value in this novel. Mr. Hoso-kawa flies to an obscure country just to hear Roxane Coss sing, the terrorists allow Roxane whatever she wants, and Cesar is accorded great respect once his musical talent is revealed. Is there something unique about the characters in this novel that allows them to be so affected by music, or is it the situation they're in that creates their response? The accompanists are merely admired, while the singers are outright worshipped. Why do you think they are treated so differently?

📖 The role of the soap opera might be considered an opposite to that of music: It is entertainment rather than art, melodrama rather than real beauty. Beatriz and President Masuda both love the soap opera, scheduling everything else in their lives around it, as the prisoners schedule around Roxane's practicing. Are Beatriz and Masuda inferior to those who like opera better, or are they simply different? Beatriz is affected by Maria's false tears but not by the hostages' real ones: Does this make her a bad person or just unaware? Both the soap opera and the soprano's music allow the people in the house to escape their situation: What is the author saying about high and low art? Is one more transporting than the other?

📖 Some characters are offered the choice to leave and instead choose to stay, like Roxane's accompanist and Father Arguedas. They stay because they feel it is their responsibility to do so. Others who might have similar responsibilities—Dr. Gomez because of his medical ability and Monsignor Rolland because of his religious background—choose to go. Are those who go cowardly or practical? Are those who stay crazy or heroic?

📖 In the United States, you must be eighteen years old to fight for your country, but the terrorists in the book are mostly young teenagers. Why do you think they want to fight for the generals? Do they genuinely care about the cause, or do they just want power or excitement? They wield weapons and take on more responsibility than most adults. Do you think children's growing up fast can ever be a good thing?

📖 Gen translates for everyone who wants him to, whether they are terrorists or hostages. Is this lack of distinction between "good guys" and "bad guys" morally wrong? Why doesn't it bother him when his irreplaceable help is taken for granted? He hesitates to translate some very personal messages. Is it a translator's right to decide whether to translate on sensitive topics, or is he simply the unhearing vessel for communication that many of the characters treat him as?

📖 Opposites attract in this book, especially opposites in terms of communication: Many of the men fall in love with Roxane, although few of them speak her language, and the linguist Gen and silent Carmen also fall in love. Can you love someone you can't communicate with in language? Are there other, more important ways to communicate than with words in this book? Is Gen's bond with Carmen based on or in spite of their differences in communication?

📖 The terrorists seem vicious and cruel when you first read about them, but by the end of the book they are a group of impressionable kids who are friendly enough with the hostages to cook and play soccer with them. Is this because they are young or because of the fantastical situation? Would any two groups of people become friends after this kind of ordeal, or is there something special about the groups in this book? Would you be able to form a bond with someone who held so much power over you?

Beyond the Book

SONG: Listen to Renée Fleming's recording of Roxane's aria from *Rusalka* by Dvořák. Does it affect you the way it does Mr. Hosokawa?

LANGUAGE: Learn a phrase from a foreign language and try to teach it to a friend without using English. Imagine communicating with others only in this way.

FOOD: The terrorists and guests collaborate on a meal with chicken, eggplant, peppers, onions, and garlic. Find a recipe with chicken and vegetables and prepare it.

GAMES: Mr. Hosokawa and General Benjamin form a bond by playing chess together. Ishmael also finds his niche by learning chess. Learn to play chess and teach a friend.

RELIGION: Learn more about the lifestyle of a Catholic priest like Father Arguedas by reading *Padre Pio: The True Story* by Bernard Ruffin. Father Arguedas is not a public figure like Padre Pio, and he doesn't have miracles to his name. Can a priest be heroic and make a difference without receiving revelations and healing the sick?

If You Liked This Book, Try . . .

The Magician's Assistant or *Patron Saint of Liars* by Ann
    Patchett
The Kite Runner by Khaled Hosseini
Reading Lolita in Tehran: A Memoir in Books by Azar
    Nafisi (a memoir but, like *Bel Canto,* also about the
    transformative power of art)

The Time Traveler's Wife by Audrey Niffenegger
How I Live Now by Meg Rosoff

About the Author

Ann Patchett was born in Los Angeles in 1963. She studied fiction writing at Sarah Lawrence College then went on to attend the University of Iowa Writers' Workshop. Her novels have received numerous awards, including a Guggenheim Fellowship in 1994 for *The Magician's Assistant.*

Big Mouth & Ugly Girl
Joyce Carol Oates

When Matt Donaghy is taken from his homeroom class by Rocky River police, the last thing he assumes is that he is about to be accused of plotting to terrorize his high school. *Big Mouth & Ugly Girl* follows the lives of popular, wisecracking Matt and the self-named Ugly Girl, Ursula Riggs, as they navigate the four difficult months that bring them together and help them discover a great deal about themselves and each other.

READING TIME: 2–3 hours, 288 pages

THEMES: coming of age, friendship, terrorism, loneliness, persecution

Discussion Questions

📖 In today's culture of tabloid news and fear, is it realistic to think that a high school administrator would ask police to enter a classroom and escort a student away for questioning based on the word of two sisters? Would this be the right thing to do?

📖 Ursula often refers to herself as Ugly Girl—however, does it sound like she is actually an unattractive person? Matt comes to call himself Big Mouth—is that name more appropriate, if not just as self-deprecating? Do Matt and Ursula see themselves as Big Mouth and Ugly Girl at the end of the novel?

📖 This story takes place in an affluent suburb outside New York City. How might the story play out differently in a Midwestern high school or in a poor urban area?

📖 Is it possible a community would so readily ostracize an

otherwise well-behaved student, even after it became overwhelmingly clear he had done nothing wrong? Did you think it strange that even Matt's parents had to ask if there was any truth to the accusations?

📖 Are you offended that the main antagonists are right-wing Christians of some presumably evangelical denomination and a popular student heading to college with a football scholarship?

📖 Matt and Ursula are both older siblings. Do you think that shapes how they respond to adversity and to each other?

📖 How did you react as you realized Matt was contemplating suicide? Is the portrayal believable? Did Ursula save Matt's life?

📖 Do you think by incorporating e-mail and fast-reacting news media into the story, Oates has changed the nature of the American coming-of-age story at the heart of this novel in a significant way?

📖 Ursula quits her basketball team after losing a big game to rival Tarrytown; she feels her team unfairly blames her for the loss, as if she had done it on purpose. Does she make the right assessment at the time? Matt feels persecuted as well, albeit for more concrete reasons—still, is this something the two of them share?

📖 After everything Matt and his family go through—possible police charges, media attention, assault, dognapping, and attempted framing—does it make sense that they dropped their lawsuit?

📖 While Matt and Ursula do eventually kiss—it is not until many weeks after they meet on the trail, and many trials that test them at their deepest levels—were you surprised it took so long?

Beyond the Book

Silly Name: While the names Big Mouth and Ugly Girl may be self-deprecating, they are also kind of cute. Try to come up with more appropriate names for Matt and Ursula. Then make up some names for yourself and for your friends. Focus on the positive things that make people stand out.

The Power of the Press: Matt found out in a very rough way how damaging gossip and bad press can be. Take on the role of a professional newspaper reporter during the first incident at Matt's high school and write a brief news piece about it. Keep in mind that the details released to the public are sketchy and that the accusations initially appear plausible. If you want to take it one step further, write a short opinion piece taking a side for Matt or against him.

Food for Thought: In honor of Matt's dog, Pumpkin, and the author of *Big Mouth & Ugly Girl,* Joyce Carol Oates—serve your friends Joyce Carol Oates oatmeal pumpkin cookies. Use a favorite oatmeal cookie recipe, but replace half the butter with canned pumpkin (you can even add sugar and replace all of the butter for a low-fat version).

If You Liked This Book, Try . . .

Speak by Laurie Halse Anderson
Freaky Green Eyes by Joyce Carol Oates
The Perks of Being a Wallflower by Stephen Chbosky
Stargirl by Jerry Spinelli

About the Author

Joyce Carol Oates is the author of numerous highly regarded short stories and novels, including the national best-sellers *We Were the Mulvaneys* and *Blonde*. Currently, she is the Roger S. Berlind Distinguished Professor of the Humanities at Princeton University.

Chu Ju's House
Gloria Whelan

Chu Ju knows every inch of her village in rural China, from the graves of her ancestors to the neat rows of peas in her garden plot. But when another girl is born into her family, Chu Ju decides she must leave behind everything she knows in order to give her new sister a chance at life. The law dictates that a family can have only two children, and it is tradition to have at least one boy. Chu Ju sets off with only her courage and cleverness to guide her. She skips from one group to another, becoming close with wildly different people through hard work and kindliness. Chu Ju creates a home for herself wherever she travels, but she longs for a family.

READING TIME: 3 hours, 240 pages

THEMES: family, integrity, courage, tradition, sacrifice

Discussion Questions

📖 Chu Ju's grandmother, her Nai Nai, openly disapproves of her. Why does Chu Ju feel responsible for her family? Why does her grandmother want a boy rather than a girl to be born into the family?

📖 Do you think Chu Ju made the right decision by leaving her family? Is she being completely selfless, or did Chu Ju have anything to gain from leaving? Will her absence make things better for her sister, Hua? Was hurting her parents worth saving her sister from the orphanage? Her grandmother is harsh, and her parents even seem cold to Chu Ju. Will she be missed?

📖 Throughout the book, Chu Ju seems to prove the saying "No good deed goes unpunished." She always appears to get herself into trouble through helping others. Could she avoid this? Is she being compassionate or impractical?

📖 Chu Ju manipulates both lies and the truth. She refuses to lie in some scenarios, but in other situations she is skilled at bending the truth. Why is she so unwilling to tell Han Na the real reason she took the money? Is it better to tell the truth or to keep a promise? Why did she feel it was acceptable to lie about her own family on the fishing boat and at the silk worm factory? Is it ever okay to lie?

📖 How does Chu Ju's education help her on her journey? How does having an education seem dangerous under the Communist Party government? Is it necessary?

📖 Chu Ju often seems far more mature than the adults in the book. She takes on the responsibility of caring for her young sister, Hua, and feels she needs to protect Han Na from the truth about her son. How has she reversed roles with the adults around her? Have the adults in the novel failed by forcing Chu Ju to grow up too fast, or is it Chu Ju's forceful nature that makes her assume grown-up roles?

📖 Chu Ju is angry at Quan for leaving his elderly mother to care for their rice paddies while he moves to Shanghai. She thinks he is selfish and is greatly sympathetic to Han Na as she yearns for her son. Does Chu Ju see the parallel between Han Na and her own parents? Why is she unable to identify with Quan? Later, she seems to forgive Quan when she sees how much he loves the bustle and chaos of Shanghai. Is this enough of a reason to leave your family behind? Is Chu Ju excused from leaving her own family because she loves the rice paddy? Does Chu Ju forgive herself for fleeing?

📖 Throughout the book, there are numerous examples of people being punished by the government for speaking the truth. The son of the woman on the train was sent away to a re-education center, and Ling must keep his books hidden in his water buffalo's stables. Why is Ling forced to hide his books? What is the value of the truth and of speaking it? Is it better to protect yourself and your family or to speak out against injustice?

📖 Chu Ju longs for a family. She finds companionship and even love at first with her own family, then on the riverboat, in the silk worm factory, and in the rice paddy with Han Na and Ling. Which family is most valuable to her? Are families more precious if you create them yourself instead of being born into one?

📖 Were you surprised to find that the third child was a girl? Does this make Chu Ju's journey worthless, or was it still necessary? Has her family accepted her? Do they accept her despite her gender, or do they welcome all of her?

📖 For a very modern girl, Chu Ju seems to have great qualms about modernity. She despises the city and the anonymity of living outside a village. However, she also treasures her pair of blue jeans and is eager to read Ling's books. How can you reconcile Chu Ju's notions of tradition and modernity? The tradition that disparages girls while favoring boys seems limiting, but modernity, with the starkness of the Communist Party, is equally unappealing. How can Chu Ju carve out a place for herself? What will she have to sacrifice?

📖 Chu Ju finds great comfort in the land around her. She begins the novel by describing the rolling hills around her village, and ends it by finding solace in planting shoots in the rice paddy. How does the constancy of the earth reassure Chu Ju? Farming seems to offer her a means of control. How does she not have control over other things in her life? How does the land affect her definition of home? How is Chu Ju able to be happy, even when she is alone?

Beyond the Book

GARDENING: If you can, grow a small garden patch like the one Chu Ju works on. If you don't have a place to garden, plant garlic, herbs, or onions in small terra-cotta pots indoors.

LANGUAGE: Chu Ju teaches Bo the Chinese character for "fish," describing it as a net with a fish leaping inside. At the library or online, find a dictionary with Chinese characters. Write out words from the book. Does the character for "earth" look like a man standing on the ground to you, as it does to Chu Ju?

FOOD: Chu Ju savors bowls of noodles in hot broth. Make a bowl of Chinese noodles (from a grocery store) in chicken or vegetable broth. Try to eat it with chopsticks, as Chu Ju does.

MAPS: Chu Ju is amazed by the map of China that covers an entire wall in her classroom at school. She pictures herself moving across the map while on the train to Shanghai. Find a map of your country or state and hang it on a wall. Put in thumbtacks for the places you have visited—or the places you would like to visit.

HELPING HAND: Chu Ju performs many small acts of kindness throughout the novel. Create a little gesture of kindness: Leave a pot of flowers on your neighbor's doorstep, put change in expired meters, bake cookies for someone in your family, clean up a room without being asked.

POLITICS: Learn more about the Chinese Communist government by reading *China's Long March* by Jean Fritz or *Red Scarf Girl: A Memoir of the Cultural Revolution* by Ji-li Jiang. Chu Ju struggles with her feelings about the government, including the law forbidding all families from having more than two children. Can you think of any unfair laws in your own government?

If You Liked This Book, Try . . .

Homeless Bird or *Once on This Island* by Gloria Whelan
A Girl Named Disaster by Nancy Farmer
Shabanu: Daughter of the Wind by Suzanne Fisher Staples
Julie of the Wolves by Jean Craighead George

About the Author

Gloria Whelan was born in Detroit, Michigan. She graduated from the University of Michigan and worked as a social worker and teacher. She is a best-selling author of books for young readers and has received numerous distinctions, including the National Book Award for *Homeless Bird.* She lives in northern Michigan.

Crystal
Walter Dean Myers

Crystal Brown is blessed with stunning good looks and a caring family and friends. When she begins a career as a model in New York City, she must decide how much she is willing to sacrifice to succeed in the cutthroat industry. The glamorous photographers, agents, and stylists humiliate Crystal even as they celebrate her beauty. They objectify her and reduce her racial identity to a passing trendy look. Crystal is torn between exploring opportunities and saving her pride. She tries to navigate both the world of her comfortable home and school and the sparkling land where anything seems possible. As Crystal is reduced to her looks alone, she fights to reconcile her image with her self, before she is lost.

READING TIME: 3 hours, 208 pages

THEMES: beauty, identity, opportunity, duty, pride, superficiality, integrity

Discussion Questions

Loretta tells Crystal that a photographer does not see her as black because she is so "beautiful and fresh." Why does her beauty affect her racial identity? Why would the photographer not want to see all of her, including her blackness? How is the way Crystal is perceived important to how she sees herself?

When Crystal meets Rowena, Rowena's career is slowing down while Crystal's is taking off. How does Crystal see Rowena at first? How is Rowena a cautionary tale for Crystal? How are Rowena and Crystal parallels?

📖 Crystal is able to convince Mr. Fishman to let her friend Pat play on the volleyball team. How are Crystal's looks helpful? Does she use them to her advantage? Is this manipulative or the same as using your intelligence to persuade people? Is it fair that Crystal is treated differently than other people? Does it make her life easier or more difficult?

📖 Crystal feels it is her responsibility to pursue modeling. How does her mother affect this outlook? It seems that the more opportunities Crystal explores, the more constrained she is. How can she find freedom? Is it Crystal's duty to help her parents by earning money through modeling? Are her parents being responsible by letting Crystal shrug off school and obligations in order to model? Are they being encouraging or careless? Would Crystal model at all if her mother did not promote it, or does she use her parents' encouragement as an excuse to justify her search for fame and glamour?

📖 In the first photo shoot Crystal describes, she is told to crawl around on the ground and act sexy. She is made to look like an animal, a tiger. Is this demeaning or artistic? Would it make a difference if Crystal was older? Crystal struggles to define her boundaries. How much is too much? Is it acceptable for her to act sexy? At what point would you stop?

📖 Crystal is furious at Pat for doing the history homework assignment and accuses her of being disloyal. Pat says that just because Crystal is pretty, not everyone is jealous and eager to put her down. How does Crystal change throughout the course of the book? Is Pat actually jealous? Or is Crystal hypersensitive? Is Crystal conceited or just aware of the power of her looks?

📖 Crystal's parents have a very tense relationship. They often disagree, and her mother seems disappointed in her father. How does Crystal mediate between her parents? What are their differing views on modeling? What do you think has happened to make her mother so bitter and her father so dejected? Is modeling a real escape for Crystal, or does it offer only false hopes?

📖 Crystal dresses up for her arranged date with a movie star, Sean Farrell. She wears a slinky white dress and impeccable makeup. Crystal twirls in front of the mirror happily. Do you think it is okay for Crystal to delight in her beauty? Or should she try to downplay it? Where is the fine line between enjoying her good looks and being superficial?

📖 Crystal bargains with Jerry for Rowena's compromising photographs. She is forced to exchange her own revealing pictures in order to obtain Rowena's. Do you think this was smart? Could Crystal have found a way to get Rowena's photos without losing her own? Is it worth the sacrifice? Do you think this gesture makes up for Crystal's poor friendship with Pat?

📖 Nearly everyone in the novel is engaged in some form of denial. Carol, Crystal's mother, ignores the dangerous implications when Crystal tries to confide in her about a photographer's advances. Crystal herself even tries to deny the humiliation of certain situations and to project confidence. Is denial a useful coping strategy, or does it only set you up for troubles? Crystal tells herself to be someone else during uncomfortable situations. Is she surviving, or could she deal more effectively with the problem at hand?

Beyond the Book

SONG: Listen to recordings of the kind of gospel music Crystal sings at her church. Try *The Forester Sisters' Greatest Gospel Hits* by the Forester Sisters, *Voices From Heaven* by the Soweto Gospel Choir, or *Amazing Grace* by Mahalia Jackson.

HIGH FASHION: Crystal is embarrassed when she is told to act like a tiger. Find a subject who already acts like a tiger—your cat! Build a backdrop like the one Crystal describes by draping fabric over chairs or even painting a jungle scene on a big piece of paper. Then photograph your pet lounging in the scene. If your pet is not patient enough for posed shots, do action photography of your dog running or fish swimming.

RUNWAY: Create your own runway show, using your friends or family as models. Put together crazy getups or elegant outfits and parade down a runway. Use a hallway or garden path as a catwalk, set up chairs along the side, and be sure to have some paparazzi taking shots at the end.

BODY IMAGE: In the novel, the modeling industry creates unattainable standards of beauty; even Crystal, who is considered gorgeous, is told she will not be thought beautiful in a few years. Cut out images of models from magazines and paste them together on a piece of paper. Do the models look realistic to you? Now assemble photographs of your friends and family. Are there differences between the women around you every day, and the media's representations of women?

If You Liked This Book, Try . . .

Another Way to Dance by Martha Southgate
Savion: My Life In Tap by Savion Glover (memoir)
Maizon at Blue Hill by Jacqueline Woodson

About the Author

Walter Dean Myers was born in West Virginia in 1937 but spent most of his young life in Harlem. He is an award-winning writer of books and poetry for young adults. Among other honors, he received the Margaret A. Edwards Award for his contribution to young adult literature and won the Coretta Scott King Award five times. He lives in Jersey City, New Jersey, with his family.

The Curious Incident of the Dog in the Night-Time
Mark Haddon

In Mark Haddon's critically acclaimed and best-selling first novel, he tells the story of fifteen-year-old Christopher John Francis Boone as he attempts to solve the mystery of who killed his neighbor's dog. Christopher, an autistic boy from a broken, working-class family, encounters much more than he bargained for in the process.

READING TIME: 3 hours, 240 pages

THEMES: family, courage, disability, choice

Discussion Questions

Did you suspect that Christopher killed Mrs. Shears's dog? Were you surprised to find out who the real killer was?

Christopher writes about a recurring dream of his where almost the entire world's population dies. It is one of his favorite dreams. Do you find this sentiment creepy or endearing?

Despite major cognitive and social obstacles, Christopher manages to escape from his father's home in Swindon and travel to his mother's apartment in London. During this adventure he escapes his father, his neighbors, police, and possibly death. What impressed you most about this epic journey? Did you find it to be realistic?

The Curious Incident is a mystery novel of a kind. Which mystery did you find most compelling: Who killed Mrs. Shears's dog, what happened to Christopher's mother, or how Christopher would perform on his A-level math examination?

📖 Do you find Christopher's mother to be a sympathetic character? How might you handle having an autistic child? Or an autistic sibling?

📖 What role, if any, does Toby the pet rat serve?

📖 Did you believe Christopher's father when he said Christopher's mother had died? How did you feel when Christopher found his mother's letters? How about when he didn't understand what they were?

📖 Christopher enjoys the Sherlock Holmes mystery stories written by Sir Arthur Conan Doyle, but he seems to be repulsed by Doyle's spiritualist beliefs. Using "The Case of the Cottingly Fairies," a real life fairy-hoax which Doyle believed to be true, Christopher illustrates this point. He also recounts Occam's razor, the assertion that the simplest explanation is generally the correct one. Christopher says it means that "a murder victim is usually killed by someone known to them and fairies are made out of paper and you can't talk to someone who is dead." Do these seem to be the thoughts of a disabled person?

📖 Does reading this story lead you to reevaluate your assumptions about mental disabilities?

📖 How did you react when Mrs. Alexander told Christopher that his mom had slept with Mr. Shears? Do you think that it was right of her to tell Christopher?

📖 Christopher thinks metaphors should be called lies and doesn't enjoy "proper novels" that use them. How important is literalness to Christopher? Can you discuss ways this fixation gives Christopher an advantage?

📖 Did you find the ending of this novel to be a satisfactory one? Do you imagine Christopher's life will follow the path he has envisioned?

📖 Christopher distrusts intuition as removed from logic. How important is intuition for someone reading this story?

📖 Does Christopher learn anything about himself as a result of his experiences? What do we learn about ourselves after seeing the world through Christopher's eyes?

Beyond the Book

TIMETABLE: After explaining that time is a mystery and not even a thing, Christopher says that one reason he likes to make timetables is so he doesn't "get lost in time." Make a timetable for today and bring it with you to discussion. See if it makes you feel any better about your day.

SEE EVERYTHING: With each new and increasingly busy location Christopher encounters on his way to his mother's apartment in London, the more difficult his journey becomes. Sometimes he has to do math problems in his head or close his eyes, put his hands over his ears, and groan in order to deal with the massive stimulus. Take some time to try to see things as Christopher must see them. Try to take into account every detail you see while maintaining a focus on the task at hand. (In Christopher's words, don't worry about silly things, like if Julie has given birth yet, or if you left the gas cooker on.)

KEEP A JOURNAL: The entire book is Christopher's journal, beginning in the investigation into the death of Wellington. Remarkably, the book is both plausibly the work of someone in Christopher's circumstances as well as easy to read and interesting. Try to write a few journal entries through the perspective of someone you know. If you are feeling especially daring, write a few entries from the point of view of a person you do not know very well.

RESEARCH: Go on the Internet or to your local library and look up information about autism and other related conditions. Compare what you discover about your past assumptions of people with such conditions. Try to see if your general attitudes toward what constitutes intelligence and disability have changed as a result.

RED FOODS: Christopher eats red foods but detests anything that is yellow or brown. Avoid yellow and brown foods today (no American cheese on wheat bread) and serve something red. Maybe tasty pasta covered in marinara sauce, or some red delicious apples, or even red raspberry syrup on strawberry ice cream.

If You Like This Book, Try . . .

> *The Complete Sherlock Holmes* by Sir Arthur Conan Doyle
> *Motherless Brooklyn* by Jonathan Lethem
> *The Dark Stairs: A Herculeah Jones Mystery* by Betsy Byars
> *Yolanda's Genius* by Carol Fenner
> *Making Peace with Autism: One Family's Story of Struggle,
>   Discovery, and Unexpected Gifts* by Susan Senator
> *My Sister's Keeper* by Jodi Picoult

About the Author

This is Mark Haddon's first novel. He currently teaches creative writing at the Arvon Foundation and lives in Oxford, England.

Extremely Loud and Incredibly Close
Jonathan Safran Foer

Oskar Schell is nine when his father dies in the World Trade Center on September 11. Weeks after his father's death, Oskar discovers a key in an envelope with the word "Black" written on the outside of it. Believing the name and the key are clues left for him by his father, Oskar sets out to contact everyone in the telephone book with the last name "Black" in hopes that one of them knows something about the key. *Extremely Loud and Incredibly Close* tells the stories of the various people Oskar meets on his journey looking for the "key" to his father's death, but it is also the story of Oskar's own family, and especially that of Oskar's grandparents (victims of the bombing of Dresden in World War II, another tragic historical event), and how connections are made or not made among people who love each other.

READING TIME: 5 hours, 368 pages

THEMES: loss, tragedy, grief, family, connection, love and communicating

Discussion Questions

🕮 Oskar's mom is a busy lawyer who seemingly doesn't keep too careful watch on her son's comings and goings. Does it bother you as a reader that the nine-year-old Oskar is allowed to roam freely all over the five boroughs of New York City? Why do you think Jonathan Safran Foer chose a child to narrate this story?

🕮 Beyond the literal question of the key and its mystery, what do you think Oskar is trying to accomplish with his search of the two hundred and sixteen different addresses listed under the name "Black" in the phone book?

📖 Oskar loves his grandmother, but he's embarrassed by her when she comes to see his performance of Hamlet: "the way she tilted her head, like she was concentrating incredibly hard on something, and how she sneezed and told herself, 'God bless me.' And how she cried and said, 'That's sad,' so everyone could hear it." Have you ever felt embarrassed in a social situation because of someone you love? Is it possible that quirks in personalities make us love someone even more on the inside, when on the outside, we might wish the person was wearing an invisibility suit?

📖 As Oskar tells his story, he tells a googolplex of lies, including many lies to his mother. He says he never had to tell lies before. Why do you think he feels it's necessary to tell lies now? Is it ever okay to tell lies?

📖 Oskar doesn't understand why he needs to go see Dr. Fein. It seems to Oskar that "you should wear heavy boots when your dad dies, and if you aren't wearing heavy boots then you need help." What does this novel tell you about grief and grieving? Are Oskar and his mother grieving the same way or differently?

📖 Near the end of the novel, Oskar says of his mother, whom he's had a rough patch with over the course of the book: "I don't believe in God, but I believe that things are extremely complicated, and her looking over me was as complicated as anything ever could be. But it was also incredibly simple. In my only life, she was my mom, and I was her son." What is complicated about Oskar's relationship with his mother? And what is simple about it? What is complicated about love? And what is simple about it? Anything?

📖 How did you react when Oskar tells his mother he would have "chosen you," meaning he would have chosen for her to have died on 9/11 rather than his father? Are you sympathetic to Oskar or to his mother at that moment? Is this a convincing moment in the story? Do you believe it?

📖 Jonathan Safran Foer uses typography, numbers, and pictures, and even blank book pages in the novel. Why do you think he uses these visual elements? Is it gimmickry? What do you think the author is suggesting about attention? How do you explain the title?

📖 What do you make of the part about the grandmother typing page after page of her life story with no ribbon in the typewriter? What do you think this means? And what do you make of the grandfather's "yes" and "no" tattoos on his hands? What other odd ways of communicating are there in this novel? What is the author trying to say about communication and connection? How does the message that Oskar's father left on the answering machine fit in with this theme?

📖 Although this story is based on one of the most tragic events in our country's history, the novel doesn't explore modern political or foreign policy themes. Why do you think neither Oskar as a character nor Jonathan Safran Foer as author are curious in this book about the cause of the disaster or who the perpetrators are?

📖 Oskar's grandparents lived by their own set of peculiar rules: eating side by side rather than across from each other and facing the window; never talking about the past; never watching a television show about sick children. Are there spoken and/or unspoken rules in your home? What are they? Why do people make up rules for everyday living?

📖 Oskar's narration is often funny, if juvenile. For example, when Oskar asks his father why he is his son and his father answers: "Because Mom and I made love, and one of my sperm fertilized one of her eggs." Oskar says, "Excuse me while I regurgitate." To which Oskar's father replies, "Don't act your age." What are some of the lines that made you laugh (or groan?) as you were reading the novel? Is humor appropriate in a story about grief? Why or why not?

📖 Oskar has quite an imagination and likes to make up inventions: "I tried to invent optimistic inventions. But the pessimistic ones were extremely loud." For example, what if the water that came out of the shower was treated so that your skin color changed according to your mood? Why does Oskar wish it was easier to read people? Name some of Oskar's other inventions. How does his inventing things help him? If you were to invent something that saves people, what would it be?

📖 Were you surprised when you learned the story behind the key?

Beyond the Book

CLUES: Oskar and his dad used to play a game they called "Reconnaissance Expedition," which was like a scavenger hunt. Make up clues related to *Extremely Loud and Incredibly Close* and have a scavenger hunt as part of your book-club meeting.

STUFF: That Happened to Me: Oskar keeps a scrapbook of everything that's happened to him. Keep a scrapbook of stuff that happens to you.

YES/NO: Use a marker to write the words "yes" and "no" on your hands. Play a game in which you try to communicate with only these words.

INVENTIONS: Invent a product that saves people. Make a drawing or model of it and give it a name. Come up with an advertising campaign, logo, or slogan for your invention.

PHOTOGRAPHS: Document a day with photographs. Take pictures of ordinary things as well as of anything extraordinary you happen to see or notice in the course of your wanderings. Make a collage or scrapbook of the pictures.

VEGAN: Oskar is a vegan, which means he doesn't eat any foods derived from animals. His one exception is dehydrated ice cream. Prepare a vegan meal or snack for your club meeting.

SAY, "I LOVE YOU.": Oskar's grandmother writes to Oskar about regret that she did not tell her sister how much she loved her. She tells Oskar it is always necessary to let people know that you love them. Say "I love you" to someone you love.

If You Liked this Book, Try . . .

> *Everything Is Illuminated* by Jonathan Safran Foer
> *The Year of Magical Thinking* by Joan Didion (memoir of
>   loss and grief)
> *The History of Love* by Nicole Krauss
> *Sun & Spoon* by Kevin Henkes

About the Author

Jonathan Safran Foer was born in 1977 and attended Georgetown Day School in Washington, D.C. As an undergraduate at
Princeton, he won the freshman, sophomore, junior, and senior
creative writing thesis prizes. He has also worked as a morgue
assistant, jewelry salesman, farm sitter, and ghostwriter. His first
book, the bestselling *Everything Is Illuminated,* was inspired by
Foer's researching his grandfather's life in the Ukraine. He lives
in New York with his wife, the novelist Nicole Krauss.

Hush
Jacqueline Woodson

Toswiah Green and her family are no longer allowed to be themselves—literally. Since Toswiah's father testified against another police officer in a murder case, the Greens have been forced to move out of Denver and start a whole new life, with new names and a new home. The family has changed, too: Toswiah's mother has become an evangelist, her father is too depressed even to take care of himself, and her sister is planning to leave town. Toswiah—now Evie—has to find a way to live away from Denver and her old life, but how can she when her new world is unfriendly and her family has fallen apart?

READING TIME: 2 to 3 hours, 192 pages

THEMES: family, discrimination, friendship, religion, depression, loss, coming of age, displacement

Discussion Questions

📖 Evie's father's decision to testify is hard for two reasons: First, the officers he testifies against are his good friends, and second, his family will have to suffer the consequences by entering the Witness Protection Program. Would you have made the same decision he did, even if it affected your family the same way? Is justice more important than your personal happiness? Do you think Mr. Thomas had the right to make a decision that affected his family like that?

📖 Mr. Thomas is very depressed after the family's move: He can't work as a police officer anymore, so he sits at home all day. Why do you think he isn't looking for a job? He gets more depressed as the days go by, stopping bathing and eventually trying to kill himself. Is he right to blame himself for his family's unhappiness? If you were in Evie's position, would you be angry at him?

📖 Evie's mother usually turns away Jehovah's Witnesses at the door, but the day the family is leaving, she accepts their books. As Evie says, "She believes God sent His Witnesses to our door that morning for a reason." Why might Evie's mother believe that? She becomes religious once the family has switched houses, reading her Bible every day and taking the family to Kingdom Hall. How does religion help her handle the change? Why doesn't it work for the rest of the family? Do you think it's right that she tries to impose her religious views on Evie and Anna?

📖 When Evie starts running, it helps her in two ways: She begins to make friends, and she forgets how much she misses Denver. Is running an unhealthy escape, or is it good for her? She is afraid to tell her mother because she won't approve. Is it good parenting to disapprove of something that's obviously good for your child? If you were Evie, would you tell your mother?

📖 Evie spends most of the time wishing she was back in Denver. Do you think it's really the city of Denver that she misses or her family and her life when she was there? Is it possible for Evie to re-create her life away from Denver, or is this new city really worse? She plans to go to college with her best friend, Lulu. Do you think her dream is practical, or would the government forbid it?

📖 Anna wants to get a scholarship and go to college early—she says "that's the prize I have my eyes on." What makes college a better choice than the family Anna has? What exactly is she running away from? Anna thinks her mother won't agree to her going away to school so young, but her mother is a schoolteacher. Did you doubt that her mother would let her go? Do you think starting to teach again will be helpful for Mrs. Thomas?

📖 The family doesn't have jobs in the place the Feds send them, so the government supplies them with money. Is this extra money part of the reason Mr. Thomas is in no rush to get a job? Instead of making the family happy, the money seems to make them sadder: Mrs. Thomas now buys Evie's coconut cakes rather than make them. Does a baked cake show more love and affection than a bought cake? Why do you think Mrs. Thomas stopped baking?

📖 Evie has trouble making friends in her new home. Do you think it's really because the new city is worse, as she claims, or because being new anywhere takes time to get used to? She begins making friends with another Toswiah, but she has to lie about her background to everyone she meets. Do you think Evie enjoys or tolerates telling these lies? Why is it harder to make friends with someone you can't tell the truth to?

📖 Evie meets Toswiah's sister, Sheila, who is handicapped. Is Toswiah ashamed of her sister? How does Evie handle the situation? Toswiah tells Evie beforehand about her sister. What makes Toswiah trust Evie? Is it just because she has no other friends to tell the secret to or because Evie seems like a good person? What kind of person should be trusted with secrets?

Beyond the Book

BAKING: Evie loves to eat her mother's special coconut cake for her birthday. Bake a coconut cake with some friends and enjoy it together.

SPORTS: Try running as Evie does. Do some laps around the outside of your house or run with a friend around the school track. Does it make you feel as good as it makes Evie feel? Why or why not?

FRIENDS: Try to get to know a new kid in school or someone who doesn't have that many friends. Do you think people don't have friends because they are bad people, or sometimes just because they are shy? Imagine if you were in a new school, and act the way you hope someone would act toward you.

MUSIC: Evie's mother loves to listen to old records on a phonograph. Listen to record albums, if you have access to them (try the library or a friend's parent's collection). How do they sound different from CDs or tapes? What do you think the appeal of records is?

BISCUITS: Evie's mother makes fried chicken and biscuits for the family, and Evie loves to eat the biscuits right out of the oven. Serve a Southern meal like Evie's mother's. Make homemade biscuits.

If You Liked This Book, Try . . .

Miracle's Boys by Jacqueline Woodson
Habibi by Naomi Shihab Nye
The Truth about Sparrows by Marian Hale

About the Author

Jacqueline Woodson was born in Ohio, grew up in South Carolina and in Brooklyn, New York, where she still lives. A former drama therapist for runaways and homeless children in New York City, she now writes full-time and has received the Kenyon Review Award for Literary Excellence in Fiction and most recently, two Coretta Scott King Honor awards.

No Laughter Here
Rita Williams-Garcia

Akilah and Victoria are true friends, even though they were born in different countries. The summer before fifth grade, Victoria goes to Nigeria, where her family is from, for a special coming-of-age ceremony. Akilah misses Victoria terribly and can hardly bear the days without her friend. But when Victoria comes home, she's not the friend Akilah remembers. She doesn't laugh. She doesn't volunteer in class. Instead she slouches at her desk and walks with a strange sliding step. Akilah is determined to find out what's wrong with Victoria, and when she does, she finds she has more questions than ever.

READING TIME: 1–2 hours, 144 pages

THEMES: cultural rituals, friendship, keeping vows, female circumcision

Discussion Questions

📖 Why does Akilah call herself Girl Warrior? Does the name suit her? Why does Victoria call herself Queen Victoria? And does the name suit her?

📖 Akilah and her mother have a little ritual of backyard tea talks that they started when Akilah was five. Now that Akilah is ten, she and her mother use the time to have real talks. What's important about rituals like backyard tea talks? Why do you suppose Akilah and her mother call each other "girl" in the backyard but nowhere else? Do you and your mom have nicknames for each other? What are some of the rituals you observe in your relationship?

📖 Akilah describes Ms. Saunders as having that "motherland" look when she heard Victoria say she had been to Nigeria over summer vacation. African cultural references abound in the book, and Akilah's mother wears the "motherland" look when she's sharing something about Africa. In what other ways do the characters let you know they are proud of their African heritage? For example, Akilah's mom has given Akilah a Swahili name that means "intelligent." She also surrounds Akilah with African dolls, has taught her African dances, and so on.

📖 Before Victoria tells Akilah what has happened to her, Victoria tells Akilah that she can no longer be made to laugh. What would it be like to lose laughter?

📖 Akilah does not look forward to getting her period, especially at age ten. After researching on the Internet, she thinks the moon must be "pulling down her period," and she shifts in her bed to get away from the moonbeams. What was your reaction to this part of the book? Did you sympathize with Akilah? Why does she not feel like a super-hero when she thinks about getting her period?

📖 How did you feel when Akilah signed the permission slip for Victoria to attend the sex education class and Paths to Discovery video? Might you have done the same thing?

📖 Were you shocked to learn what had really happened to Victoria? Had you ever heard of female genital mutilation before?

📖 What was your reaction to the scene in which Akilah hit Juwan?

📖 What's ironic about the fact that Akilah's parents, and

especially her father, immediately assumed that Juwan threw the first punch? What's ironic about his statement, "That boy needs to learn how to treat a young lady"?

📖 What do you think about the different reactions of Akilah's parents to the Juwan incident? With whom do you relate more?

📖 Akilah says her mom is something of a "snob": She always points out other kids' public behavior—especially black kids—and says, "There's no reason for you to behave like that." Akilah thinks this is why her mom likes the Ojikes, because they're quiet and refined. What is ironic about this, by appearances, so regal family?

📖 Why does Akilah refuse to apologize in Vice Principal Skinner's office? How would you characterize this? Is it audacious? Stubborn? True to her convictions?

📖 What makes Akilah feel like "the true Girl Warrior" her dad always says she is?

📖 It's very difficult for Akilah to keep her vow to Victoria and not tell her parents the true story. Would you have been able to keep the secret the way Akilah does?

📖 How did you react to the scene in which Akilah's mom confronts Mrs. Ojike, telling her what the Ojikes have done to Victoria is "barbaric" and "inhumane"? Do you have any sympathy for the Ojikes?

📖 Akilah is furious with her mom for confronting the Ojikes. Would it have been better for Akilah's mom not to have done so? Why or why not?

📖 Does the scene in which Akilah confronts Nelson help clarify the Nigerian practice? Do you agree with Akilah that no one has told her anything yet that makes sense?

📖 Akilah has always had a crush on Nelson, but she's so angry about what has happened to Victoria that she doesn't even look after Nelson when he walks away. How do you feel about Akilah at that moment in the story?

📖 Mrs. Saunders knows about female circumcision from her work in Kenya. She says it was a challenge for her to understand and is hard for Akilah to understand because it is not part of their world. Do you agree?

📖 Akilah says, "I refused to let my mind bend in any direction where mutilating girls was okay." Is she right not to see or try to understand the other side? What did you think when Mrs. Saunders suggests that had Victoria grown up in the village in Nigeria, she would have been prepared for the ritual? Would this have made a difference for Victoria? Does being prepared for it and accepting it as part of your culture make it okay?

Beyond the Book

TEA TALKS: Enjoy the simple ritual of a "tea talk" as Akilah and her mother do. Serve juice and animal crackers as they did when Akilah was young or the more grown-up version of iced herbal tea with tuna sandwiches cut in quarters. The point is to dedicate regular time together, enjoy a simple snack, and just talk.

ALI BABA: Akilah and her friends play a game called Ali Baba and the Forty Thieves. Play this game at your club meeting; see instructions at www.creativedrama.com.

NAMES: Akilah means "intelligent" in Swahili. Before your club meeting, have members each research the meaning and etymology of their own name and be prepared to share what they learn with the group.

INFORMATION: If you're interested in learning more about the issue or female circumcision, you may write to Rita Williams-Garcia at ritawg@aol.com.

If You Liked This Book, Try:

Every Time a Rainbow Dies by Rita Williams-Garcia
Chanda's Secrets by Allan Stratton
Lucy Forever and Miss Rosetree Shrinks by Susan Shreve

About the Author

Rita Williams-Garcia is also the award-winning author of the young adult novels *Every Time a Rainbow Dies*, *Fast Talk on a Slow Track*, *Blue Tights*, and *Like Sisters on the Homefront*. She works as a manager in a marketing and media company and lives in Jamaica, New York, with her two daughters.

A Northern Light
Jennifer Donnelly

Mattie Gokey dreams of going to college in New York City and someday becoming a writer. But her mother's recent death and the responsibility Mattie feels toward her sisters and her father as he struggles to keep up their farm, make the truths of Mattie's life more real than she is able to express in her stories. And what does she really think about handsome Royal Loomis, the young man who says he wants to marry her? When Mattie gets a summer job at a fancy hotel near Big Moose Lake in the Adirondacks, a woman's mysterious drowning and the love letters she leaves behind give Mattie the strength to follow her heart and lead her own life.

READING TIME: 3–4 hours, 408 pages

THEMES: family, love, coming of age

Discussion Questions

Why does the inscription "Almighty God, give us serenity to accept what cannot be changed, courage to change what should be changed, and wisdom to know the one from the other" on Mattie's aunt's angel figurine anger Mattie so much?

Weaver advises Mattie: "Go round cringing like a dog, Matt . . . and folks will treat you like one. Stand up like a man, and they'll treat you like a man." Mattie wonders if it's possible to stand like a man while being a girl. By the end of the novel, has Mattie learned to stand?

At one point in the novel, Mattie concludes that hope is

the "Eighth Deadly Sin." What events lead Mattie to this bitter realization? How does Mattie's opinion of hope evolve throughout the book?

📖 Miss Wilcox tells Mattie that "voice" is not just "sound that comes from your throat but the feeling that comes from your words." What does she mean by that? What gives Mattie the courage to use her voice and the confidence to go to New York?

📖 When Uncle Fifty visits, he brings presents, laughter, and good meals. However, he leaves the Gokey family on a sour note. In what way is Uncle Fifty a disappointment? Why is his leaving without fulfilling promises worse than admitting he cannot keep promises in the first place?

📖 Weaver hates the town of South Otselic and claims that it "kills everything." Is Weaver right? What good things come out of this small town in the Adirondacks?

📖 The Gokey children's relationships with their father are very strained. Pa is distant and sometimes callous. However, Pa has shown fierce loyalty to his family. Is Pa a good father? How does your opinion of him change during his illness?

📖 Miss Wilcox says Mattie's writing is a "true gift." Why does Mattie think her writing may be more of a burden than a gift?

📖 The members of the Gokey family are constantly reminded of Lawton's absence. How would things have been different had Lawton remained at home instead of running away? Was Lawton's decision to leave irresponsible? Can some of the family's struggles be blamed on Lawton's desertion?

📖 What is Weaver's reaction to the man at the train station who calls him a "darky"? How did the situation's similarity to the circumstances surrounding his father's death affect Weaver? How might Weaver have handled the situation differently?

📖 What do you think about Mattie's relationship with Royal Loomis? Despite Royal's utter lack of interest in Mattie's passion for reading and writing, Mattie still finds herself drawn to him. Did Mattie ever really like Royal? Why does she agree to marry him?

📖 Promises are made and broken in *A Northern Light*. Make a list of all the promises you remember from the novel. Should some have been kept and others not? For example, do you agree with Weaver that Mattie's mom should not have exacted that promise from Mattie? How would you advise Mattie when she asks Ada, "When you make a promise, do you always have to keep it?"

Beyond the Book

WORD OF THE DAY: Challenge book-club members to find their own "word of the day" as Mattie does. Open a dictionary to a random page and pick a word. Learn the meaning of the word and then try to use the word sometime that day. Be able to report back to the group about your word and how you used it.

PASSIONS: Share one thing you're truly passionate about with the book group. Describe what you've done to follow your heart and feed that passion.

$$$$$: In the novel, Mattie picks fiddleheads for hours and sells them for a grand total of sixty cents. She then uses this

money to buy a quality notebook for her writing. Come up with a lucrative scheme of your own, and use the money you make to reach for a dream.

WOMEN'S STUDIES: Mattie struggles to find meaningful work in a time when women had few opportunities. Read up on women's work in the Adirondacks during the time of this novel at www.adirondackhistory.org

COUNTRY BREAKFAST: Prepare cream of wheat to mimic the "mush" Mattie makes to feed her siblings every morning. In contrast, someone else could prepare pancakes with maple sugar, bacon, potatoes, and biscuits, as Uncle Fifty does.

If You Liked This Book, Try . . .

> *An American Tragedy* by Theodore Dreiser. (Like *A Northern Light,* this American classic is also based on the real-life murder of Grace Brown.)
> *Walk Two Moons* by Sharon Creech

About the Author

Jennifer Donnelly is also the author of *The Tea Rose,* a novel, and *Humble Pie,* a picture book for children ages four to eight. For *A Northern Light,* she drew on stories she heard from her grandmother while growing up in upstate New York. She lives in Brooklyn, New York.

Replay
Sharon Creech

Twelve-year-old Leo gets a small part in his school play, but he dreams he's a great Broadway star. His big, boisterous family sometimes makes him feel like a sardine packed in a tin, but in his imagination, Leo is the center of attention and the pride of both his mother and father. Nicknamed "Fogboy" because he's always dreaming and replaying everyday scenes in his mind, Leo discovers a box in the attic that leads him to discover something real about growing up and something about his father and himself as well.

READING TIME: 2 hours; 240 pages

THEMES: dreams, imagination, family, family history

Discussion Questions

📖 Leo's brothers and sisters all vie for attention in their big Italian family, playing sports, singing, acting in school plays. Sometimes Leo feels anonymous among all the other family members. How different would it be if Leo was an only child? Can you relate to how he feels? In contrast, Leo's friend, Ruby, now an only child, says her life is like being under a microscope. With whom do you identify more, Leo or Ruby?

📖 Leo has lots of nicknames in the book. Fogboy. Sardine. Dreamer. What does Fogboy mean and how is it different from Dreamer?

📖 Leo's father is upset when he discovers Leo has found the box of childhood memorabilia in the attic. Why does Papa not want Leo to know what's inside? Would it have been better for Leo to ask his father directly for permission to read the journal?

📖 Mr. Beeber tells the cast to think about one of their siblings when the sibling was young and to compare that young version to the way the sibling is now. Try this same exercise with one of your own siblings or someone else you know well. Think about yourself when you were younger. How have you changed? Are there similarities between your young and your older selves?

📖 Leo has always thought that being a grown-up was the greatest thing in the world: "All that freedom to do whatever you want! You don't have a bunch of teachers telling you what to do, and you don't have to follow everyone else's rules, and you can stay up late and eat as many doughnuts as you want, and you can be whatever you want." What's wrong with this picture?

📖 Why was it so surprising for Leo to learn from his father's journal that his father used to tap-dance? Is there something in your life that you always do when you're happy? Or something in your life that always makes you happy when you do it?

📖 Why does Leo equate his father's not being happy now to being a father? Is Leo right or wrong about this?

📖 Leo says reading his father's journal is like reading a story about someone else. Why do you think this is so? How might the relationship with his children have been different if Papa had shared more of his childhood with them?

📖 Leo imagines himself to be many things—a great actor, writer, dancer, physicist, Nobel Prize–winner. How do these dreams help Leo in his everyday life?

📖 Leo remembers when he was little and his father used to tell him, Contento, and Pietro a story called "What We Did Today," making whatever they had done that day seem exciting and adventurous. How is this storytelling similar to Leo's own "replays"? What do you think the author is trying to say about storytelling?

📖 When Leo himself tells a "What We Did Today" story to Nunzio to stop him from crying, Papa says, "Leo, you make gold from pebbles." How else does Leo make gold from pebbles? How does his ability to do this affect the people around him?

📖 How does Leo's reading about his father's interests and goals in the journal help him to understand his father more? What is surprising to Leo about his father's childhood goals? Why does Leo scratch out all the goals on the list he makes for himself and change them all to "to be a father"?

📖 Leo imagines himself giving a press conference after having invented an automated house-cleaning robot and a cure for heart attacks. In his imagination, Leo accepts the Nobel Prize for these discoveries, saying he did it all "for his parents." If you could make discoveries to help specific members of your own family, what would those discoveries be?

📖 Leo is surprised to learn from Grandma that his father used to do plays when he was younger. What reason would the author have had for leaving this interest of Papa's off the list in the journal? What do you suppose Leo learns from this omission? When was Papa finally moved to tell Leo about his interest in plays as a child? Was this the right time for Papa to tell Leo?

📖 Why do you suppose Papa doesn't want to tell Leo how he got the scar on his neck?

📖 Why is it good for Leo and his grandmother to finally have a talk about Rosaria? What does Leo learn then about Papa and the family he grew up in? What does Grandma mean when she says of her conversation with Leo, "It upset me, yes, but it was a little good, too."

📖 How is Leo's friendship with Ruby important in this story? How are their lives similar? How are they different?

📖 Mr. Beeber asks the cast to do a banana rehearsal two days before the performance, with each cast member substituting the word banana in any one line of the play. How does this messing with the script help the players in their rehearsal? Would this work in real life?

📖 During the performance of *Rumpopo's Porch*, Leo worries that Rumpopo's sister might remind Papa, Grandma and Grandpa Navy of Rosaria and upset them. Name some other parallels between the characters in the novel and the characters in the story of Rumpopo?

📖 There are a number of symbols used throughout the novel. What do the tap shoes symbolize? What about the sardine? At the end of *Autobiography, Age Thirteen*, Leo sees a picture of his father standing on his front porch, smiling, with his arms spread. What does the porch symbolize? Does it mean the same thing in the play *Rumpopo's Porch*?

Beyond the Book

BANANA: Play a game in which book-club members substitute the word "banana" once each throughout the book discussion.

(It's important that each club member do the banana thing only once each so your meeting doesn't turn into a sillyfest!)

MEMORABILIA: In advance of your book-club meeting, ask members to create boxes filled with favorite childhood memorabilia. Bring the boxes to the discussion of *Replay*, and discuss how your younger selves are different from your older selves.

BROWNIES AND ICE CREAM: When Leo upsets Grandma at dinner, he imagines he is quarantined with no visitors allowed and that he doesn't speak ever again. When the doctor examines Leo's throat, he finds nothing that brownies and ice cream won't cure. Serve brownies and ice cream at your discussion of *Replay*.

If You Liked this Book, Try . . .

> *Walk Two Moons* and *Chasing Redbird*, also by Sharon Creech
> *The Penderwicks: A Summer Tale of Four Sisters, Two Rabbits, and a Very Interesting Boy* by Jeanne Birdsall
> *Criss Cross* by Lynne Rae Perkins

About the Author

Sharon Creech is the author of the Newbery Medal winner *Walk Two Moons* and the Newbery Honor winner *The Wanderer*. After spending eighteen years teaching and writing in Europe, she and her husband have returned to the United States to live.

The Skin I'm In
Sharon G. Flake

The kids tease Maleeka about her dark black skin and her homemade clothes. When Maleeka meets the new seventh-grade teacher, who has a prominent birthmark on her face, Maleeka thinks she has finally met someone who is worse off than she. Eager to improve her social standing, Maleeka makes a deal with Charlese Jones, a popular girl in the grade, who promises to hang out with Maleeka and let her borrow fashionable clothes if Maleeka will do Charlese's homework. Charlese's dealings with Miss Saunders also bring about some trouble, especially for Maleeka, who gets caught in a dangerous prank that was all Charlese's idea.

READING TIME: 2 hours; 176 pages

THEMES: bullying, self-esteem, peer pressure, skin color bias

Discussion Questions

Maleeka says she is "the kind of person folks can't help but tease." In your school, what causes people to tease others? Are there certain people in your peer group who can't seem to escape torment and bullying? Why do you think this is so?

Why does Maleeka identify with Miss Saunders?

When Maleeka looks at herself in her father's mirror, she says, "I don't get it. I think I'm kind of nice-looking." Why, then, do you suppose Maleeka begins to doubt herself?

When Miss Saunders first meets Maleeka, she compliments her pretty skin. Caleb, the popular boy in Maleeka's grade, also thinks Maleeka is pretty and says he likes her "sweet cocoa brown skin." Why do their opinions and Maleeka's own opinion of herself seem to have less influence on Maleeka than the taunts she hears from John John and others?

Why did Maleeka assume at first that Caleb saw her as the other kids did?

How did you react to the way the kids at school responded to Maleeka's new haircut?

Maleeka says kids like John John only "see what they want to see" and never look for the real person underneath an outside appearance. Have you ever judged someone on appearance? Are you aware of others judging you? What other characters in the book are guilty of seeing only what they want to see? Is Maleeka one of them, too?

Were you surprised that in a school such as Maleeka's, which is predominantly African American, kids are taunted because of their skin tone? Why do you think this happens? Where might the prejudices come from?

Maleeka's friend Sweets goes to a school where the girls have skin the color of "potato chips and cashews and Mary Jane candies." Sweets says it's not about skin color, but it's about "how you feel about who you are that counts." Why is it so hard for Maleeka to be confident when she knows she's just as smart if not smarter than Sweets and the girls at that school? Why is Sweets's attitude so much more positive than Maleeka's?

Why did Miss Saunders give up a high-paying job with a company to teach in Maleeka's school?

🕮 Maleeka gets up early one Saturday morning and starts to work on her writing assignments for Miss Saunders, "for fun." Have you ever been surprised at how much you enjoyed working on a school assignment? Did it make you feel good about yourself?

🕮 Caleb says, "Char's the kind of friend that will get you locked up or shot up." So why does Maleeka go along with trashing Miss Saunders's room when she knows better? What is she afraid Char will do if she refuses? What should Maleeka have done instead?

🕮 What does Maleeka think will happen when she wears Char's nice clothes? Does she actually feel better about herself when she wears them? Do people treat Maleeka differently when she's wearing Char's clothes? Do nice clothes, hairstyles, and jewelry have an actual effect on our self-esteem? Do they make us more confident? Why do you think this is so, or not so?

🕮 What is the significance of Maleeka writing in her diary as herself rather than as Akeelma? What does she get out of keeping the diary?

🕮 How did you feel when Caleb moved seats on the bus on the trip to Washington? Have you ever been in a situation where you should have stood up for a friend but weren't able to because of peer pressure? What does that feel like?

🕮 Were you glad that Maleeka decided to forgive Caleb and give him another chance? Did he deserve it?

🕮 Were you relieved when Maleeka told the truth about Char, Raise, and Raina being responsible for vandalizing the classroom? Was this the right thing to do?

📖 At what point does Maleeka finally decide that enough is enough and she wants to take a stand against the treatment she's been getting? What really gets through to her?

Beyond the Book

SWEETS: Caleb's poem asks of Maleeka: "Would you be my Almond Joy / My chocolate chip, my Hershey Kiss / My sweet dark chocolate butter crisp?" Serve any or all of these sweets at your book club meeting.

DREAM BOX: Maleeka's mom keeps a shoebox in the closet filled with memorabilia of Gregory. Make a dream box in honor of someone you love.

KEEPSAKE MIRRORS: Maleeka's father told her she needed to see herself with her own eyes and that that would be the only way to know who she really is. Decorate a small hand mirror with beads or paints or fabric or fancy paper. Give as a gift or keep as a reminder to see yourself with your own eyes and know who you are.

ALTER EGO: Maleeka makes up a diary entry as a class assignment for a girl named Akeelma. Make up a character name based on your name and write a diary entry for her. Set the diary entry in historical times.

If You Liked This Book, Try . . .

> *Begging for Change* by Sharon G. Flake
> *Monster* by Walter Dean Myers
> *Child of the Owl* by Laurence Yep

White Lilacs by Carolyn Meyer
Incidents in the Life of a Slave Girl by Harriet Jacobs (the
    book Miss Saunders suggests Maleeka read to help
    with her writing)

About the Author

Sharon G. Flake is a public relations director at the University of Pittsburgh. She is a former youth counselor for the Center for the Assessment and Treatment of Youth in Pittsburgh, Pennsylvania. She lives in Pittsburgh with her daughter, Brittney. *The Skin I'm In* is her first novel.

Speak
Laurie Halse Anderson

Melinda's friends won't speak to her, her parents don't notice her, and her entire high school is out to make her life miserable. This is her punishment for calling the cops on a wild party the summer before her freshman year. But Melinda can't reveal what really happened at that party, so she is forced to come to terms with it on her own. To return to her friends and to the world, she must learn to forgive herself and admit what happened—but in a place where she is nothing but Outcast, who will listen?

READING TIME: 2–3 hours, 208 pages

THEMES: art, friendship, popularity, family, identity, depression

Discussion Questions

The main character, Melinda, jumps right into the book in the first person, with no introduction or dialogue. What is the effect of this abrupt beginning? Are you more or less sympathetic to the character because of the way the narrative begins? What does the first paragraph tell you to expect about the character?

Art class is the first thing Melinda is positive about at all—she even calls it "too much fun." But she manages to modify this bit of optimism with negative comments and sarcasm about Mr. Freeman and his strangeness: She harps on his looks, noting that, "This guy is weird." Is her worldview realistic or overly pessimistic? Is it safer to assume things are bad, because there will be less disappointment when they turn out that way?

Would you be sadder if you lived like this? Can you think of any instances when you have been overly negative?

📖 Melinda's family is not close: They communicate by leaving notes on the refrigerator. When her parents actually pay attention to her, she is so happy she starts crying. Is this neglect a symptom of lack of love within the family, or are they caring and simply uncommunicative? Do you think Melinda would have told her parents what happened to her if she could trust them more or if they paid more attention to her?

📖 Melinda uses Heather's friendship as a way to feel better about herself, even though she doesn't seem to like Heather much, calling her a "disposable friend" and an "accessory." Is this unkind or deceptive? Does the fact that Heather uses Melinda too make it acceptable that Melinda uses Heather? Are there any characters in the novel who would have more in common with Melinda and make better friends?

📖 When IT is mentioned for the first time, what did you think had happened between him and Melinda? Did you figure it out before the end of the book? What part of the book specifically helped you to realize what happened? Were there any parts that threw you off track?

📖 David Petrakis is a role model to Melinda: He stands up for himself and his opinions, and he won't let Mr. Neck push him around. But because he is a good student, David is a member of the "Cybergenius" clan. Is it fair or correct to simplify a complicated person like David and to categorize him as just another member of a "brainy" group? Why do you think high school cliques try to label and categorize people like that? Does it serve any purpose?

📖 Melinda goes from thinking her art "stinks" to confidently rearranging and re-creating it based on what "feels right." Does this make her an artist? When asked about her sculpture, she still can't speak. Art is a way for her to communicate feelings without using words. Why is art linked so closely to pain for her? Would she have become interested in art if she had been able to share her feelings verbally? If not, do you think the horrible thing that happened to her is somehow made less horrible because of what she gained from it?

📖 The gym teacher gives Melinda special treatment when she demonstrates her foul shot skills. Are you surprised when Melinda realizes she has a very good foul shot? Why does Melinda try to pursue her artistic talent but not her athletic talent? Is it a waste for her not to use all her talents? What do you think of the gym teacher as compared to Mr. Freeman?

📖 Melinda enjoys symbolism because analyzing a writer's work is like "breaking into his head and finding the key to his secrets." It seems like she wants her secrets to be decoded, but she is also terrified of it at the same time. Why is she too scared to speak? What finally triggers her to tell Rachel? How does Melinda feel when Rachel doesn't believe her?

📖 One day Melinda cuts school and takes a trip to the mall—something any teenaged girl would do. Another day, though, she visits the hospital instead. Why is she drawn to the hospital? She leaves when she realizes there are people there who are physically ill, "sick that you can see." Would a hospital really help her, or are there other ways of curing the kind of sick that Melinda is?

📖 How do you feel when Melinda finally confesses what

happened? Did you feel sorry for her, proud, or both? Do you think her confession is enough to make her better, or is there more progress she needs to make?

📖 Melinda explores the possibility of her being raped by using the voices of talk show hosts, perhaps because it's easier for her than admitting it in her own voice. Do you think this is an effective strategy for dealing with trauma like Melinda's? She uses several other strategies, like hiding in a closet, making sarcastic jokes, and writing on the bathroom wall. Which of these strategies are helpful to her, and which make her problems worse?

Beyond the Book

TURKEY SOUP: Make turkey soup as Melinda's father tries to do. He ends up throwing his out. Do his good intentions make up for the failure in Melinda's eyes?

ART: Look at some of Picasso's cubist paintings online or in a book. Why was Melinda drawn to cubism? How does his art make you feel? Do you like the same things about it that Melinda does?

MAYA ANGELOU: Read a poem by Maya Angelou, like "Still I Rise." Maya Angelou is a positive role model for Melinda because of her strong messages about women. Find a poster of a woman who inspires you and put it on your wall.

SPORTS: Make foul shots until you sink one. Is it hard or easy for you to do? Would you be proud to make forty-one like Melinda?

GARDENING: If you can, grow a small garden like Melinda. Put in flowers or vegetables, whatever you like. Take care of it and see what the seeds yield.

If You Liked This Book, Try . . .

> *Fever 1793* or *Catalyst* by Laurie Halse Anderson
> *Stargirl* by Jerry Spinelli
> *The Perks of Being a Wallflower* by Stephen Chbosky

About the Author

Laurie Halse Anderson was born in Potsdam, New York, in 1961. She was a 1999 National Book Award Finalist in Young People's Literature for *Speak*.

True Believer
Virginia Euwer Wolff

LaVaughn has it pretty good: two best friends from childhood, a loving mother with great ambitions for her, college dreams, and a gorgeous next-door neighbor. But suddenly everything starts to go wrong. Her friends turn to religion and away from LaVaughn, her mother finds a new man to take the place of LaVaughn's father, her education distances her from the people she loves, and she isn't sure if dreamy Jody feels the same way she does. LaVaughn must learn to accept her skills and weaknesses, to stand up for herself, and to fight for her dreams.

READING TIME: 3–4 hours, 272 pages

THEMES: religion, family, education, homosexuality

Discussion Questions

It turns out that LaVaughn's father is absent not because of a divorce but because he was shot and killed. What effect do you think LaVaughn's father's death had on her? What about on her mother? LaVaughn's mother starts dating another man, Lester, and LaVaughn isn't sure how she feels about him. Is her response to Lester understandable, or is she overreacting? How do you think she feels when her mother kicks him out?

Myrtle and Annie join a religious group and encourage LaVaughn to join, but she refuses because she can't believe in what their group preaches. As she says, "I don't mean to be mean to Jesus in my thoughts . . . but I don't get how he hates so many millions of people and sends them down to Hell." Is there a reason Myrtle and Annie's group keeps getting kicked out of churches? Why don't Myrtle and Annie see that their views are too extreme?

📖 LaVaughn has very mixed feelings about her sexuality. On the one hand, she is terrified of getting pregnant because she wants to go to college. But on the other hand, she desperately wants Jody to kiss her. Can these two feelings be reconciled? When LaVaughn finds out that Jody isn't interested in girls, she is heartbroken and refuses to talk to him. Why does she react this intensely? Do you think she should be more understanding of Jody and continue to be friends with him?

📖 LaVaughn is good with children—she helps Jolly out, rescues a little girl on the bus, and folds clothes in the Children's Hospital. Do you think this affects her desire to be a nurse? Even though her mother tells her not to, she gets involved in Jolly's problems again. Does this make her a good person or just naïve?

📖 When LaVaughn starts taking accelerated classes, it creates a rift between her and some of the people she cares about: She begins noticing the grammar mistakes her mother and Lester make, and Patrick, Myrtle, and Annie think she's getting conceited. Is an education worth the distance it can create between you and less educated people? Ronell tells her that she's allowed to be "uppity," and losing friends is a price to pay for gaining education. Do you think there is a way to keep friends and get educated at the same time? Or is it true that LaVaughn's friends just can't "appreciate" her and that their friendship is doomed?

📖 Patrick has a crush on LaVaughn, but she doesn't feel the same way—she is happy just to be friends with him. Do you think LaVaughn would have been nicer to him if she hadn't been so crazy about Jody? He makes her feel guilty for ignoring him and being arrogant. Is there anything she could have done to be kinder to him without letting him think she was interested in him? Is Patrick's accusation correct, or is LaVaughn simply acting like a friend instead of a girlfriend?

At the beginning of the book, LaVaughn is losing the few friends she has, but by the end, she has enough friends for a great party. How did she make friends if she wasn't even trying to? Her new friends seem to reflect her complicated personality better: There are people from her past, like Jolly, Myrtle, and Annie, but ambitious scholars as well, like Patrick and the Brain Cells. Does LaVaughn have to choose one of these two paths, or can she continue to have friends from both worlds? Do you think she will continue to be friends with Myrtle and Annie, considering their "limits" and their exclusive church group?

LaVaughn paints a tree on her ceiling when she is in elementary school, even though the apartment she's living in is a rental. What do you think this tree means to LaVaughn? Can you think of a better symbol for her? Jody tells her it's like Michelangelo's art, and later buys her a book of his works. What does it say about Jody that he knows about the Sistine Chapel and Michelangelo? Is he a good person for LaVaughn to be friends with and learn from, even after she learns he doesn't want to date her?

LaVaughn's time at the dance is a magical experience for her. Did Jody make the night special for her, or was it simply that it was her first dance? Would she be able to have as much fun with someone else—say, Patrick? When she learns Jody isn't interested in her, she cuts up her dress. Is the gesture simply wasteful, or is it necessary for LaVaughn to do? What could it have meant to her?

Beyond the Book

ART: LaVaughn paints a tree on her ceiling both as a symbol of herself and as a decoration. Find an image to symbolize you, and paint or draw it.

THANKSGIVING: LaVaughn's mother generously feeds many people on Thanksgiving. Have a Thanksgiving feast like hers, with turkey, gravy, yams, and cider.

MUSIC: Jody and LaVaughn sing together "We're a Couple of Swells" by Judy Garland at the dance. Find a copy of the song or read the lyrics. What do you think the song means to La-Vaughn?

CRAFTS: Myrtle, Annie, and LaVaughn make Valentines for each other every year. Exchange handmade cards with a friend for any occasion you can think of. Start a tradition of making and exchanging cards.

If You Liked This Book, Try . . .

Make Lemonade by Virginia Euwer Wolff
The Friends by Rosa Guy
Like Sisters on the Homefront by Rita Williams-Garcia

About the Author

Virginia Euwer Wolff was born in 1937. She received her Bachelor's degree from Smith College in 1959, and afterward taught elementary school and later high school English. She has written many acclaimed young adult novels, earning the Golden Kite Award for Fiction and the Jane Addams Book Award for Children's Books That Build Peace. She lives in Oregon, which is where she is from originally.

Whirligig
Paul Fleischman

Brent Bishop wants nothing more than to be one of the cool kids in his new private school in Chicago. But after a humiliating and public rejection at a party at which he had been drinking, Brent attempts to commit suicide while driving home. Though he survives the crash, Lea, an innocent girl whom Brent has never met, is killed. After the criminal proceedings, Lea's parents ask that Brent place whirligigs in the four corners of the United States to honor her memory and let loose her spirit. In his "second life" he comes to see the good and bad consequences to every action.

READING TIME: 2–3 hours, 133 pages.

THEMES: drinking, loss, learning, maturation, race, community

Discussion Questions

📖 *Whirligig* begins with the whirling violence of rejection and anger, something Brent sees as a kind of death, and ends with twirling celebration, what he takes to be a rite of passage in his second life. What is it about the building of the whirligigs that enables Brent to change so much?

📖 What kind of person did you take Brent to be after reading the first chapter? Are many adolescents similar to Brent and just lucky enough not to have been provoked to a high degree?

📖 What kinds of things does Brent do to try to impress his peers? Could the embarrassment he suffers at Chaz's party have been avoided?

How do you react when Brent's parents try to buy his way out of trouble?

Can you imagine your own life as a series of swirling, invisibly connected events—like the movements of a whirligig in the wind? Is the metaphor that life is a whirligig limiting?

What would you include on a whirligig about you?

Despite thinking of himself as a stranger in strange lands, Brent makes new friends along every point in his journey—and these seemingly incidental encounters both alter and define his experience. Which encounter did you enjoy reading about the most? Which one had the biggest impact on Brent's life?

How do you think you would be able to handle knowing that while driving drunk and attempting suicide, you had unwittingly taken an innocent young person's life?

In the story of Alexandra and Stephanie, Alexandra says there are invisible forces, like electricity, that bind us and are always around. At one point, Brent takes a while to consider the word "karass," which he learned from a Kurt Vonnegut novel, to describe a group of disparate people linked together in some special way. Do you believe such a binding force exists? What kind of role would something like a whirligig play in such a system? What about the mediator Miss Gill's comment that our actions "reach into places we can't see"—how does that fit into this scheme?

Is Lea's mother's request that Brent build and place whirligigs at the four corners of the country a reasonable one? What, if anything, would you have requested from Brent if you found yourself in her position?

Beyond the Book

PAPERGIG: Using paper and pencil, design a whirligig of your own. Take the various models Brent used—a girl playing the harp, a whale with a mermaid, a marching band—or be like Brent in Maine on his final whirligig and design whatever you want to.

STRANGE LANDS: During his journey through America, Brent had numerous chance encounters and sightseeing experiences. Go out and explore somewhere you have never been before—as long as you are safe, of course. Take along a friend and go to that new store down the block, or that exhibition in the city you have been meaning to see, or simply to the park to have a picnic.

SUNDAEGIG: Whirligig whipped-cream sundae swirl. Make a chocolate-vanilla swirl sundae with all of your favorite toppings in honor of *Whirligig*. Don't forget to twirl the hot fudge and whipped cream.

VISUALIZATION: Even if you think it is total junk as Stephanie did at first, try Alexandra's visualization method. You don't need wind or even a whirligig to do it; just close your eyes and picture the things that you want most to come to fruition. Sometimes visualizing helps—at least, it probably can't hurt!

CONSTELLATIONS: Brent becomes interested in the stars and their names. Research constellations in a book or on the Internet. Draw one of the constellations that Brent sees on his journey.

If You Liked This Book, Try . . .

Seek or *Breakout* by Paul Fleischman
Speak by Laurie Halse Anderson
Tears of a Tiger by Sharon M. Draper

About the Author

Paul Fleischman grew up in Santa Monica, California, where he remembers hearing his father, author Sid Fleischman, read his books aloud chapter by chapter, as they were written. Sid Fleischman won the Newbery Medal for *The Whipping Boy* in 1987. Paul Fleischman won the Newbery Medal for *Joyful Noise: Poems for Two Voices* in 1989.

APPENDIX

BOOK LISTS FROM THE ORIGINAL MOTHER-DAUGHTER BOOK CLUB

YEAR ONE 1995–1996   4TH GRADE

The Ear, the Eye, the Arm, *Nancy Farmer*
The Man in the Ceiling, *Jules Feiffer*
Charlie Pippin, *Candy Boyd*
The House of Dies Drear, *Virginia Hamilton*
Cousins, *Virginia Hamilton*
The Shimmershine Queen, *Camille Yarbrough*
Her Stories, *Virginia Hamilton*

YEAR TWO 1996–1997   5TH GRADE

The Mystery of Drear House, *Virginia Hamilton*
Julie of the Wolves, *Jean Craighead George*
The Friends, *Rosa Guy*
Homesick: My Own Story, *Jean Fritz*
Life in the Ghetto, *Anika Thomas*
Time Cat, *Lloyd Alexander*
Mama's Girl, *Veronica Chambers*
Rites of Passage, *Tonya Bolden*
Walk Two Moons, *Sharon Creech*

YEAR THREE 1997–1998   6TH GRADE

Absolutely Normal Chaos, *Sharon Creech*
The View from Saturday, *E. L Konigsburg*
Barrel of Laughs, Vail of Tears, *Jules Feiffer*
The Westing Game, *Ellen Raskin*
Something Terrible Happened, *Barbara Ann Porte*
Maizon at Blue Hill, *Jacqueline Woodson*
Another Way to Dance, *Martha Southgate*
A Warm Place, *Nancy Farmer*

YEAR FOUR 1998–1999   7TH GRADE

A Girl Named Disaster, *Nancy Farmer*
Sweet Whispers, Brother Rush, *Virginia Hamilton*
Confessions of a Wayward Preppie, *Stephen Roos*
African American Christmas Stories, *Betty Collier-Thomas*
The Red Scarf Girl, *Ji-Li Jiang*
Running Out of Time, *Margaret Peterson Haddix*
The True Confessions of Charlotte Doyle, *Avi*
Ella Enchanted, *Gail Carson Levine*
The Dark Side of Nowhere, *Neal Shusterman*
The Woman in the Wall, Patrice Kindl

YEAR FIVE 1999–2000   8TH GRADE

Holes, *Louis Sachar*
Bud, Not Buddy, *Christopher Paul Curtis*
Killing Mr. Griffin, *Lois Duncan*
Bluish, *Virginia Hamilton*
Habibi, *Naomi Shihab Nye*
The Moorchild, *Eloise McGraw*

Farewell to Manazanan, *Jeanne Wakatsuki Houston*
    & James Houston
The Skin I'm In, *Sharon Flake*
Death on the Nile, *Agatha Christie*

YEAR SIX 2000–2001   9TH GRADE

She Said Yes, *Misty Bernall*
A Ring of Endless Light, *Madeleine L'Engle*
Sugar in the Raw, *Rebecca Carroll*
Kindred, *Octavia Butler*
The Wedding, *Dorothy West*
Send Me Down a Miracle, *Han Nolan*
Rules of the Road, *Joan Bauer*
Lives of Our Own, *Lori Hewitt*
Whirligig, *Paul Fleischman*

YEAR SEVEN 2001–2002   10TH GRADE

Blanche Passes Go, *Barbara Neely*
If You Come Softly, *Jacqueline Woodson*
Calling the Swan, *Jean Thesman*
River Cross My Heart, *Breena Clarke*
A Stranger Is Watching, *Mary Higgins Clarke*
Speak, *Laurie Halse Amderson*

YEAR EIGHT 2002–2003   11TH GRADE

Searching for David's Heart, *Cherie Bennett*
White Oleander, *Janet Fitch*
The Just Us Girls, *Evelyn "Slim" Lambright*

Born Blue, *Han Nolan*
The Best American Mystery Stories of the Century, *Tony Hillerman*
The Sisterhood of the Traveling Pants, *Ann Brashares*
Kit's Wilderness, *David Almond*

BOOK LISTS FROM SKYLAR'S MOTHER-DAUGHTER BOOK CLUB

YEAR ONE 2004–2005   9TH GRADE

The Curious Incident of the Dog in the Night-Time, *Mark Haddon*
Prom, *Laurie Halse Anderson*
Extremely Loud and Incredibly Close, *Jonathan Safran Foer*

YEAR TWO 2005–2006   10TH GRADE

The Lovely Bones, *Alice Sebold*
Go Ask Alice, *Anonymous*
A Long Way Down, *Nick Hornby*
Bee Season, *Myla Goldberg*
Girl in Hyacinth Blue, *Susan Vreeland*
A Northern Light, *Jennifer Donnelly*
The Liar's Club, *Mary Carr*
The Ice Queen, *Alice Hoffman*

RESOURCES ON CHILDREN'S AND YOUNG ADULT BOOKS

ALAN Review
http://scholar.lib.vt.edu/ejournals/ALAN
The Assembly on Literature for Adolescents of the National

Council of Teachers of English publishes The ALAN Review three times each year (fall, winter, and spring). The journal contains articles on YA literature and its teaching, interviews with authors, reports on publishing trends, current research on YA literature, a section of reviews of new books, and ALAN membership news. An Electronic Archive of Past Issues is available. ALAN is made up of teachers, authors, librarians, publishers, teacher-educators and their students, and others who are particularly interested in the area of young adult literature.

Amazon.com
http://www.amazon.com

Berkeley Public Library Teen Services Booklists
http://www.infopeople.org/bplcent.html
Prepared by the Teen Services staff of Berkeley Public Library

Booklist
http://www.ala.org/booklist
A basic tool for adult, young adult, and children's books and media. Only titles recommended by the American Library Association are included.

Booklists for Young Adults on the Web
http://seemore.mi.org/booklists/
An index compiled from the many YA-related Web pages created by librarians, educators, and others serving young adults.

Boston Book Review
http://www.bookwire.com/
BookWire is the most comprehensive online portal into the book industry for librarians, publishers, booksellers, authors, and general book enthusiasts. The site provides articles on the latest industry news, access to literary journals and reviews, and

an expansive directory of book sites around the world. Users can also search updated bestseller lists, find listings of literary events, and read author interviews.

Children's Literature
http://www.carolhurst.com
Carol Hurst reviews great books for kids and provides ways to use them in the classroom, plus collections of books and activities about particular subjects, curriculum areas, themes and professional topics all adaptable to book club use.

Children's Book Council
http://www.cbcbooks.org/
Seventy-five authors/illustrators everyone should know. List originally compiled by Bernice E. Cullman, noted reading specialist.

Children's Book Watch
http://www.midwestbookreview.com
Established in 1976, the Midwest Book Review publishes several monthly publications for community and academic library systems in California, Wisconsin, and the upper Midwest. The Midwest Book Review gives priority consideration to small press publishers, self-published authors, academic presses.

Children's Classics: A Booklist for Parents
http://www.hbook.com.childclass1.shtml
Horn Book's most popular booklist, Children's Classics, prepared by Mary Burns, has achieved its own classic status as essential reading for all new parents, teachers, and librarians.

Children's Literature Web Guide
http://www.acs.ucalgary.ca/~dkbrown/
The Children's Literature Web Guide is an attempt to gather together and categorize the growing number of Internet

resources related to books for Children and Young Adults. Much of the information that you can find through these pages is provided by others: fans, schools, libraries, and commercial enterprises involved in the book world. Complied by David K. Brown Director, Doucette Library of Teaching Resources.

Fairrosa Cyberlibrary
http://www.fairrosa.info
Fairrosa Cyber Library is New York Middle School Librarian, Roxanne Hsu Feldman's personal collection of materials found on the Web related to Children's Literature.

HarperCollins
www.harpercollins.com/readersgroups.asp
HarperCollins provides discussion guides for many titles, plus an "Invite the Author" program that lets you see interviews with favorite authors and use them in your club meetings. There's also a monthly newsletter and resource listing of author events near you.

HarperCollins Canada
http://www.harpercollins.ca/readers.asp?ACT=SEARCH&
a=Mother-Daughter&search_type=subject
Mother-Daughter Reading Guides—stay on top of the best books for your book club.

International Reading Association Choices Booklists
http://www.reading.org/choices/
Each year, thousands of children, young adults, teachers, and librarians around the United States select their favorite recently published books for the "Choices" booklists. These lists are used in classrooms, libraries, and homes to help young readers find books they will enjoy.

New York Times Book Reviews
http://www.nytimes.com/book

Overbooked
http://www.overbooked.org/
A site for ravenous readers. Overbooked specializes in providing timely information about literary and genre fiction as well as readable nonfiction.

Reading Group Choices
http://www.readinggroupchoices.com/
Reading Group Choices is an opinionated guide of great books to read and discuss that have been published by independent presses as well as major publishers.

St. Louis Library Books Reviewed by Teens
http://www.slcl.org/teens/reviews/reviews.htm

Vandergrift's Children's Literature Page
http://scils.rutgers.edu/~kvander/
Kay E. Vandergrift, Associate Dean, School of Communication, Information and Library Sciences, Rutgers University, shares ideas and information related to literature for children and young adults.

YALSA (Young Adult Library Services Association) Booklists
http://ala.org/yalsa/booklists/index/html
The annual list of "Best Books for Young Adults" makes up a diverse list that features science fiction and fantasy, nonfiction, novels in verse, cutting-edge contemporary fiction and graphic novels. The committee also selected a top-ten list of titles that showcases the quality and diversity of literature being published for teens.

AWARDS

Alex Award

http://www.ala.org/yalsa/booklists/alex/
Given annually since 1998 to ten adult books that will be enjoyed by young adults, ages twelve through eighteen.

Américas Book Award for Children's and Young Adult Literature

http://www.uwm.edu/Dept/CLACS/outreach/americas.html
The Américas Award is given in recognition of U.S. works of fiction, poetry, folklore, or selected nonfiction published in the previous year.

Coretta Scott King Book Award

http://www.ala.org/ala/emiert/corettascottkingbookawards/corettascott.htm
The Coretta Scott King Book Award is presented annually by the Coretta Scott King Committee of the American Library Association's Ethnic Multicultural Information Exchange Round Table. The award (or awards) is given to an African American author and an African American illustrator for an outstandingly inspirational and educational contribution.

Margaret A. Edwards Award

http://www.ala.org/ala/yalsa/booklistsawards/margaretaedwards/margaretedwards.htm
Honors an author's lifetime achievement for writing books that have been popular over a period of time.

Newbery Medal Award

http://www.ucalgary.ca/~dkbrown/newbery.html
The Newbery Medal was named for eighteenth-century British bookseller John Newbery. It is awarded annually by the Association for Library Service to Children, a division of the

American Library Association, to the author of the most distinguished contribution to American literature for children.

Michael L. Printz Award
http://www.ala.org/ala/yalsa/booklistsawards/printzaward/
Printz,_Michael_L__Award.htm
An award for a book that exemplifies literary excellence in young adult literature.

Winning Titles
http://www.ala.org/yalsa/booklists/index.html
American Library Association (ALA) and Young Adult Library Services Association (YALSA) Award lists for all major awards.

ORGANIZATIONS WITH SPECIFIC SUPPORT FOR BOOK CLUBS AND BOOK CLUB LISTS

The American Association of University Women
www.aauw.org

American Library Association
www.ala.org

The Center for the Book
www.loc.gov/loc/cfbook/

ACKNOWLEDGMENTS

I am especially grateful to the following people, for helping to make this book possible and helping to ensure its long life.

My mother, Charlotta, for instilling in me an appreciation of reading; and to all the mothers and daughters in the original Mother-Daughter Book Club, Bookworms, and Skylar's Mother-Daughter Book Club for allowing me to share our collective journeys; Jewell Stoddard, for her willingness to share her in-depth knowledge of books with us these past ten years—your book recommendations are always perfect; Lisa, for her faith in this book and for being a rock and a refuge during every phase of the project; and the entire staff at Lark Productions, particularly Robin, for all their hard work; my editor, Gail Winston at HarperCollins, for belief in the ongoing life of mother-daughter book clubs, and to the wonderful team she put together that helped make this special anniversary edition possible; Teresa Barker, for her creative energy and ability to insightfully give my thoughts and experiences a resting place on these pages; and to my friends Gail, Kim, Conni, and Anita, for being such a ready, willing, and able flow of advice and encouragement.

Thanks also to my friend and colleague, Barbara Blum, for believing I could do this; and to my best friend, Joanne Williams, for being a sounding board and counsel on every leg of every journey.

Special thanks to all the African American writers who have provided through their work the inspiration that shaped many of the original book club's discussions. And finally, a warm heartfelt thank-you to the many people who responded to my request for help on the book by contributing a book list or an interview, recommending a resource or just lending an ear. I'll never be able to thank you enough.

Shireen Dodson,
JANUARY 2007

For their contributions of time, thought, and inspiration, I extend my thanks to the following people:

To my mother, Maxine, and my father, George, who created in our family life a haven for creative thought and for reading, writing, exploring and sharing ideas; my sister Susan, a busy designer and mother of two daughters, who really didn't have time, but made time anyway, to bring her talents to the book; Beth, who forwarded the publishers my way; to Leslie, for allowing me to learn from her experience; to our goodhearted staff at Readmore Communications, particularly to Karen, for her research and organization; to Lisa, Robin, Julie, and Sarah for introducing me to Shireen and this special opportunity, and for their work.

To Shireen, for starting her Mother-Daughter Book Club, for asking me to help her share the idea with others, and for bringing candor and good humor to our partnership; to Shireen's husband, Leroy, and my Steve, for their technical assistance at all hours of day and night; and to all the mothers and daughters in Shireen's club as well as my own—Hannah and Anne Clark; Hannah, Rebecca, and Wendy Hartz; Sierra and Donna Patterson; Stephanie and Helen Shum; Kate and Jamie Sullivan; Lynae and Darlene Turner; and Stephanie and Karen Wesolowski—for sharing their thoughts and ideas; to Elizabeth Debold and her coauthors, for the inspiration that came of reading their *Mother-Daughter Revolution: From Good Girls to Great Women,* and to the other generous contributors who spoke so enthusiastically in our interviews—Susan Bailey, Nina Baym, Carolyn Collins, Martha Decherd, Bonnie Diamond, Sumru Erkut, Rosa Guy, Virginia Hamilton, Alice Letvin, Ann Martin, Harriet Mosatche, Connie Porter, Whitney Ransome, Pam Sacks, Ellen Silber, Joan Franklin Smutny, Lee Temkin, Bertha Waters, and Elizabeth Wheeler; to all my friends who came or called—or refrained from both—at all the right times, whose experience and enthusiasm are an ongoing theme in my life.

And finally, to my own treasure of a family—Steve, Rachel, Rebecca, and Aaron—each one of whom accommodated this project in so many ways every day, through birthdays and holidays, nights and weekends; my younger sister Holly, with whom I have shared books and book talk from the beginning; to Steve's cousin Martha, a gifted media library teacher who has helped build our family library and our interest in the widest world of authors and stories; and to Steve's mom, Dolly, with whom I have shared books and thoughts about them for twelve happy years. The important thing about appreciation is to truly feel it. I do.

Teresa Barker,
JANUARY 2007

INDEX

Didion, Joan, 317
Dinner at the Homesick Restaurant, 79
discussion guides
    sample, 285–355
    sources of, 363
discussions, 135–160
    book groups as forum for, 21–22
    books and authors as partners in, 156–158, 160, 265, 268–269, 271
    continuity of, 151–156
    discussion guides for, 285–355, 363
    family stories in, 154
    importance of, 8–11, 14, 140–142
    leadership of, 121–124, 139, 160
    mother-daughter dialogue in, 144, 161–192
    questions for. *See* questions
    shared inquiry method, 138, 145–147
    sharing in. *See* sharing
    speaking from experience, 155
    strategies for, 145–146
    unspoken dialogue in, 144
Doctor Doolittle series, 100
Donaldson, Tiffany, 18–19, 32
Donaldson, Winnie, 18–19
Donnelly, Jennifer, 283–284, 329–332
Double Helix, The, 239
Douglass, Frederick, 99, 168

Dove, Rita, 26–27, 114, 197
Down in the Piney Woods, 234
Downright Dencey, 20
Drabble, Margaret, 79
Dragonflight, 235
Draper, Sharon M., 355
Dreiser, Theodore, 332
Drop Dead, 14
DuBois, W. E. B., 99, 168
Du Bois, William P., 67

Ear, the Eye, and the Arm, The, 5
Earth is Painted Green, The, 236
Eastman, Philip D., 16
eating disorders, 196–201, 204
Edelman, Marian Wright, 161, 224
Edith Jackson, 234
Egypt Game, The, 242
Eiseley, Loren, 239
Elidor, 14
Ella Baker, 224
Ellen Foster, 140
e-mail, invitations sent by, 56–57
Emma Willard School, 260
English Fairy Tales, 20
Enright, Elizabeth, 242
Ephron, Nora, 67
Erdrich, Louise, 146
Erkut, Sumru, 68–69, 97, 208
Estes, Clarissa Pinkola, 172
Estes, Eleanor, 105, 257
Everything Is Illuminated, 317
Every Time a Rainbow Dies, 328
experience, versus objectives, 30

About the Author

SHIREEN DODSON is a special assistant to the director of the Office of Civil Rights, U.S. Department of State. She is also active in her community, serving on the Board of Directors of the Anthony Bowen YMCA of Metropolitan Washington; Board of Trustees, Zion Baptist Church; and is Chair of the District of Columbia Retirement Board. She is an active member of the Washington Chapter of Jack and Jill of America, Inc., and was founding member of the Coalition of 100 Black Women of D.C., Inc. She lives in northwest Washington, D.C., and she is the mother of three children: Leroy III, twenty-five; Morgan, twenty; and Skylar, fifteen.

About the Writer

TERESA BARKER is a writer, editor, and communications consultant. She has written extensively about issues related to family, culture, education, and health. Her work has appeared in the *Chicago Tribune,* the *Chicago Sun-Times*, the *Eugene Register-Guard*, the *Nashville Tennessean,* and in other newspapers, magazines, and nationally syndicated publications. She is vice president and creative director of Readmore Communications in Chicago, which she founded with her husband, Steve Weiner. They live in Buffalo Grove, Illinois, with their three children—Rachel, Rebecca, and Aaron.

ALSO BY
SHIREEN DODSON

100 BOOKS FOR GIRLS TO GROW ON

ISBN 0-06-095718-2 (paperback)

Shireen Dodson, author of the acclaimed *The Mother-Daughter Book Club*, offers a selection of both new and classic titles. Each book has been handpicked because it is a joy to read, because it inspires mother-daughter dialogue, and because it encourages creativity beyond the book experience. Included are brief plot summaries for each book, as well as thought-provoking discussion questions, inspired field trip ideas, fun crafts and activities, and biographies of the authors. You don't need to form a book club to use and enjoy *100 Books for Girls to Grow On*. Shireen Dodson offers stimulating ideas that will spark your daughter's creativity and nurture a love for books.